INSTRUCTOR-LED TRAINING

MICROSOFT® OFFICE SPECIALIST

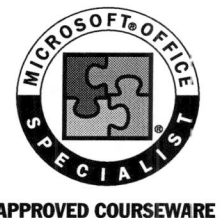

APPROVED COURSEWARE

Step by Step Courseware

Microsoft® Office XP

Microsoft®

Access

Version 2002
Core Skills
Student Guide

PUBLISHED BY
ITS-Feda Ltd under licence from Microsoft Press
ITS-Feda Ltd is a Division of Reading College and School of Arts & Design
Coombe Lodge
Blagdon, Bristol, BS40 7RG,UK

Printed and bound in the UK by Basingstoke Press.

ISBN 1-904644-09-0

1 2 3 4 5 6 7 8 9   QWT   6 5 4 3 2

Microsoft Press books are available through booksellers and distributors worldwide. For further
information about International editions contact your local Microsoft Corporation Office or contact
Microsoft Press International directly at fax (425) 936-7329 or visit the Microsoft Press web site at
mspress.Microsoft.com.
For further details of materials available from ITS-Feda Ltd please fax (44) 1761 461230 or visit
www.itservices.org.uk. For comments regarding these materials please contact
books@itservices.org.uk.

FoxPro, FrontPage, IntelliMouse, Microsoft, MSN, Office Logo, Outlook, PivotChart, PivotTable,
PowerPoint, Visual Basic, Visual FoxPro, Windows and Windows NT are either registered trademarks
or trademarks of Microsoft Corporation in the United States and /or other countries. Other product and
company names mentioned herein may be the trademarks of their respective owners.

The example companies, organizations, products, domain names, e-mail addresses, logos, people,
places and events depicted herein are fictitious. No association with any real company, organization,
product, domain names, e-mail addresses, logos, people, places or events is intended or should be
inferred.

Acknowledgements
Original Material

For Microsoft Press
Acquisitions Editor: Kong Cheung
Project Editor: Jenny Moss Benson
Technical Editor: Marc Young
Manuscript Editor: Shawn Peck
Principal Compositor: Paula Gorelick

Revision to Instructor Led

For TESI Automazione srl
Managing Editor: Sebastiano Certo
Project Manager: Elisa Donzella
Technical Editor: Vito Burgì
Mous Master Instructor: Roberto Ferraù and
Antonino Terranova
Production Team: Elio Di Mauro, Valerio
Mirabella and Josephine Casaccio.

ITS-Feda Ltd
Project Manager: Penny Price
Technical Authors: G.E.T. I.T. Solutions Ltd

Contents

Quick Reference C.1

Course Overview

Welcome to the *Office Specialist XP Courseware* series for Microsoft Office XP. This series facilitates classroom learning, letting students develop competence and confidence in using an Office application or operating system software. In completing courses taught with *Microsoft Office Specialist XP Courseware,* students learn to use the software productively and discover how to make the software work for them. This series addresses core-level and expert-level skills in Microsoft Word 2002, Microsoft Excel 2002, Microsoft Access 2002, Microsoft Outlook 2002 and Microsoft FrontPage 2002. The *Microsoft Office Specialist XP Courseware* series includes only one level for Microsoft PowerPoint 2002 called *comprehensive* and *Windows XP.*

The *Microsoft Office Specialist XP Courseware* series provides:

■ Task-based, results-oriented learning strategies.

■ Exercises based on business scenarios.

■ Complete preparation for Microsoft Office Specialist certification.

■ Attractive student guides with full-featured lessons.

■ Lessons with accurate, logical and sequential instructions.

■ Comprehensive coverage of skills from the basic to the expert level.

■ A CD-ROM with practice files.

A Task-Based Approach Using Business Scenarios

The *Microsoft Office Specialist XP Courseware* series builds on the strengths of the time-tested approach that Microsoft developed and refined for its Microsoft Office Specialist XP series. Even though the Microsoft Office Specialist XP series was created for self-paced training, instructors have long used it in the classroom. For the first time, this popular series has been adapted specifically for the classroom environment. By studying with a task-based approach, students learn more than just the features of the software. They learn how to accomplish real-world tasks so that they can immediately increase their productivity using the software application.

The lessons are based on tasks that students might encounter in the everyday work world. This approach allows students to quickly see the relevance of the training. The task-based focus is woven throughout the series, including lesson organization within each unit, lesson titles and scenarios chosen for practice files.

An Integrated Approach for Training

The *Microsoft Office Specialist XP Courseware* series distinguishes itself from other series on the market with its consistent delivery and completely integrated approach to learning. With the addition of the *Microsoft Office Specialist XP Courseware* series, which supports classroom instruction, the *Microsoft Office Specialist XP* training suite now provides a flexible and unified training solution.

Preparation for Microsoft Office Specialist Certification

This series has been certified as approved courseware for the Microsoft Office Specialist certification program. Students who have completed this training are prepared to take the related Microsoft Office Specialist exam. By passing the exam for a particular Office application, students demonstrate proficiency in that application to their employers or prospective employers. Exams are offered at participating test centres. For more information, see *www.microsoft.com/OfficeSpecialist.*

A Sound Instructional Foundation

All products in the *Microsoft Office Specialist XP Courseware* series apply the same instructional strategies, closely adhering to adult instructional techniques and reliable adult learning principles. Lessons in the *Microsoft Office Specialist XP Courseware* series are presented in a logical, easy-to-follow format, helping the student find information quickly and learn as efficiently as possible. To facilitate the learning process, each lesson follows a consistent structure.

Designed for Optimal Learning

The following "Lesson Features" section shows how the colourful and highly visual series design makes it easy for students to see what to read and what to do when practicing new skills.

Lessons break training into easily assimilated sessions. Each lesson is self- contained and lessons can be taught in sequences other than the one presented in the table of contents. Sample files for the lessons don't depend on completion of other lessons. Sample files within a lesson assume only that students are working sequentially through a complete lesson.

The *Microsoft Office Specialist XP Courseware* series features:

- **Lesson objectives**. Objectives clearly state the instructional goals for each lesson so that students understand what skills they will master. Each lesson objective is covered in its own section and each section or topic in the lesson is covered in a consistent way. Lesson objectives preview the lesson structure, helping students grasp key information and prepare for learning skills.

- **Informational text for each topic**. For each objective, the lesson provides easy-to-read, technique-focused information.

- **Hands-on practice**. Numbered steps give detailed, step-by-step instructions to help students learn skills. The steps also show results and screen images to match what students should see on their computer screens. Student and instructor CDs contain sample files used for each lesson.

- **Full-colour illustrations in colour student guides**. Illustrated screen images give visual feedback to students as they work through exercises. The images reinforce key concepts, provide visual clues about the steps and bolster students' confidence by giving them something to check their progress against.

- **Microsoft Office Specialist icon**. Each section or sidebar that covers a Microsoft Office Specialist certification objective has a Microsoft Office Specialist icon in the margin at the beginning of the section. The number of the certification objective is also listed.

- **Tips**. Helpful hints and alternate ways to accomplish tasks are located throughout the lesson text.

- **Important**. If there is something to watch out for or something to avoid, this information is added to the lesson and indicated with this heading.

- **Margin notes**. Margin notes (grey background) contain parenthetical topics or additional information that students might find interesting.

- **Button images in the margin**. When the text instructs students to click a particular button, an image of the button and its label appear in the margin.

- **Glossary**. Terms with which you might not be familiar are defined in the glossary in the back of this guide. Terms in the glossary appear in boldface type within the lesson and are defined upon their first use within lessons.

- **Quick Quiz**. You can use the short-answer quick quiz questions to test or reinforce your understanding of key topics within the lesson.

■ **Quick Reference**. A complete summary of steps for tasks taught in each lesson is available in the back of the guide. This is often the feature that students find most useful when they return to their workplaces. The expert-level guides include the references from the core-level guides so that you can review or refresh basic and advanced skills on your own whenever necessary.

■ **Index**. Student guides are completely indexed. All glossary terms and application features appear in the index.

Conventions and Features

This manual uses special forms, symbols and heading conventions to highlight important information or to call your attention to special steps. For more information about the features available in each lesson, refer to the "Course Overview" section.

Convention	Meaning
1 2	Numbered steps guide you through hands-on exercises in each topic.
●	A round bullet indicates an exercise that has only one step.
(CD icon)	This icon at the beginning of a lesson lists the files that the lesson will use and explains any file preparation that needs to take place before starting the lesson.
FileName (CD icon)	Practice files that you'll need to use in a topic's procedure are shown above the CD icon.
(Microsoft Office Specialist icon) W2002-3-2	This icon indicates a section that covers a Microsoft Office Specialist exam objective. The numbers above the icon refer to the specific Microsoft Office Specialist objective.
new for **Office**XP	This icon indicates a new or greatly improved feature in this version of Microsoft Word.
tip	This section provides a helpful hint or shortcut that makes working through a task easier.
important	This section points out information that you need to know to complete the procedure.

Convention	Meaning
troubleshooting	This section shows you how to fix a common problem.
Save 🖫	When a button is referenced in a topic, a picture of the button appears in the margin area with a label.
Ctrl + End	A plus sign (+) between two key names means that you must hold down the first key while you press the other key. For example, "Press Ctrl + End" means that you hold down the Ctrl key while you press End.
Boldface	Program features that you click or press, terms that are explained in the glossary at the end of the book and the text that you are supposed to type appear in boldface type.
Practice files	All files that you need to practice the new skills taught in the lesson are located on the CD that is provided with each student guide. Instructions for installing the practice files are in the "Using the Book's CD" section near the beginning of the student guides.
Glossary	The glossary helps you to understand key terms. Terms that are defined in the glossary are shown in boldface type text in the lesson.
Margin notes	The notes contain additional information that might be useful to you.

Using the Book's CD

The CD-ROM included with this student guide contains the practice files that you'll use to perform the exercises in the books. By using the practice files, you won't waste time creating the samples used in the lessons and you can concentrate on learning how to use Microsoft Word 2002.

important

This book does not contain the Access 2002 software. You should purchase and install that program before using this book.

System Requirements

■ **Computer/Processor**

Computer with a Pentium 133-megahertz (MHz) or higher processor

■ **Memory**

RAM requirements depend on the operating system used:

■ **Windows 98, or Windows 98 Second Edition**

24 MB of RAM plus an additional 8 MB of RAM for each Office program (such as Microsoft Word) running simultaneously

■ **Windows Me, or Microsoft Windows NT**

32 MB of RAM plus an additional 8 MB of RAM for each Office program (such as Microsoft Word) running simultaneously

■ **Windows 2000 Professional**

64 MB of RAM plus an additional 8 MB of RAM for each Office program (such as Microsoft Word) running simultaneously

■ **Hard Disk**

Hard disk space requirements will vary depending on configuration; custom installation choices may require more or less hard disk space.

245 MB of available hard disk space with 115 MB on the hard disk where the operating system is installed. (Users without Windows 2000, Windows Me, or Office 2000 Service Release 1 [SR-1] require an extra 50 MB of hard disk space for System Files Update.)

An additional 6 MB of hard disk space is required for installing the practice files.

■ **Operating System**

Windows 98, Windows 98 Second Edition, Windows Millennium Edition (Windows Me), Windows NT 4.0 with Service Pack 6 (SP6) or later, or Windows 2000 or later. (On systems running Windows NT 4.0 with SP6, Microsoft Internet Explorer must be upgraded to at least version 4.01 with SP1.)

■ **Drive**

CD-ROM drive

■ **Display**

Super VGA (800 × 600) or higher-resolution monitor with 256 colours

■ **Peripherals**

Microsoft Mouse, Microsoft IntelliMouse, or compatible pointing device

■ **Software**

Microsoft Access 2002, Microsoft Word 2002, Microsoft Excel 2002, Microsoft Outlook 2002 and Microsoft Internet Explorer 5 or later

Installing the Practice Files

You need to install the practice files on your hard disk before you use them in the lessons' exercises. Follow these steps to prepare the CD's files for your use:

1   Insert the CD-ROM into the CD-ROM drive of your computer.

A menu screen appears

troubleshooting

If the menu screen does not appear, start Windows Explorer. In the left pane, locate the icon for your CD-ROM and click this icon. In the right pane, double-click the **StartCD** file.

2   Click **Install Practice Files**.

3   Click **OK** in the initial message box.

4   If you want to install the practice files to a location other than the default folder (C:\SBS\Word), click the **Change Folder** button, select the new drive and path and then click **OK**.

5   Click the **Continue** button to install the selected practice files.

6   After the practice files have been installed, click **OK**.

Within the installation folder are subfolders for each lesson in the book.

7   Remove the CD-ROM from the CD-ROM drive and return it to the envelope at the back of the book.

Using the Practice Files

Each lesson's introduction lists the files that are needed for that lesson and explains any file preparation that you need to take care of before you start working through the lesson.

OpenDoc

Each topic in the lesson explains how and when to use any practice files. The files that you'll need are indicated in the margin at the beginning of the procedure above the CD icon:

The following table lists each **Core** lesson's practice files.

Chapter	Folder	Files
1	GettingToKnowXL	FileOpen, ZeroIn, DataEntry and Replace
2	SettingUpWorkbook	Easier, DataRead, AddPicture
3	PerformingCalculations	Formula
4	ChangingDocAppearance	Formats, CreateNew, Follow, and Margins
5	MultipleSources	TemplateStart, January, February, March, Linking, 2001Q1, Y2001Q1
6	Charts	CreateChart and Customize
7	Printing	Printing and Part
8	OtherPrograms	Include, YearEndSummary, WorkSheet, SalesByCategory, Hyperlink, ProductList, PasteChart and ChartTarget
9	Web	Saving and Publish
10	Collaborating	Comments

Uninstalling the Practice Files

After you finish working through this book, you should uninstall the practice files to free up hard disk space.

1   On the Windows taskbar, click the **Start** button, point to **Settings** and then click **Control Panel**.

2   Double-click the **Add/Remove Programs** icon

3   **In the list of installed programs, click Microsoft Access 2002 SBS Files** and then click **Add/Remove**. (If you're using Windows 2000 Professional, click the **Remove** or **Change/Remove** button.)

4   Click **Yes** when the confirmation dialog box appears.

tip

If you need additional help installing or uninstalling the practice files, please see the section "Getting Help" earlier in this book. Microsoft's product support does not provide support for this book or its CD-ROM.

Locating the Practice Files

After you have installed the practice files, all files that you need for this course will be stored in a folder named Word that is located on your hard disk. To navigate to this folder from within Word:

1   On the Standard toolbar, click the **Open** button.

2   Click the **Look In** down arrow and click the icon for your hard disk.

3   Double-click the folder named Access.

All the files for the lessons appear within this folder.

On the first page of each lesson, look for the margin icon *Practice files for this lesson.* This icon points to the paragraph that explains which file(s) you will need to work through the lesson exercises.

Microsoft Office Specialist Objectives

Each Microsoft Office Specialist certification level has a set of objectives, which are organised into broader skill sets. To prepare for the Microsoft Office Specialist certification exam, you should confirm that you can meet its objectives.

W2002-3-2

This book will prepare you fully for the Microsoft Office Specialist exam at the core level because it addresses all the objectives for this exam. Throughout this book, content that pertains to a Microsoft Office Specialist objective is identified with the Microsoft Office Specialist logo and objective number in the margin:

Core Microsoft Office Specialist Objectives

Ac2002-1	**Creating and Using Databases**
Ac2002-1-1	Create Access databases
Ac2002-1-2	Open database objects in multiple views
Ac2002-1-3	Move among records
Ac2002-1-4	Format datasheets
Ac2002-2	**Creating and Modifying Tables**
Ac2002-2-1	Create and modify tables
Ac2002-2-2	Add a predefined input mask to a field
Ac2002-2-3	Create Lookup fields
AC2002-2-4	Modify field properties
Ac2002-3	**Creating and Modifying Queries**
Ac2002-3-1	Create and modify select queries
Ac2002-3-2	Add calculated fields to select queries
Ac2002-4	**Creating and Modifying Forms**
Ac2002-4-1	Create and display forms

Ac2002-4-2	Modify form properties
Ac2002-5	**Viewing and Organizing Information**
Ac2002-5-1	Enter, edit, and delete records
Ac2002-5-2	Create queries
Ac2002-5-3	Sort records
Ac2002-5-4	Filter records
Ac2002-6	**Defining Relationships**
Ac2002-6-1	Create one-to-many relationships
Ac2002-6-2	Enforce referential integrity
Ac2002-7	**Producing Reports**
Ac2002-7-1	Create and format reports
Ac2002-7-2	Add calculated controls to reports
Ac2002-7-3	Preview and print reports
Ac2002-8	**Integrating with Other Applications**
Ac2002-8-1	Import data into Access
Ac2002-8-2	Export data from Access
Ac2002-8-3	Create a simple data access page

Taking a Microsoft Office Specialist Exam

As desktop computing technology advances, more employers rely on the objectivity and consistency of technology certification when screening, hiring and training employees to ensure their competence. As an employee, you can use technology certification to prove that you meet the standards set by your current or potential employer. The Microsoft Office Specialist program is the only Microsoft-approved certification program designed to assist employees in validating their competence at using Microsoft Office applications.

About the Microsoft Office Specialist Program

A Microsoft Office Specialist is an individual who has certified his or her skills in one or more of the Microsoft Office desktop applications: Microsoft Word, Microsoft Excel, Microsoft PowerPoint, Microsoft Outlook, Microsoft Access, Microsoft FrontPage, or Microsoft Project. The Microsoft Office Specialist program typically offers certification exams at the "core" and "expert" skill levels. (The availability of Microsoft Office Specialist certification exams varies by application, application version and language. Visit *http://www.microsoft.com/traincert/mcp/officespecialist* for exam availability.) The Microsoft Office Specialist Program is the only Microsoft-approved program in the world for certifying proficiency in Microsoft Office desktop applications and Microsoft Project. This certification can be a valuable asset when searching for a job or for career advancement.

If you want to take a Microsoft Office Specialist exam go to your nearest IQ CENTER® (IQ CENTER locations are listed at our Web site: www.certiport.com/IQCenters/IQCenterlocatorinternal.asp)

For Microsoft Office Specialist training courses go to you nearest Microsoft IT Academy Centre details of which can be found at the Microsoft web site.

A Microsoft IT Academy uses official Microsoft Office Approved Courseware and trains students to undertake the Microsoft Office Specialist exams, providing the end-user with a guaranteed high standard and quality of training. Courses are presented by Microsoft Certified Instructors, who are qualified in and have the know-how and experience to train students to this the industry gold standard for Office applications.

What Does This Logo Mean?

APPROVED COURSEWARE

It means this courseware has been approved by the Microsoft Office Specialist Program because it is the finest available for learning each Office XP application. It also means that upon completion of this courseware, you may be prepared to become a Microsoft Office Specialist.

Selecting a Microsoft Office Specialist Certification Level

In selecting the Microsoft Office Specialist certification levels that you would like to pursue, you should assess the following:

- The Office application and versions of the application with which you are familiar

- The length of time you have used the application

- Whether you have had formal or informal training

Candidates for the core-level Microsoft Office Specialist certification exams are expected to successfully complete a wide range of standard business tasks, such as formatting a document. Successful candidates generally have six or more months of experience with the application, including either formal instructor-led training with a Microsoft Office Specialist Authorized Instructor or self-study using Microsoft Office Specialist-approved books, guides, or interactive computer-based materials.

Candidates for expert-level certification, by comparison, are expected to complete more complex business-oriented assignments utilizing the application's advanced functionality, such as importing data and recording macros. Successful candidates generally have two or more years of experience with the application, again including formal instructor-led training with a Microsoft Office Specialist Authorized Instructor or self-study using Microsoft Office Specialist-approved materials.

Microsoft Office Specialist Exam Objectives

Every Microsoft Office Specialist certification exam is developed from a list of exam objectives, which are derived from studies of how the Office application is actually used in the workplace. Because these objectives dictate the scope of each exam, they provide you with critical information on how to prepare for Microsoft Office Specialist certification.

Microsoft Office Specialist Approved Courseware, including the Microsoft Press Step by Step series, is reviewed and approved on the basis of its coverage of the Microsoft Office Specialist exam objectives.

The Exam Experience

The Microsoft Office Specialist certification exams are unique in that they are performance-based examinations that allow you to interact with a "live" version of the Office application as you complete a series of assigned tasks. All the standard menus, toolbars and keyboard shortcuts are available—even the **Help** menu. Microsoft Office Specialist exams for Office XP applications consist of 25 to 35 questions, each of which requires you to complete one or more tasks using the Office application for which you are seeking certification. For example:

Prepare the document for publication as a Web page by completing the following three tasks:

1 Convert the memo to a Web page.

2 Title the page **Revised Company Policy**.

3 Name the memo **Policy Memo.htm**.

   The duration of Microsoft Office Specialist exams ranges from 45 to 60 minutes, depending on the application. Passing percentages range from 70 to 80 percent correct.

The Exam Interface and Controls

After you fill out a series of information screens, the testing software starts the exam and the respective Office application. You will see the exam interface and controls, including the test question, in the dialog box in the lower right corner of the screen.

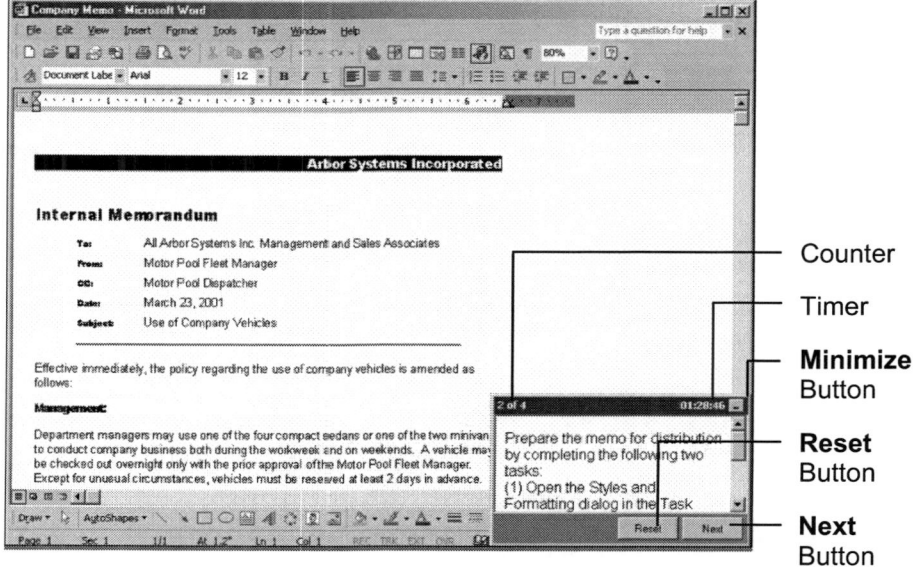

■ If the exam dialog box gets in the way of your work, you can hide it by clicking the Minimize button in the upper right corner, or you can drag it to another position on the screen.

■ The timer starts when the first question appears on your screen and displays the remaining exam time. The timer will not count the time required for the exam to be loaded between questions. It keeps track of only the time you spend answering questions. If the timer and the counter are distracting, click the timer to remove the display.

■ The counter tracks how many questions you have completed and how many remain.

■ The Reset button allows you to restart work on a question if you think you have made an error. The Reset button will not restart the entire exam or extend the exam time limit.

■ When you complete a question, click the **Next** button to move to the next question.

important

It is not possible to move back to a previous question on the exam.

Test-Taking Tips

■ Follow all instructions provided in each question completely and accurately.

■ Enter requested information as it appears in the instructions but without duplicating the formatting. For example, all text and values that you will be asked to enter will appear in the instructions as bold and underlined; however, you should enter the information without applying this formatting unless you are specifically instructed to do otherwise.

■ Close all dialog boxes before proceeding to the next exam question unless you are specifically instructed otherwise.

■ There is no need to save your work before moving on to the next question unless you are specifically instructed otherwise.

■ Do not cut and paste information from the exam interface into the application.

■ For questions that ask you to print a document, spreadsheet, chart, report, slide and so forth, nothing will actually be printed.

■ Responses are scored based on the result of your work, not the method you use to achieve that result (unless a specific method is explicitly required) and not the time you take to complete the question. Extra keystrokes or mouse clicks do not count against your score.

■ If your computer becomes unstable during the exam (for example, if the application's toolbars or the mouse no longer functions) or if a power outage occurs, contact a testing centre administrator immediately. The administrator will then restart the computer and the exam will return to the point before the interruption occurred.

Certification

At the conclusion of the exam, you will receive a score report, which you can print with the assistance of the testing centre administrator. If your score meets or exceeds the minimum required score, you will also be mailed a printed certificate within approximately 14 days.

For More Information

To learn more about becoming a Microsoft Office Specialist, visit *http;//www.microsoft.com/traincert/mcp/officespecialist.*

To purchase a Microsoft Office Specialist certification exam contact your nearest IQ testing centre.

Glossary

action query A type of query that updates or makes changes to multiple records in one operation.

Active Server Pages (ASP) Pages stored on a server that generate different views of the data in response to choices users make on a Web page.

aggregate function A function that groups and performs calculations on multiple fields.

arithmetic operator An operator that performs an arithmetic operation: + (addition), - (subtraction), * (multiplication), or / (division).

ASCII Acronym for *American Standard Code for Information Interchange*, a coding scheme for text characters developed in 1968. ASCII files have the extension *.asc*.

ASP Acronym for *Active Server Pages*.

AutoForm A feature that efficiently creates forms using all the available fields and minimal formatting.

back-end database The part of a split database that is stored on a server for security reasons, and which usually consists of the tables and other objects that you don't want people to be able to modify. *See also* front-end database.

binary file A file coded so that its data can be read by a computer.

Boolean A data type that can hold either of two mutually exclusive values, often expressed as *yes/no*, *1/10*, *on/off*, or *true/false*.

Bound Linked, as when a form used to view information in a table is linked to that table.

Briefcase A replication folder that you use to keep files in sync when you work on different computers in different locations.

class module One of two types of modules in Microsoft Visual Basic for Applications (VBA). A class module is associated with a specific form or report. *See also* standard module.

code VBA programs; also called *procedures*, referred to in Access as modules. *See also* class module; standard module.

combo box A control in which you can either select from a drop- down list or type an option.

comma-delimited text file A data file consisting of fields and records, stored as text, in which the fields are separated from each other by commas.

command button A control shaped like a button to which you can attach code that runs when the button is clicked.

comment A note embedded in code that helps people reading the code understand its purpose.

comparison operator An operator that compares values, such as < (less than), > (greater than), and = (equal to).

component A part of a database that is used to store and organize information. Also known as a database object.

compression A means of compacting information for more efficient means of transportation.

constant A named item that retains a constant value throughout the execution of a program, as opposed to a variable, whose value can change during execution.

control An object such as a label, text box, option button, or check box in a form or report that allows you to view or manipulate information stored in tables or queries.

control property A setting that determines the appearance of a control, what data it displays, and how that data looks. A control's properties can be viewed and changed in its Properties dialog box.

control source The source of a control's data—the field, table or query whose data will be displayed in the control.

criteria The specifications you give to Access so that it can find matching fields and records. Criteria can be simple, such as all the records with a postal code of 98052, or complex, such as the phone numbers of all customers who have placed orders for over $500 worth of live plants within the last two weeks and who live in postal codes 98052, 98053, and 98054.

crosstab query A query that calculates and restructures data for easier analysis. *See also* select query, parameter query, and action query.

data access page A dynamic Web page that allows users to directly manipulate data in a database via the Internet.

data source A database or file to which a data access page is connected.

data type The type of data that can be entered in a field: text, memo, number, date/time, currency, AutoNumber, Boolean (Yes/No), OLE object, and hyperlink. You set the data type by displaying the table in Design view.

data warehouse A company that serves as a data repository for a variety of data and that may make use of replication to keep each database synchronized when more than one version of the database is updated in more than one remote location.

database application A database that is refined and made simpler for the user by the sophisticated use of queries, forms, reports, a switchboard, and various other tools.

database program A program that stores data. Programs range from those that can store one table per file (referred to as a flat database) to those that can store many related tables per file (referred to as a relational database).

database security The protection of database information from accidental damage, destruction, or theft through the use of encryption, passwords, access permissions, replication, and other security measures.

database window The window from which all database objects can be manipulated or accessed.

Datasheet view The view in which the information in a table or query can be viewed and manipulated. *See also* views.

decrypting "Unscrambling" a database that has been encrypted for security reasons.

delimited text file A type of text file format in which each record and each field is separated from the next by a known character called a *delimiter*.

delimiter A character such as a comma (,), semicolon (;), or backslash (\), or pairs of characters such as quotation marks (" ") or braces ({}), that are used to separate records and fields in a delimited text file.

design grid The name given to the structure used in Design view to manually construct and modify advanced filters and queries.

Design Master In replication, the term for the version of the database from which replicas are made and where changes made to replicas are copied and synchronized.

Design view The view in which the structure of a table or query can be viewed and manipulated. *See also* views.

DHTML Acronym for *Dynamic Hypertext Markup Language.*

Dynamic Hypertext Markup Language (DHTML) A new version of the standard authoring language, HTML, that includes codes for dynamic Web page elements.

dynamic Web page A page whose content is created in response to some action on the part of a user who is viewing the page over the Internet. *See also* static HTML page.

encrypting "Scrambling" data for security reasons.

event An action performed by a user or by Access, to which a programmed response can be attached. Common user events include Click, Double Click, Mouse Down, Mouse Move, and Mouse Up. You can use macros or VBA modules to determine how Access responds when one of these events occurs.

exclusive use A setting used when you want to be the only person who currently has a database open. You must open a database for exclusive use when setting or removing a password that limits database access.

exporting The process of creating a file containing the information in a database table in a format that can be used by other programs.

expression A combination of functions, field values, constants, and operators that yield a result. Expressions can be simple, such as *>100*, or complex, such as *((ProductPrice*Quantity)*.90)+(Shipping+Handling).*

Expression Builder A feature used to create formulas (expressions) used in query criteria, form and report properties, and table validation rules.

Extensible Markup Language (XML) A refined language developed for Web documents that describes document structure rather than appearance.

field An individual item of the information that is the same type across all records. Represented in Access as a column in a database table. *See also* record.

fixed-width text file A common text file format that is often used to transfer data from older applications. Each record is always the same number of characters long, and the same field within the records is always the same number of characters. In other words, the same field always starts the same number of characters from the beginning of each record, and any characters not occupied by real data are filled with zeros.

flag A marker that can be set to true or false to indicate the state of an object.

flat database A simple database consisting of one table. *See also* relational database.

form A database object used to enter, edit, and manipulate information in a database table. A form gives you a simple view of some or all of the fields of one record at a time.

Form view The view in which you can enter and modify the information in a record. *See also* views.

front-end database The part of a split database that is distributed to the people who analyze and enter data. The actual data tables are stored on a server for security reasons. *See also* back-end database.

function A named procedure or routine in a program, often used for mathematical or financial calculations.

function procedure In VBA, a procedure that is enclosed in Function and End Function statements and returns a value. *See also* sub procedure.

group One of four elements—the other three being object, permission, and user—on which the Access user-level security model is based.

grouping level The level by which records are grouped in a report. For example, records might be grouped by state (first level), then by city (second level), and then by postal code (third level).

HTML Acronym for *Hypertext Markup Language*.

HTML tag An HTML command that determines how the tagged information looks and acts.

Hypertext Markup Language (HTML) The authoring language used to create Web documents.

importing The method whereby data is brought into an Access database from a different database or program. *See also* exporting.

input mask A field property that determines what data can be entered in the field, how the data looks, and the format in which it is stored.

intranet A secure, proprietary Web-based network used within a company or group and accessible only to its members.

keyword A word that is part of the VBA programming language.

label control An area on a form that contains text that appears on the form in Form view.

LAN Acronym for *local area network.*

Layout Preview A view of a report that shows you how each element will look but without all the detail of Print Preview.

linking The process of connecting to data in other applications.

local area network (LAN) A computer network that connects computers, printers, and other hardware to a server or group of servers.

logical operator One of the Boolean operators: AND, OR and NOT.

Lookup Wizard The wizard in Access that simplifies the creation of a Lookup list.

macro A set of automated instructions that perform a sequence of simple tasks.

main form One form that is linked to one or more tables. *See also* subform.

main report One report that displays records from one or more tables. *See also* subreport.

many-to-many relationship A relationship formed between two tables that each have a one-to-many relationship with a third table. *See also* one-to-many relationship; one-to-one relationship.

mapped network drive A drive to which you have assigned a drive letter. Used for quickly accessing files stored in locations that are not likely to change. *See also* UNC path.

mask A field property that determines what data can be entered in a field, how the data looks, and the format in which it is stored.

Microsoft Database Executable (MDE) A compiled version of a database. Saving a database as an MDE file compiles all modules, removes all editable source code, and compacts the destination database.

Microsoft Visual Basic for Applications (VBA) A high- level programming language developed for the purpose of creating Windows applications.

MDE Acronym for *Microsoft Database Executable.*

module A VBA program.

named range A group of cells in an Excel spreadsheet.

native format The file format an application uses to produce its own files.

navigation button One of the buttons found on a form or navigation bar that helps users display specific records.

network server A central computer that stores files and programs and manages system functions for a network.

object One of the components of an Access database, such as a table, form, or report.

one-to-many relationship A relationship formed between two tables in which each record in one table has more than one related record in the other table. *See also* many-to-many relationship; one- to-one relationship.

one-to-one relationship A relationship formed between two tables in which each record in one table has only one related record in the other table. *See also* many-to-many relationship; one-to- many relationship.

operator *See* arithmetic operator; comparison operator; logical operator.

optimistic locking Locking a record only for the brief time that Access is saving changes to it.

option button A control on a form that allows users to select preferred settings.

page *See* data access page.

parameter query A query that prompts for the information to be used in the query, such as a range of dates.

parsing In Access, the process of analyzing a document and identifying anything that looks like structured data.

password A secret sequence of letters and other symbols needed to log on to a database as an authorized user.

permission An attribute that specifies how a user can access data or objects in a database.

pessimistic locking Locking a record for the entire time it is being edited.

PivotChart An interactive chart that is linked to a database.

PivotTable An interactive table that is linked to a database.

populate To fill a table or other object with data.

primary key One or more fields that determine the uniqueness of each record in a database.

Print Preview A view of a report that allows users to see exactly how the report will look when printed.

procedure VBA code that performs a specific task or set of tasks.

property A setting that determines the content and appearance of the object to which it applies.

query A database object that locates information so that the information can be viewed, changed, or analyzed in various ways. The results of a query can be used as the basis for forms, reports, and data access pages.

record selector The grey bar along the left edge of a table or form.

record source The place from which information derives between two bound objects, such as a field that pulls information from a table. *See also* control source.

record All the items of information (fields) that pertain to one particular entity, such as a customer, employee, or project. *See also* field.

referential integrity The system of rules Access uses to ensure that relationships between tables are valid and that data cannot be changed in one table without also being changed in all related tables.

relational database A sophisticated type of database in which data is organized in multiple related tables. Data can be pulled from the tables just as if they were stored in a single table.

relationship An association between common fields in two tables.

replica A copy of the Design Master of a database.

replicating The process of creating a Design Master so that multiple copies of a database can be sent to multiple locations for editing. The copies can then be synchronized with the Design Master so that it reflects all the changes.

report A database object used to display a table or tables in a formatted, easily accessible manner, either on the screen or on paper.

row selector The grey box at the left end of a row in a table that, when clicked, selects all the cells in the row.

running a query The process of telling Access to search the specified table or tables for records that match the criteria you have specified in the query and to display the designated fields from those records in a datasheet (table). *See also* criteria; query.

saving The process of storing the current state of a database or database object for later retrieval. In Access, new records and changes to existing records are saved when you move to a different record; you don't have to do anything to save them. You do have to save new objects and changes to existing objects.

schema A description of the structure of XML data, as opposed to the content of the data. Applications that export to XML might combine the content and schema in one .xml file or might create an .xml file to hold the content and an .xsd file to hold the schema.

select query A query that retrieves data matching specified criteria from one or more tables and displays the results in a datasheet.

selector A small box attached to an object that you click to select the object.

sharing a database Providing access to a database so more that one person can access it to add or alter its information.

splash screen An introductory screen containing useful or entertaining information. Often used to divert the user's attention while data is loading.

SQL Acronym for *Structured Query Language*.

SQL database A database that supports SQL and that can be accessed simultaneously by several users on a LAN.

standard module A VBA program that contains general procedures that are not associated with any object.

static HTML page A Web page that provides a snapshot of some portion of the database contents at one point in time.

string A series of characters enclosed in quotation marks.

sub procedure A series of VBA statements enclosed by Sub and End Sub statements.

subdatasheet A datasheet that is embedded in another datasheet.

subform A form inserted in a control that is embedded in another form.

subreport A report inserted in a control that is embedded in another report.

switchboard A form used to navigate among the objects of a database application so that users don't have to be familiar with the actual database.

synchronizing The process of comparing the information in a database replica with the database's Design Master and merging any changes.

syntax The format that expressions must conform to in order for Access to be able to process them.

table Information organized in columns (records) and rows (fields).

Table Wizard The Access tool that helps users construct tables.

tags Codes in HTML that give instructions for formatting or other actions.

task pane A pane that provides a quick and easy way of initiating common tasks.

template A ready-made database application that users can tailor to fit their needs.

text box control A control on a form or report where data from a table can be entered or edited.

transaction record The written record of transactions.

unbound Not linked, as when a control is used to calculate values from two or more fields and is therefore not bound to any particular field. *See also* bound.

UNC Acronym for *universal naming convention.*

universal naming convention (UNC) path A path format that includes the computer name, drive letter, and nested folder names. *See also* mapped network drive.

update query A select query that changes the query's results in some way, such as by changing a field.

user A person authorized to access a database but who generally is not involved in establishing its structure.

validation rule A field property that tests entries to ensure that only the correct types of information become part of a table.

variable A name or symbol that stands for a value that can change.

VBA Acronym for *Microsoft Visual Basic for Applications.*

VBA procedure A VBA program.

view The display of information from a specific perspective.

Visual Basic Editor The environment in which VBA code is written.

Visual Basic Integrated Development Environment (IDE) *See* Visual Basic Editor.

Web browser An application used to view Web pages on the World Wide Web.

WIF Acronym for *workgroup information file.*

wildcard character A placeholder for an unknown character or characters in search criteria.

wizard A helpful tool that guides users through the steps for completing a specific task.

workgroup information file (WIF) The file where information about the objects, permissions, users, and groups that comprise a specific workgroup is stored.

worksheet A page in a Microsoft Excel spreadsheet.

XML Acronym for *Extensible Markup Language.*

LESSON 1: Getting to Know Microsoft Access 2002

After completing this chapter, you will be able to:

✓ *Open an existing database*

✓ *Open tables in different views*

✓ *Open and run queries*

✓ *Open a form in different views*

✓ *Open a report in different views*

This book gives you straightforward instructions for using Microsoft Access 2002 to create databases. It takes you from knowing little or nothing about Access—or, for that matter, about databases—to a level of expertise that will enable you to develop database applications for use by one person or by many.

This chapter introduces the concept of a database, explains a little about Access, and then takes you on a tour. The database you will use for the tour belongs to The Garden Company, a fictional garden supply and plant store. (You will be working with this database throughout this book.) Although looking at someone else's work might not be as exciting as jumping in and creating your own database, this tour will give you a firm foundation from which to begin working with Access to create your own databases.

In this chapter, you will open the GardenCo database, explore its structure, and look at some of the objects used to store and manipulate the data it contains. You will be working with the GardenCo database files that are stored in the following subfolders of the *SBS\Access\KnowAccess* folder: *Open, Tables, Queries, Forms,* and *Reports.*

tip

To follow along with the exercises in this book, you need to install the practice files from the companion CD. (You cannot just copy the files.) You will find instructions for installing the files in the "Using the Book's CD" section at the beginning of the book.

What Is a Database?

In its most basic form, a database is the computer equivalent of an organized list of information. Typically, this information has a common subject or purpose, such as the list of employees shown here:

ID	LastName	FirstName	Title	Hire Date
1	Dale	Martha	Sales Rep	May 1, 1992
2	Fuller	Joanna	V.P., Sales	Aug 14, 1992
3	Lee	Mark	Sales Rep	Apr 1, 1992
4	Penn	Daniel	Sales Rep	May 3, 1993

This list is arranged in a **table** of columns and rows, called **fields** and **records** in database terms. Each column (field) stores a particular type of information about an employee: first name, last name, date of hire, and so on. Each row (record) contains information about a different employee.

If a database did nothing more than store information in a table, it would be as useful as a paper list. But because the database stores information in an electronic format, you can manipulate the information in powerful ways to extend its utility.

For example, a phone book for your city is probably sitting on a shelf within a few feet of you. If you want to locate a person or a business in your city, you can do so, because the information in the telephone book is organized in an understandable manner. If you want to get in touch with someone a little further away, you can go to the public library and use its collection of phone books, which probably includes one for each major city in the country. However, if you want to find the phone numbers of all the people in the country with your last name, or if you want the phone number of your grandmother's neighbour, these phone books won't do you much good because they aren't organized in a way that makes that information easy to find.

When the information published in a phone book is stored in a database, it takes up far less space, it costs less to reproduce and distribute, and, if the database is designed correctly, the information can be retrieved in many ways. The real power of a database isn't in its ability to store information; it is in your ability to quickly retrieve exactly the information you want from the database.

What's Special About Access?

Simple **database programs**, such as the Database component of Microsoft Works, can store information in only one table, which is often referred to as a flat file. These simple databases are often called **flat databases**. More complex database programs, such as Microsoft Access, can store information in multiple related tables, thereby creating what are often referred to as **relational databases**If the information in a relational database is organized correctly, you can treat these multiple tables as a single storage area and pull information electronically from different tables in whatever order meets your needs.

A table is just one of the types of **objects** . that you can work with in Access. The following graphic shows all the Access object types:

The table is the most important database object and all the other objects are based on it. The table contains all the information used by the other objects.

Objects

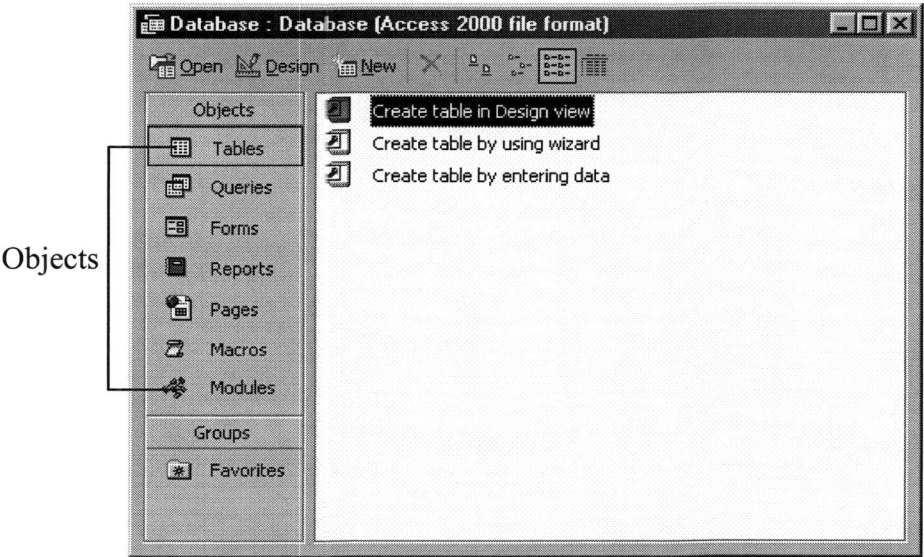

tip

For maximum compatibility with existing databases, the default format for new databases created with Access 2002 is Access 2000.

Of all these object types, only one—tables—is used to store information. The rest are used to manage, manipulate, analyze, retrieve, display, or publish the table information—in other words, to make the information as accessible and therefore as useful as possible.

Over the years, Microsoft has put a lot of effort into making Access not only one of the most powerful consumer database programs available, but also one of the easiest to learn and use. Because Access is part of the Microsoft Office suite of programs, you can use many of the techniques you know from using other Office applications, such as Microsoft Word and Microsoft Excel, when using Access. For example, you can use familiar commands, buttons, and keyboard shortcuts to open and edit the information in Access tables. And because Access is integrated with other members of the suite, you can easily share information between Access and Word, Excel, or other programs.

Opening an Existing Database

The database for The Garden Company, which is called *GardenCo*, contains information about its employees, products, suppliers, and customers that is stored in a series of tables. As you complete the exercises in this book, you will work with these tables and develop an assortment of queries, forms, reports, data access pages, macros, and modules that can be used to enter, edit, and manipulate the information in the tables in many ways.

GardenCo

In this exercise, you will open the GardenCo database, explore some of its objects, and then close the database. You won't find a lot of detailed explanation here, because this is just an overview. The working folder for this exercise is *SBS\Access\KnowAccess\Open*. Follow these steps:

1   At the left end of the taskbar at the bottom of your screen, click the **Start** button, point to **Programs**, and then click **Microsoft Access**.

When Access first opens, your screen looks like this:

Menu Bar   Toolbar   Task Pane

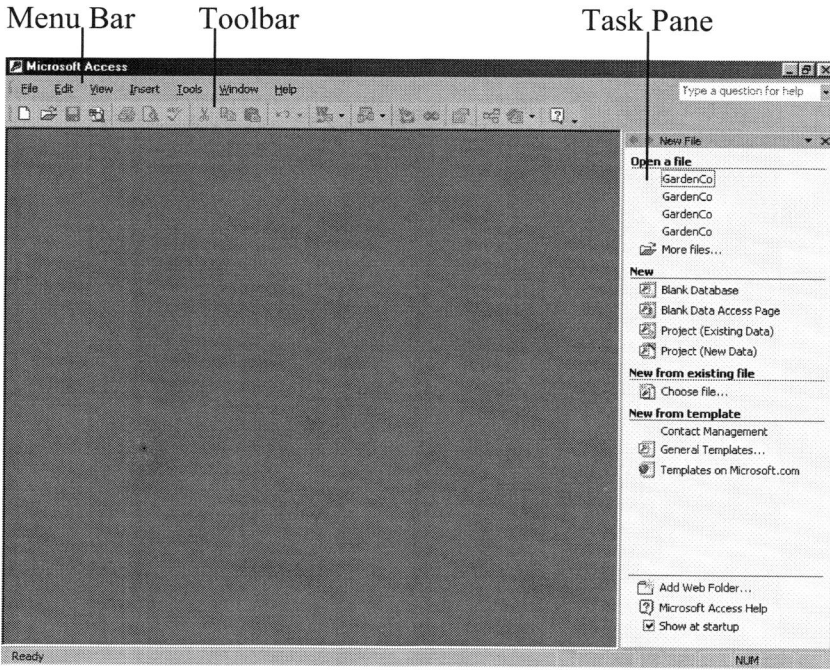

important

What you see on your screen might not match the graphics in this book exactly. The screens in this book were captured on a monitor set to 800 x 600 resolution with 24-bit colour and the Windows Standard colour scheme. The book starts with the Access default settings, and the screens reflect any changes to those settings that are called for by the steps in the exercises.

Task Pane
new for
OfficeXP

As with other Microsoft Office applications, Access has a menu bar and one or more toolbars across the top of the window. New to programs in Microsoft Office XP is the **task pane** shown at the right side of this window. In Access, a different version of the task pane appears when you click either **New** or **Search** on the **File** menu, or click **Office Clipboard** on the **Edit** menu.

Open

2   Click the **Open** button on the toolbar, and then browse to the *SBS\Access\KnowAccess\Open* folder, and double-click **GardenCo**.

The Garden Company introductory screen, called a **splash screen**, appears.

tip

You will normally open a database by double-clicking its file name in Windows Explorer. (Access databases have a file name extension *.mdb.*) Or you can start Access and click **New** on the **File** menu to display the **New File** task pane, which offers a variety of options for opening new or existing databases.

3   Select the **Don't show this screen again** check box, and then click **OK**.

You see this **switchboard**, which is used to easily access the database objects needed to perform common tasks:

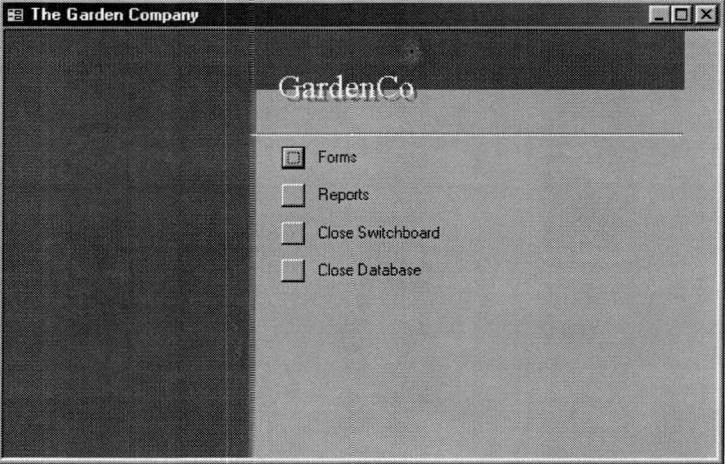

4   Click **Close Switchboard** to close the switchboard.

Restore

5   The database window is minimized as a small title bar in the lower left corner of your screen. Click the **Restore** button in this title bar to expand the database window.

The GardenCo **database window** looks like this:

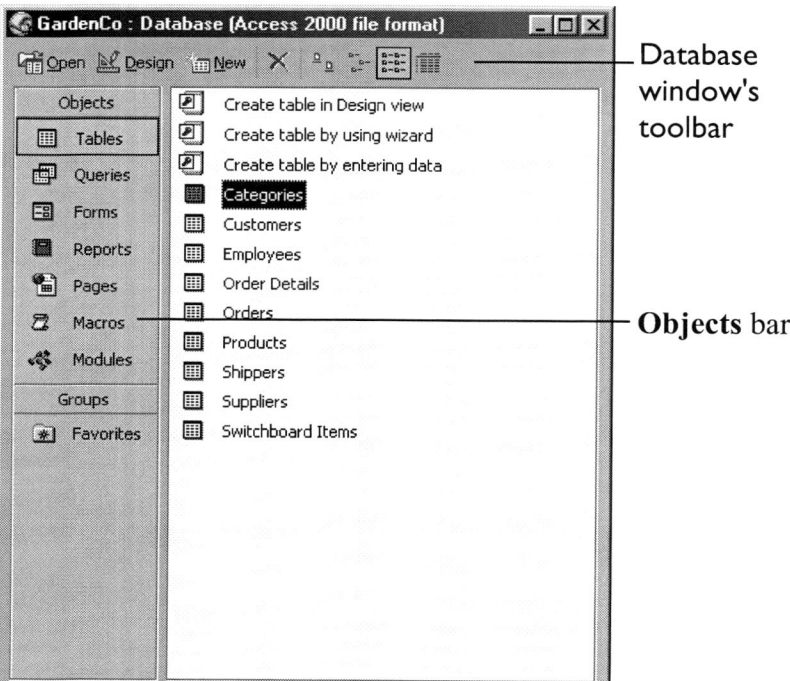

Database window's toolbar

Objects bar

Across the top of the window is a toolbar and along the left edge is the **Objects** bar, which lists the Access database objects. Because **Tables** is selected, the right pane of the window lists the tables contained in the database.

6   Close the **GardenCo** database by clicking **Close** on the **File** menu.

Exploring Tables

Ac2002-1-2
Ac2002-5-3
Ac2002-5-4

Tables are the core database objects. Their purpose is to store information. The purpose of every other database object is to interact in some manner with one or more tables. An Access database can contain thousands of tables, and the number of records each table can contain is limited more by the space available on your hard disk than anything else.

tip

For detailed information about Access specifications, such as the maximum size of a database or the maximum number of records in a table, click the Ask A Question box at the right end of the menu bar, type **Access specifications**, and press ⌷Enter⌷.

The Design view allows you to modify the type of information which the fields can contain.

Every Access object has two or more **views**. For tables, the two most common views are **Datasheet view**, where you can see and modify the table's data, and **Design view**, where you can see and modify the table's structure. Clicking the **View** button toggles the view of the open table between Datasheet and Design views. You can also click the down arrow to the right of the **View** button and select a view from the drop-down list.

When you view a table in Datasheet view, you see the table's data in columns (fields) and rows (records), as shown here:

Row selector   Column header

Row (record)   Column (field)

Products : Table

Product ID	Product Name	Latin Name	Supplier	Category
1	Magic Lily	Lycoris squamigera	The Bulb Basket	Bulbs
2	Autumn crocus	Colchicum	The Bulb Basket	Bulbs
3	Compost Bin		Garden Hardware Mfg.	Tools
4	Cactus Sand Potting Mix		Soil and Sand Supplier	Soils/Sand
5	Weeping Forsythia	Forsythia suspensa	The Shrub Club	Shrubs/Hedges
6	Bat Box		NoTox Pest Control	Pest Control
7	Electronic Insect Killer		NoTox Pest Control	Pest Control
8	Beneficial nematodes	Neoaplectana carpocaps	NoTox Pest Control	Pest Control
9	Crown Vetch	Coronilla varia	Cover Up Stuff	Ground Covers
10	English Ivy	Hedera helix	Cover Up Stuff	Ground Covers
11	Austrian Copper	R. foetida bicolor	Rosie's Roses	Roses
12	Persian Yellow Rose	R. foetida 'Persiana'	Rosie's Roses	Roses
13	Indoor Magic Potting Soil		Soil and Sand Supplier	Soils/Sand
14	GrowGood Potting Soil		Soil and Sand Supplier	Soils/Sand
15	Sterilized Soil		Soil and Sand Supplier	Soils/Sand
16	Winterberry	Ilex verticillata	The Shrub Club	Shrubs/Hedges
17	Anise	Pimpinella anisum	The Herb House	Herbs
18	Crushed Rock		Wholesale Rock & Gravel	Soils/Sand
19	Chamomile	Anthemis nobilis	The Herb House	Herbs
20	English lavender	Lavandula angustifolia	The Herb House	Herbs
21	Peppermint	Mentha piperita	The Herb House	Herbs

Record: 1 of 189

New Record button
Last Record button
Next Record button
Previous Record button
First Record button

When tables have fields in common a relationship exists between them.

If two tables have one or more fields in common, you can embed the datasheet for one table in another. The embedded datasheet, which is called a **subdatasheet**, allows you to see the information in more than one table at the same time. For example, you might want to embed an Orders datasheet in a Customers table so that you can see the orders each customer has placed.

GardenCo

In this exercise, you will open existing tables in the GardenCo database and explore their structure in different views. The working folder for this exercise is *SBS\Access\KnowAccess\Tables*. Follow these steps:

1 Open the **GardenCo** database located in the working folder.

2 Click **Tables** on the **Objects** bar.

Details

Because the **Details** button is active on the toolbar at the top of the database window, a description of each of the objects listed in the window is displayed to the right of its name.

tip

You can resize the columns in the database window by dragging the vertical bar that separates columns in the header. You can set the width of a column to the width of its widest entry by double-clicking the vertical bar.

Maximize

3 Click the **Maximize** button in the upper right corner of the database window.

The database window expands to fill the Access window, and you can now read the table descriptions. Note that the first three items in the **Name** column are not tables; they are shortcuts to three commands you can use to create a new table.

Restore

4   Click the **Restore** button to shrink the database window again.

5   Click the **Categories** table, and then click the **Open** button at the top of the database window.

The table opens in Datasheet view, as shown here:

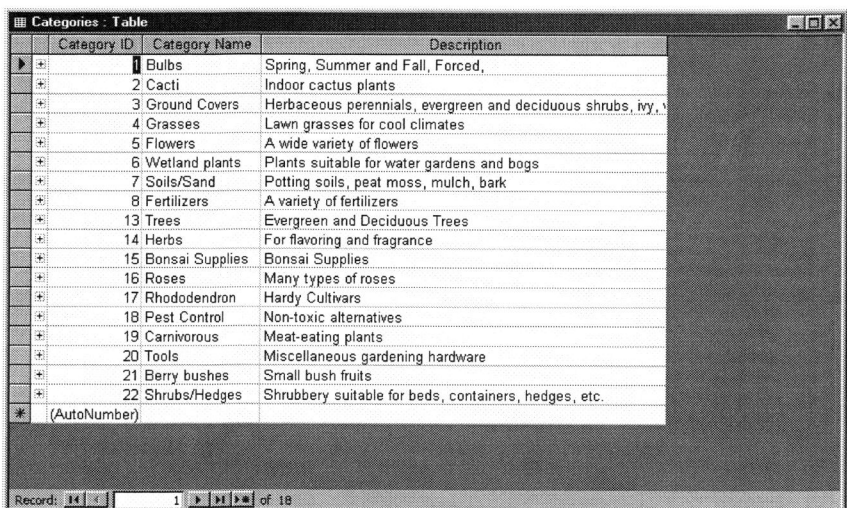

This datasheet contains a list of the categories of products sold by The Garden Company. As you can see, there are fields for Category ID, Category Name, and Description.

6   Click the plus sign to the left of the record for the Bulbs category.

Clicking the plus sign expands an embedded subdatasheet. You are now looking at category records from the Categories table and product records from the Products table simultaneously, as shown here:

Notice that the plus sign has changed to a minus sign.

7   Click the minus sign to the left of the Bulbs record to collapse the subdatasheet.

8   Close the **Categories** table by clicking **Close** on the **File** menu. If you are prompted to save changes to the table layout, click **Yes**.

tip

You can also close a window by clicking the **Close** button in the window's upper right corner. When an object window is maximized, this button is called the **Close Window** button to avoid confusion with the **Close** button at the right end of the Access window's title bar. Be careful to click the correct button, or else you will quit Access.

9   On the **Objects** bar, double-click the **Orders** table to open it in Datasheet view, like this:

The navigation area at the bottom of the window indicates that this table contains 87 records and that the active record is number 1.

Next Record

10 Move the selection one record at a time by clicking the **Next Record** button several times.

The selection moves down the OrderID field, because that field contains the insertion point.

tip

You can move the selection one record at a time by pressing the ⬆ or ⬇ key, one screen at a time by pressing the Page Up or Page Down key, and to the first or last field in the table by pressing Ctrl ✛ Home or Ctrl ✛ Enter .

11 Move directly to record 40 by selecting the current record number, typing **40**, and pressing Enter .

12 Close the **Orders** table, clicking **No** if you are prompted to save changes to the table's layout.

13 Double-click **Products** in the list of tables to open it in Datasheet view.

Notice that this table contains 189 records.

View

14 Click the **View** button on the toolbar to switch the view of the Products table to Design view.

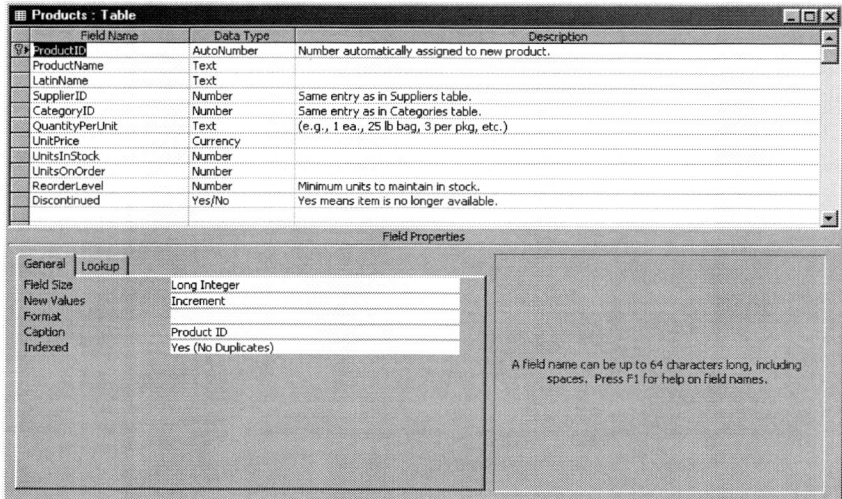

In Datasheet view, you see the data stored in the table, whereas in Design view, you see the underlying table structure.

Close

15 Close the **Products** table by clicking its **Close** button. If prompted to save changes to the table layout, click **No**.

16 Close the **GardenCo** database by clicking its **Close** button.

Exploring Queries

One way you can locate information in an Access database is to create **queries**. You use queries to locate information so that you can view, change, or analyze it in various ways. You can also use the results of queries as the basis for other Access objects.

A query is a request to view or analyze data from specific fields.

A query is essentially a question. For example, you might ask, "Which records in the Customer table have the value 98052 in the Postal Code field?" When you **run a query** (the equivalent of asking a question), Access looks at all the records in the table or tables you have specified, finds those that match the criteria you have defined, and displays them in a datasheet.

In order for Access to be able to answer your questions, you have to structure queries in a very specific way. Each type of question has a corresponding type of query. The primary query types are select, crosstab, and parameter. Less common types are action, AutoLookup, and SQL (Structured Query Language). Access includes wizards that quickly guide you through the creation of the more common queries; the less common ones have to be created by hand in a **design grid** in Design view. Here's what a typical query looks like:

Relationship between tables Table field list Table area

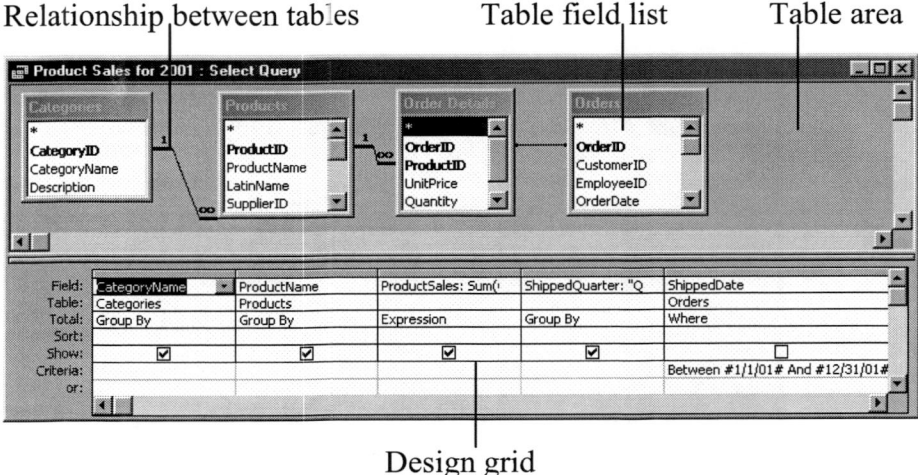

Design grid

At the top of this query window are four small windows, listing the fields in the four tables that will be included in this query. The lines connecting the tables indicate that they are related by virtue of common fields. The first row of the grid contains the names of the fields to be included in the query, and the second row shows which table each field belongs to. The third row (labelled **Total**) enables you to perform calculations on the field values, and the fourth indicates whether the query results will be sorted on this field. A check mark in the check box in the fifth row (labelled **Show**) means that the field will be displayed in the results datasheet. (If the check box is not selected, the field can be used in determining the query results, but it will not be displayed.) The sixth row (labelled **Criteria**) contains criteria that determine which records will be displayed, and the seventh row (labelled **or**) sets up alternate criteria.

Don't worry if this all sounds a bit complicated at the moment. When you approach queries logically, they soon begin to make perfect sense. And don't worry if they sound like a lot of work. The **Query Wizard** is available to help you structure the query, and if you create a query that you are likely to run more than once, you can save it. It then becomes part of the database and is displayed in the database window when you click **Queries** on the **Objects** bar.

GardenCo

In this exercise, you will explore a few of the queries that have already been defined and saved in the GardenCo database. The working folder for this exercise is *SBS\Access\KnowAccess\Queries*. Follow these steps:

1 Open the **GardenCo** database located in the working folder.

2 Click **Queries** on the **Objects** bar.

The database window displays all the queries that have been saved as part of the GardenCo database.

3 Double-click the title bar of the database window to maximize the window.

Your screen looks like this:

Command icon   Delete query icon

Update query icon   Select query icon

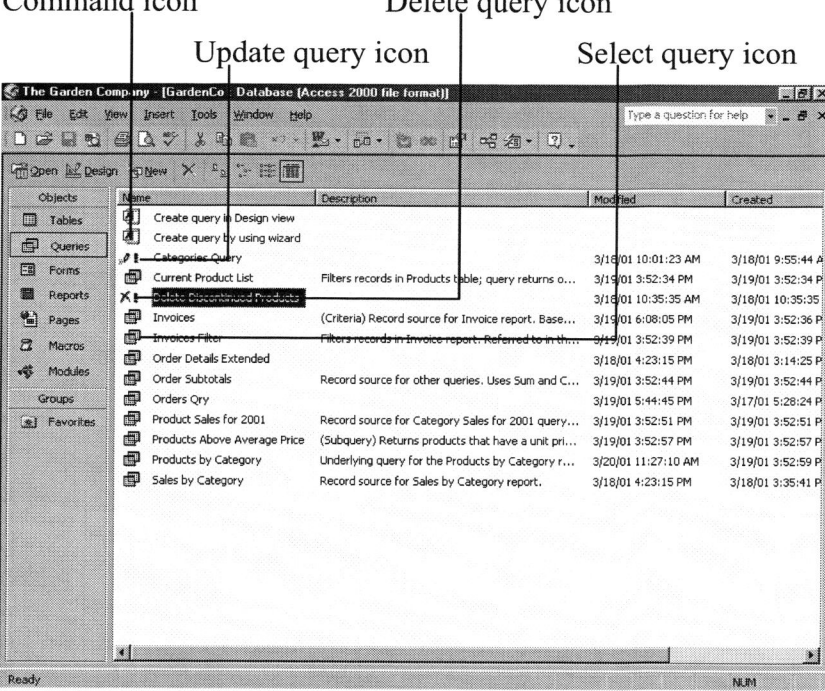

The top two entries in this window are commands for creating queries. The remaining entries are queries that have already been created. The description of each query explains its purpose. The icon in the **Name** column is an indication of the query's type, as is the information in the **Type** column, which you can see by scrolling the window to the right.

Restore

4   Restore the database window to its original size by clicking the **Restore** button at the right end of the menu bar (not the title bar).

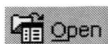

5   Open the **Products by Category** query in Datasheet view by selecting it and clicking the **Open** button at the top of the database window.

When you open the query, Access processes, or *runs*, it and produces a datasheet that displays the results shown on the next page.

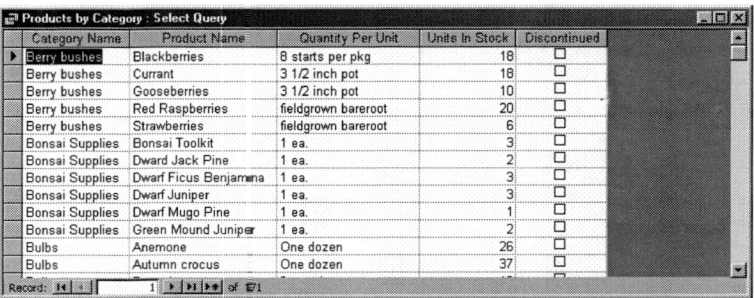

The navigation bar tells you that 171 records are displayed. The Products table contains 189 records. To find out why 18 of the records are missing, you need to look at this query in Design view.

View

6   Click the **View** button on the toolbar to view the query in Design view, where it looks like this:

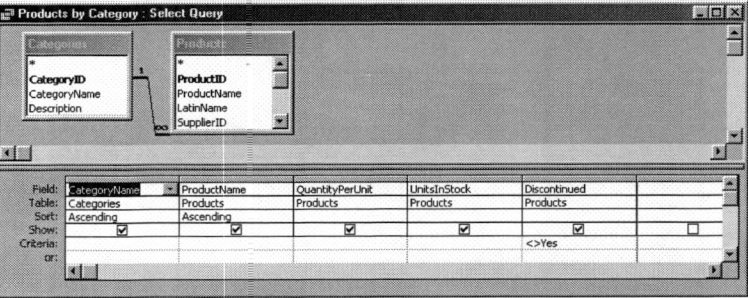

In the top part of the query window, two boxes list the fields of the tables this query is designed to work with. The bottom part is the design grid, where the query is formed. Each column of the grid can refer to one field from one of the tables above. Notice that <> Yes (*not equal to Yes*) has been entered in the **Criteria** row for the Discontinued field. This query therefore finds all the records that don't have a value of *Yes* in that field (in other words, that have not been discontinued).

Run

7   As an experiment, select **<>Yes** in the **Criteria** row for **Discontinued**, type =Yes, and then click the **Run** button on the toolbar.

> ## tip
> You can also run a query by switching to Datasheet view.

You changed the query so that it finds all the records that have a value of *Yes* in the Discontinued field (in other words, that have been discontinued). Here are the results:

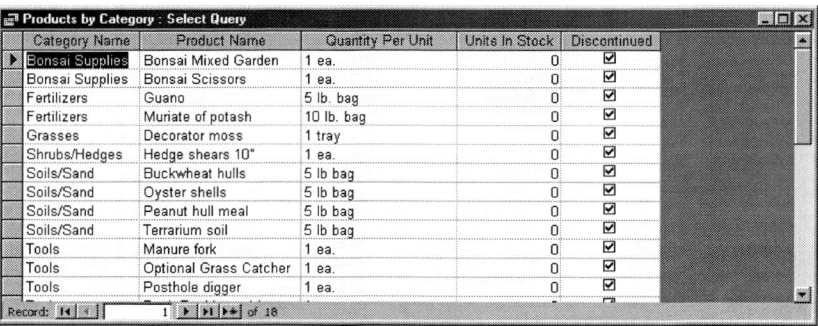

The 18 discontinued products account for the difference in the number of records in the Products table and the number of records displayed by the original query.

8   Close the query window, clicking **No** when prompted to save the design changes.

9   Close the **GardenCo** database.

Exploring Forms

Access tables are dense lists of raw information. If you create a database that only you will use, you will probably be very comfortable working directly with tables. But if you create a database that will be viewed and edited by people who don't know much about it—and don't necessarily want to know about it—working with your tables might be overwhelming. To solve this problem, you can design **forms** to guide users through your database, making it easier for them to enter, retrieve, display, and print information.

A form adds graphic elements to a table and is used primarily to enter or display data in a database.

A form is essentially a window in which you can place **controls** that either give users information or enable them to enter information. Access provides a toolbox that includes many standard Windows controls, such as labels, text boxes, option buttons, and check boxes. With a little ingenuity, you can use these controls to create forms that look and work much like the dialog boxes in all Microsoft Windows applications.

Form view allows you to add, delete or search for records. Design view allows you to make changes to formats or controls.

You use forms to edit the records of the underlying tables or enter new records. As with tables and queries, you can display forms in several views. The three most common views are **Form view**, where you enter data; **Datasheet view**, which looks essentially like a table; and **Design view**, where you work with the elements of the form to refine the way it looks and works. The graphic on the next page shows what a form looks like in Design view.

Form title

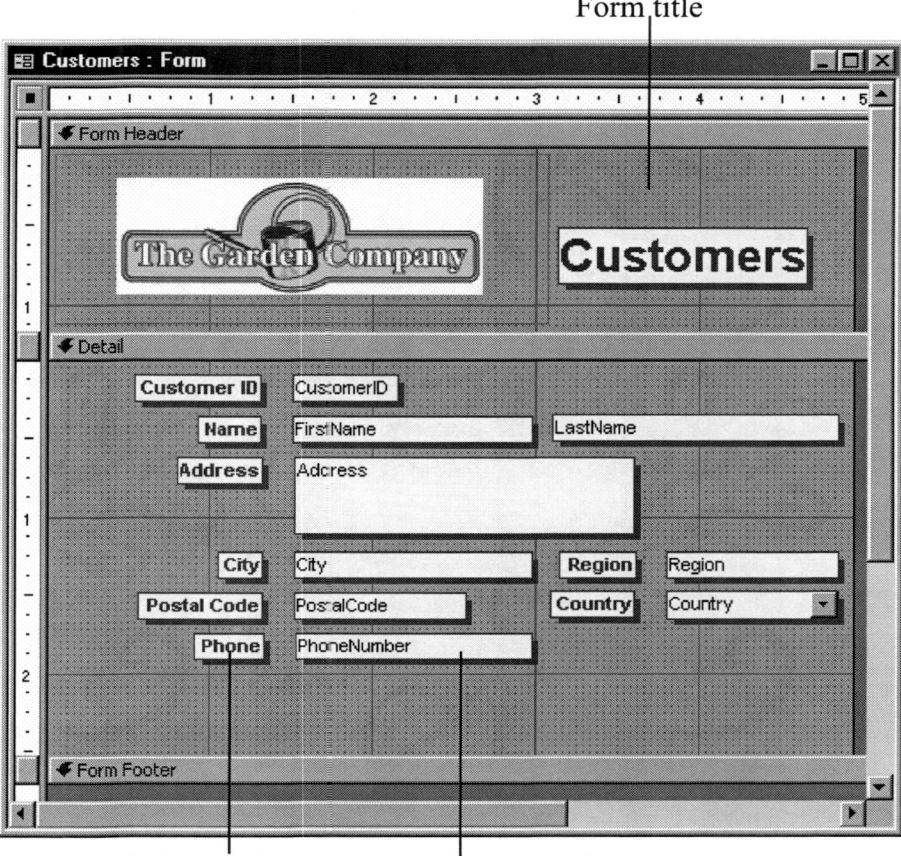

Label control   Text box control

This form consists of a **main form** that is linked to just one table. But a form can also include **subforms** that are linked to other tables. Arranged on the form are **label controls** containing text that appears on the form in Form view, and **text box controls** that will contain data from the table. Although you can create a form from scratch in Design view, you will probably use this view most often to refine the forms you create with a wizard.

GardenCo

In this exercise, you will take a look at a few of the forms in the GardenCo database that have been designed to make viewing tables, editing existing information, and adding new information easier and less error-prone. The working folder for this exercise is *SBS\Access\KnowAccess\Forms*. Follow these steps:

The bound controls contain table information; the non-bound controls are the field names.

1 Open the **GardenCo** database located in the working folder.

2 Click **Forms** on the **Objects** bar, and then double-click **Switchboard** to open the main switchboard, which looks like this:

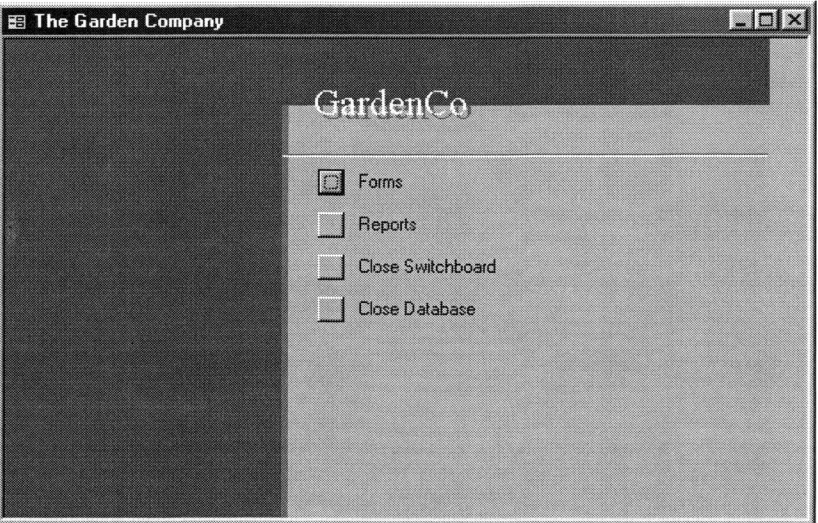

The Switchboard form has a customized title bar at the top, a title for the GardenCo database, and four command buttons. The first two buttons open switchboards—other forms—that have the same name as the button.

3 Click the **Forms** button on the switchboard to display the Forms switchboard.

4 Click **Edit/Enter Orders** to display this Orders form:

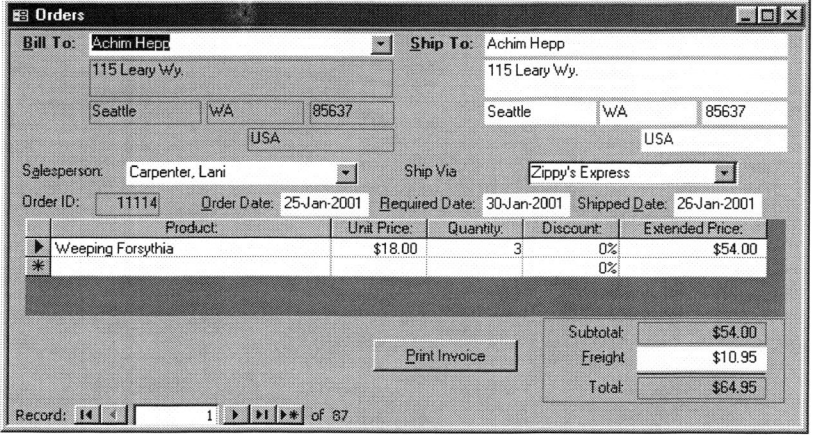

This form consists of a main form and a subform.

Next Record

5 Click the **Next Record** button on the navigation bar to display that record's information, and then click the **New Record** button (the asterisk) to display a blank form where you could enter a new order.

New Record

6 Close the **Orders** form, and click **Return** in the **Forms** switchboard to redisplay the main switchboard.

7 Click the **Close Switchboard** button.

8 In the database window, double-click **Products** in the **Forms** list to open this form:

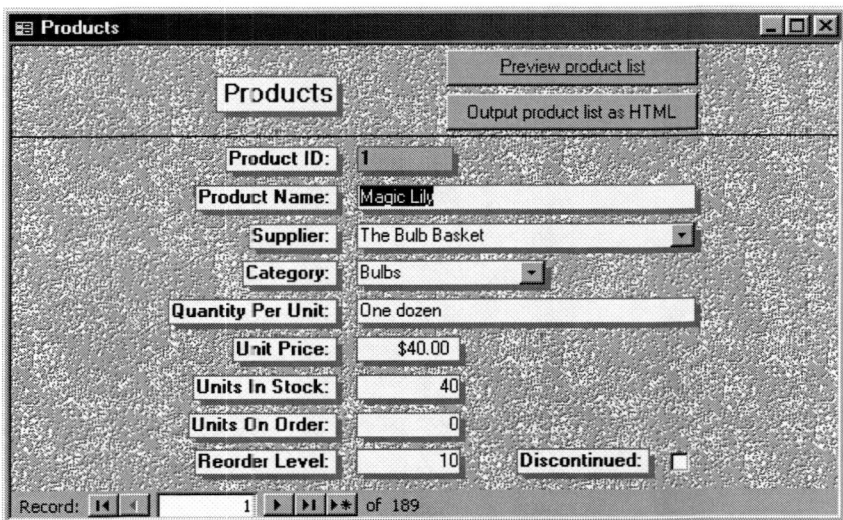

You use this form to edit the records of current products or enter new ones.

View

9 You are currently looking at the form in Form view. On the toolbar, click the **View** button's down arrow, and click **Datasheet View**.

Now the form looks essentially like the Products table in Datasheet view but without gridlines, as shown here:

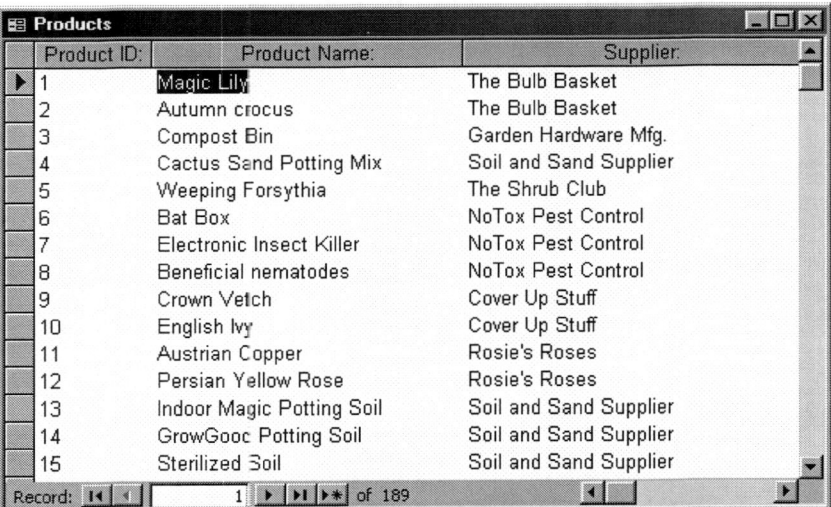

10 Click the **View** button again to switch to Design view, and then maximize the form window.

Toolbox

11 If the toolbox is not displayed, click the **Toolbox** button on the toolbar.

Your screen now looks like this:

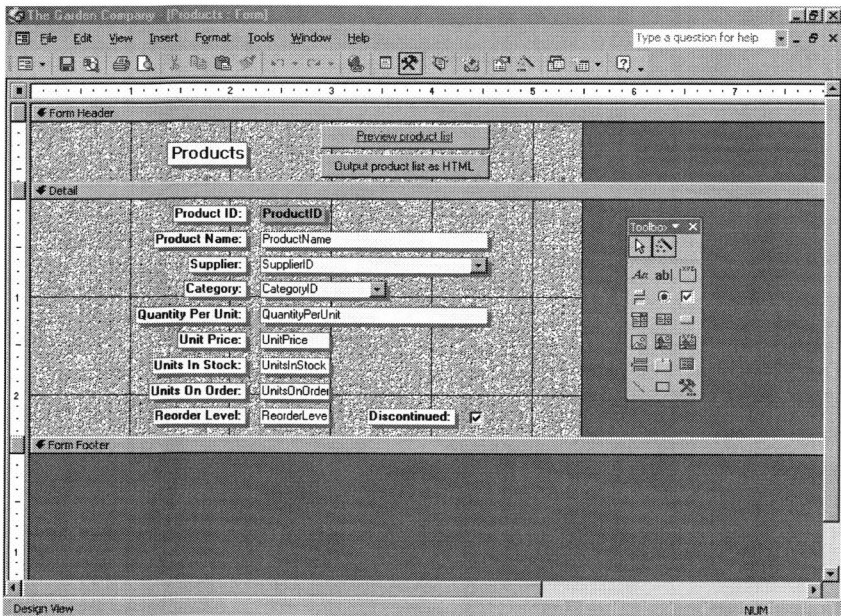

tip

If the toolbox is in the way, drag it by its title bar to where it's not obscuring anything, as shown above.

12 Point to each of the icons in the toolbox until the name of the tool is displayed.

These are the tools you use to build custom forms for your database.

13 Close the **Products** form, and then close the database.

Exploring Reports

Ac2002-7-3

You use **reports** to display the information from your tables in nicely formatted, easily accessible ways, either on your computer screen or on paper. A report can include items of information selected from multiple tables and queries, values calculated from information in the database, and formatting elements such as headers, footers, titles, and headings.

You can look at reports in three views: Design view, where you can manipulate the design of a report in the same way that you manipulate a form; **Print Preview,** where you see your report exactly as it will look when printed; and **Layout Preview**, which shows you how all each element will look but without all the detail of Print Preview. A report in Design view looks as shown on the next page.

Label control   Report title (appears on first page)

Products by Category : Report

Report Header

Products by Category

=Format(Date()," dd-mi

Page Header

CategoryName Header

Category: CategoryName

Product Name: Units In Stock:

Detail

ProductName   UnitsIr

CategoryName Footer

Number of Products: Vame])

Page Footer

="Page " & [Pa|

Report Footer

Text box control   Page number (appears on
                                     every page)

GardenCo

In this exercise, you will take a look at a report that has been saved as part of the GardenCo database, just to get an idea of what is possible. The working folder for this exercise is *SBS\Access\KnowAccess\Reports*. Follow these steps:

1   Open the **GardenCo** database located in the working folder.

2   Click **Reports** on the **Objects** bar.

    The top two entries in this window are commands you can use to create reports. The remaining entries are reports that have already been created.

3   Click **Customer Labels**, and then click the **Preview** button at the top of the database window to display the report.

    This report prints customer names and addresses in a mailing label format. You are looking at it in a view that is much like Print Preview in other Microsoft Windows programs.

tip

Access provides a wizard that can help you create a mailing label report. You can also use the Customer table in this database with Word's mail merge feature to create these labels.

4   Click in the form to change the zoom level.

tip

If the report is too small to read in Print Preview, you can also select a zoom level in the **Zoom** box on the toolbar.

5 Close the **Customer Labels** report.

6 In the database window, click the **Invoice** report, and click the **Preview** button to see the invoice shown here:

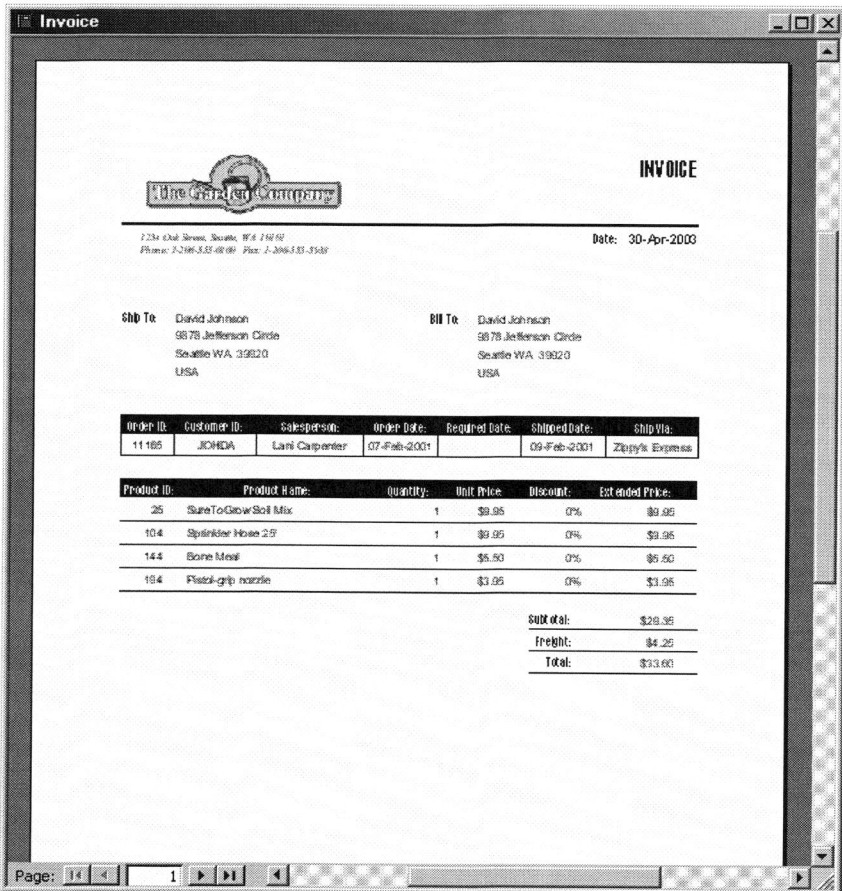

7 Check out each page by clicking the navigation buttons at the bottom of the window.

View

8 Click the **View** button on the toolbar to display the report in Design view, and then maximize the report window so that your screen looks like the one shown on the following page.

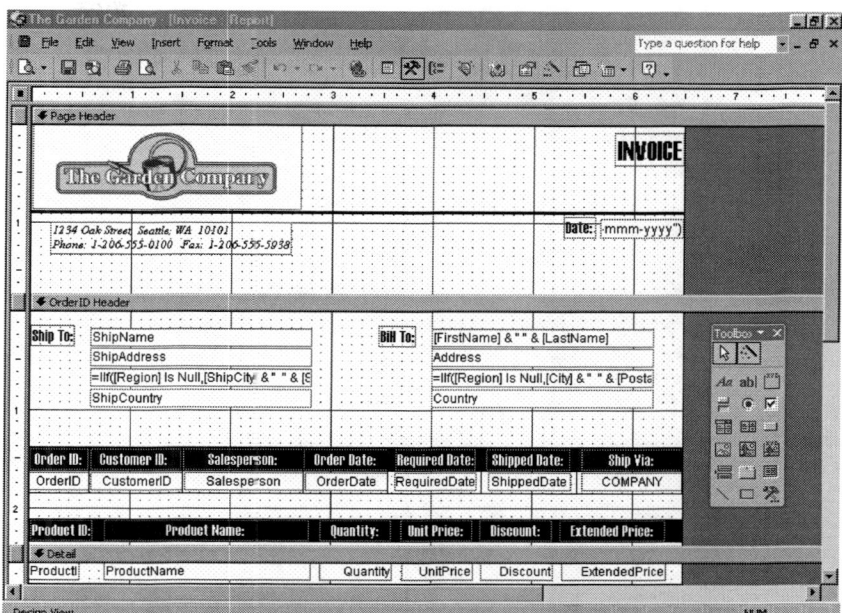

In this view, the report looks similar to a form, and the techniques you use to create forms can also be used to create reports.

9 Close the **Invoice** report, and then close the **GardenCo** database.

10 If you are not continuing on to the next chapter, quit Access.

Exploring Other Access Objects

Tables, queries, forms, and reports are the objects you will use most frequently in Access. You can use them to create powerful and useful databases. However, if you need to create a sophisticated database, you can use data access pages, macros, and modules to substantially extend the capabilities of Access. To round out this introduction to Access databases, this section provides a brief overview of these objects.

Pages

To enable people to view and manipulate your database information via an intranet or the Internet, you can create **pages**, also known as **data access pages**. Working with a data access page on the Web is very much like working directly with a table or form in Access—users can work with the data in tables, run queries, and enter information in forms.

Although publishing database information on the Web seems like a fairly difficult task, Access provides a wizard that does most of the tedious work of creating data access pages for you. You can use a wizard-generated page as is, or you can add your own personal touch in Design view.

Macros

You use **macros** to have Access respond to an event, such as the click of a button, the opening of a form, or the updating of a record. Macros can be particularly handy when you expect that other people who are less experienced with Access than you will work in your database. For example, you can make routine database actions, such as opening and closing forms or printing reports, available as command buttons on switchboards. And by grouping together an assortment of menu commands and having users carry them out via a macro with the click of a button, you can ensure that everyone does things the same way.

Modules

More powerful than macros, **modules** are Microsoft Visual Basic for Applications (VBA) programs. VBA is a high-level programming language developed by Microsoft for the purpose of creating Windows applications. A common set of VBA instructions can be used with all Microsoft Office programs, plus each program has its own set. Whereas macros can automate four to five dozen actions, VBA includes hundreds of commands and can be extended indefinitely with third-party add-ins. You could use VBA to carry out tasks that are too complex to be handled with macros, such as opening an Excel spreadsheet and retrieving specific information.

tip

The Microsoft Office XP installation CD-ROM includes several sample databases that illustrate many of the principles of creating and using a database. One of these, the Northwind Traders database, is used as an example in many topics in Access online Help, so it is a particularly good database for you to explore. You'll find a link to this database on the Access **Help** menu, under **Sample Databases**.

Quick Quizzes

- What is a database?

- What are records?

- What is a field?

- What are the objects in Access?

- What is the design view?

- What are controls?

- What is a macro?

- What do you use Queries for?

LESSON 2:

Creating a New Database

After completing this chapter, you will be able to:

✔ *Create a new database structure using a wizard*

✔ *Check the work of the wizard*

✔ *Create an empty database, and add tables using a wizard*

✔ *Refine the way your data is displayed*

✔ *Manipulate columns and rows in tables*

Creating the structure for a database is easy. But an empty database is no more useful than an empty Microsoft Word document or an empty Microsoft Excel worksheet. It is only when you fill, or **populate**, a database with data in tables that it starts to serve a purpose. As you add queries, forms, and reports, it becomes easier to use. If you customize it with a switchboard and your tools, it moves into the realm of being a **database application**.

Not every database has to be refined to the point that it can be classified as an application. Databases that only you or a few experienced database users will work with can remain fairly rough- hewn. But if you expect an administrative assistant to enter data or your company's executives to generate their own reports, then spending a little extra time in the beginning to create a solid database application will save a lot of work later. Otherwise, you'll find yourself continually repairing damaged files or walking people through seemingly easy tasks.

Microsoft Access takes a lot of the difficult and mundane work out of creating and customizing a database by providing **wizards** that you can use to create entire databases or individual tables, forms, queries, and other objects. It is generally easier to use a wizard to create something that is similar to what you need and then modify it than it is to create the same thing by hand.

In this chapter you will first use a wizard to rapidly create the structure for a sophisticated contact management database, complete with tables, queries, forms, and reports. After exploring this database and entering a few records to get an idea of what a wizard can provide in the way of a starting point, you will discard this database and start working on a simpler contacts database for The Garden Company. By the end of this chapter, you will have a GardenCo database containing three tables that will serve as the foundation for many of the exercises in this book.

In this chapter, you'll be creating a couple of databases from scratch in the working folder for this chapter, *SBS\Access\CreateDB\CreatingDB*. You will also use the Contacts and GardenCo database files that are stored in the following subfolders of the working folder: *CheckingDB*, *Refining*, and *Manipulating*.

Creating a Database Structure the Simple Way

Ac2002-1-1

In the distant past (a few years ago in computer time), creating a database structure from scratch involved first analyzing your needs and then laying out the database design on paper. You would decide what information you needed to track and how to store it in the database. Creating the database structure could be a lot of work, and after you had created it and entered data, making changes could be difficult. Wizards have changed this process. Committing yourself to a particular database structure is no longer the big decision it once was. Using the **Database Wizard**, you can create a dozen database applications in less time than it used to take to sketch the design of one on paper. Access wizards may not create exactly the database application you want, but they can quickly create something very close.

In this exercise, you will use the **Database Wizard** to create a new database structure. In this case, the new database will contain the structure for a contact management database. The working folder for this exercise is *SBS\Access\CreateDB \CreatingDB*. Follow these steps:

Access allows you to save a database before adding information to it. Every object you create subsequently will become part of the same file.

New

1   If the **New File** task pane is not displayed, open it by clicking the **New** button on the Access toolbar.

2   In the **New from template** section of the task pane, click **General Templates**, and then click the **Databases** tab to display these options:

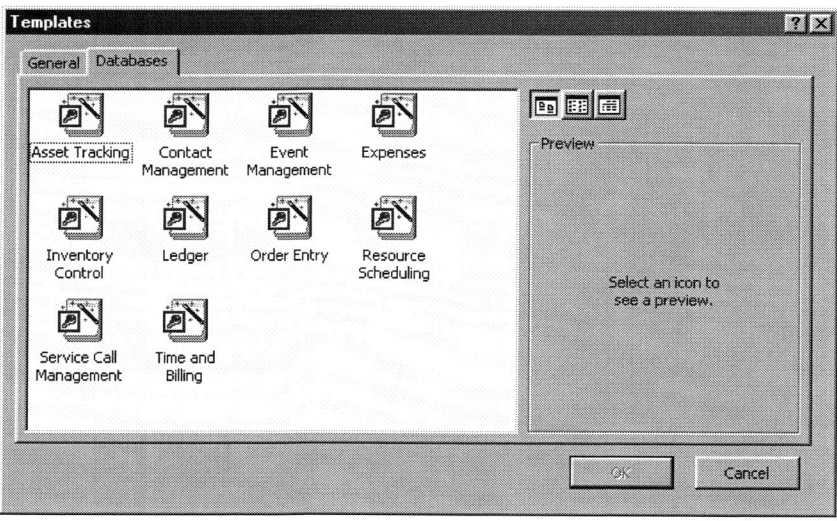

tip

The **Database Wizard** uses predefined **templates** to create fairly
sophisticated database applications. In addition to the templates provided with
Access, if you are connected to the Internet, you will find additional templates
and other resources by following the link to **Templates on Microsoft.com**
that is in the **New from template** section of the **New File** task pane.

3   Double-click **Contact Management**.

The **File New Database** dialog box appears so that you can
provide a name for your new database and specify where to store
it:

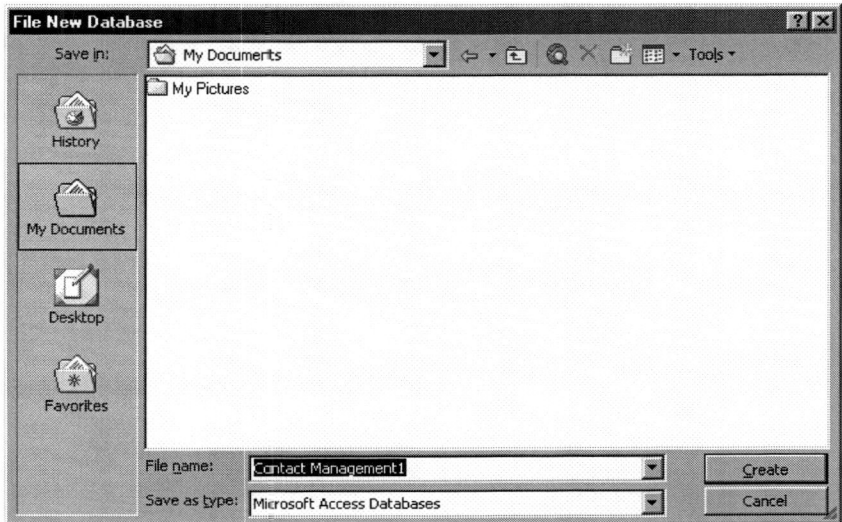

tip

The default folder for storing Access database files is *My Documents*. You
can change this default to any other folder by clicking **Options** on the **Tools**
menu when a database file is open, entering a new path in the **Default
database folder** box on the **General** tab, and clicking **OK**.

4   Browse to *SBS\Access\CreateDB\CreatingDB* (the working folder
for this exercise), replace *Contact Management* with **Contacts** in
the **File Name** box, and click **Create**.

tip

Naming conventions for an Access database file follow those for Microsoft
Windows files. A file name can contain up to 215 characters including spaces,
but creating a file name that long is not recommended. File names cannot
contain the following characters: \ / : * ? " < > |. The extension for an Access
database file is *.mdb*.

First the database window is displayed, and then you see the first
page of the **Database Wizard**, which tells you the type of
information that will be stored in this database.

5   This page requires no input from you, so click **Next** to move to
the second page of the **Database Wizard**:

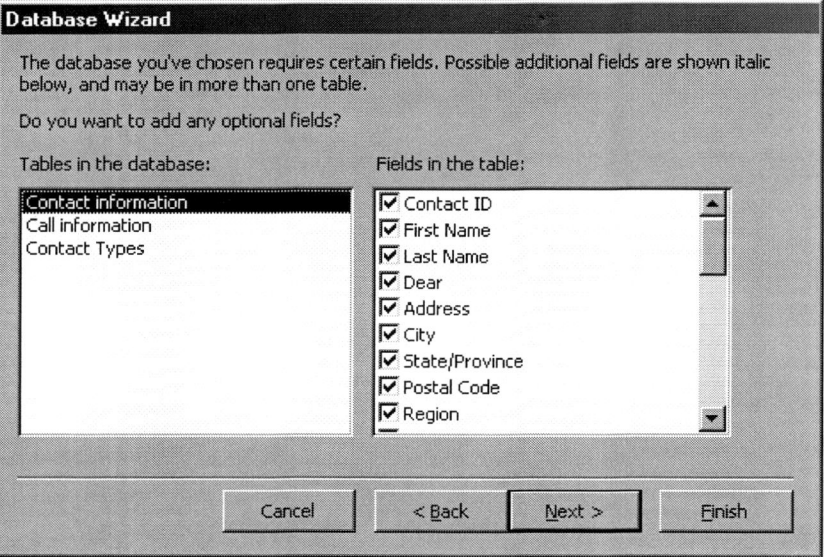

This page lists the three tables that will be included in the Contact Management database. The box on the right lists the fields you might want to include in the table selected in the box on the left. Required fields have a check mark in their check boxes. Optional fields are italic. You can select the check box of an optional field to include it in the selected table.

6   Click each table name, and browse through its list of fields, just to see what is available. Then indicate that you want to include all the selected fields in the three tables by clicking **Next** to move to the next page of the wizard.

On this page, you can select from a list of predefined styles that determine what the elements of the database will look like.

tip

Whenever the wizard's **Back** button is active (not grey), you can click it to move back through previous pages and change your selections. If the **Finish** button is active, you can click it at any time to tell a wizard to do its job with no further input from you. Most of the options set by a wizard can be modified later, so clicking **Finish** does not mean that whatever the wizard creates is cast in stone.

7   Click each of the styles to see what they look like. Then click **Blends**, and click **Next**.

8   Click each of the report styles to see what they look like. Then click **Bold**, and click **Next**.

9   Change the proposed database name to **Contacts**, leave the **Yes, I'd like to include a picture** check box clear, and click **Next**.

The **Next** button is unavailable on this page, indicating that this is the wizard's last page. By default, the **Yes, start the database** check box is selected, and the **Display Help on using a database** check box is clear.

19 Leave the default settings as they are, and click **Finish**.

The process of creating a database can take from several seconds to a minute. While the wizard creates the database, an alert box tells you what is happening and how far along the process is. When the wizard finishes, it opens the newly created Contacts database with this switchboard displayed:

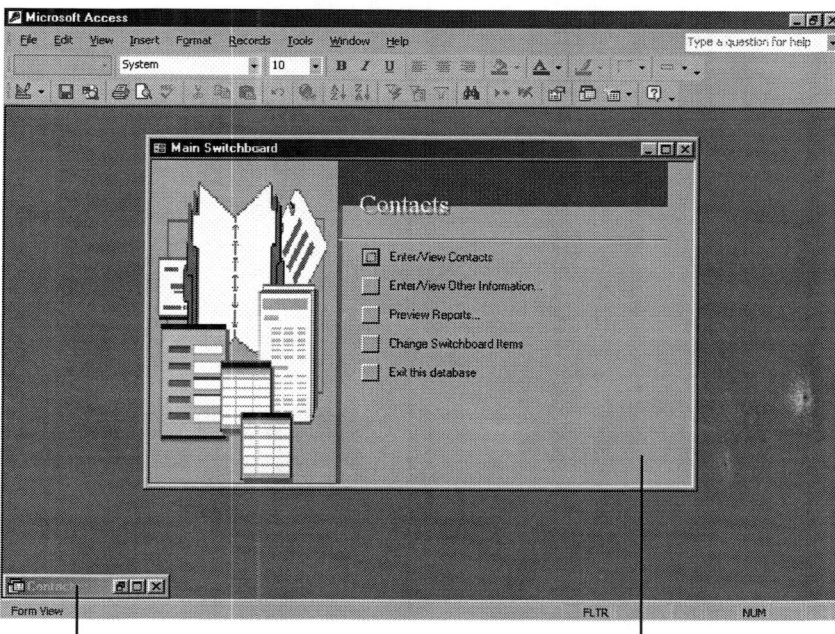

Contacts database window title bar   Switchboard

Close

11   Click the **Close** button at the right end of the Main Switchboard window's title bar.

12   When the switchboard opened, the Contacts database window was minimized. (You can see its title bar in the lower left corner of the Access window.) Click the **Close** button at the right end of this title bar to close the database.

Checking the Work of a Wizard

Ac2002-1-3
Ac2002-5-1

Using a wizard to create a database is quick and painless, but just what do you end up with? The **Database Wizard** creates a database application, complete with a switchboard, several tables, and some other objects. In many cases, all you have to do to have a working database application is add the data. If the wizard's work doesn't quite suit your needs, you can modify any of the database objects or use another type of wizard to add more objects.

For example, if you tell the **Database Wizard** to create a contact management database, it creates three tables. It doesn't create any queries for this type of database, but it does for some of the other types. It creates forms that you can use to enter or view data, and two reports that you can use to list contacts or summarize the calls made or received during the week. Finally, it creates a switchboard so that users can quickly access the parts of the database needed to perform specific tasks.

Contacts

In this exercise, you'll use the switchboard to take a quick tour of the Contacts database that the **Database Wizard** has created. You can't check out some of the objects unless the database contains data, so along the way, you will enter information in several of the tables. The working folder for this exercise is *SBS\Access\CreateDB \CheckingDB*. Follow these steps:

1 Open the **Contacts** database located in the working folder.

2 In the switchboard, click the **Enter/View Other Information** button to display the Forms Switchboard window.

This switchboard has two buttons: the first opens a form you can use to enter or view contact types, and the second returns you to the Main Switchboard window.

3 Click **Enter/View Contact Types** to display this Contact Types form:

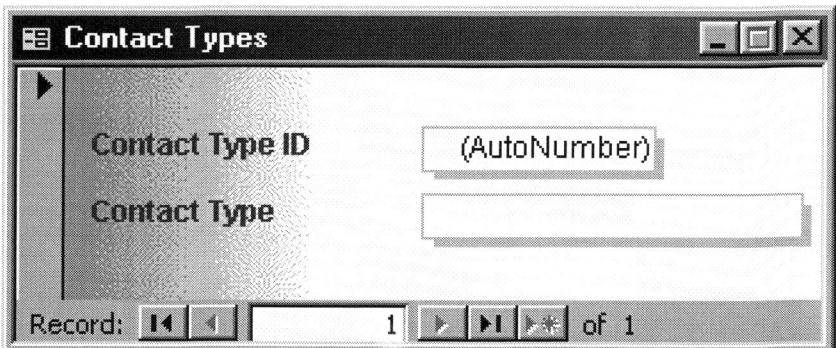

If the underlying Contact Types table contained any records, you could use this form to view them. The only action you can take now is to add a new record.

4 Type **Supplier** in the **Contact Type** box, and press 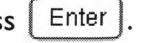.

As you typed, Access supplied the entry for the **Contact Type ID** field. Access keeps track of this number and enters the next available number in this field whenever you add a new record.

5 Repeat the previous step to enter records for **Customer** and **Shipper**.

6 Now that the underlying Contact Types table contains a few records, use the **navigation buttons** at the bottom of the form to scroll through them. Then click the **Close** button to close the Contact Types form.

important

With most computer applications, **saving** your work often is important to avoid losing it if your computer crashes or the dog chews through the power cord. With Access, it is not only *not* important to save your data, it is *not possible* to manually save it. When you move the insertion point out of a record after entering or editing information, Access saves that record. This mixed blessing means that you don't have to worry about losing your changes, but you do have to remember that any data entry changes you make are permanent and can be undone only by editing the record again.

7   Click **Return to Main Switchboard**.

8   Click **Enter/View Contacts** to display this Contacts form:

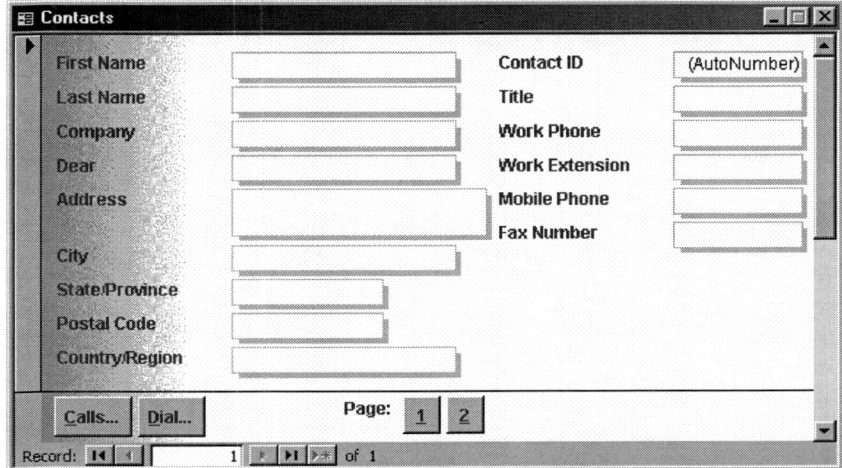

You use this two-page form to enter records in the underlying Contacts table or to view records that are already there. The form has buttons at the bottom to switch between pages and to open other forms from which you can place calls (**Dial**) or where you can record information about communications you've had with the contact (**Calls**).

9   Enter some information on this form-your own first and last name will do-and notice that when you enter your name, Access provides a contact ID.

10 Click the **2** button at the bottom of the form to move to page 2, and then expand the list of contact types.

   The list contains the three types you just entered in the Contact Types table through the Contact Types form.

11 Select one of the contact types.

12 Return to the first page, click in the **Work Phone** box to place the insertion point there, type **555-0100**, and press ⌈ Enter ⌋.

13 Click in the **Work Phone** box again, and click the **Dial** button.

   The **AutoDialer** dialog box appears, with the contents of the box that is currently selected on the form displayed as a potential number to dial.

tip

This dialog box is not part of Access; it is a Windows utility. When you click the **Dial** button, VBA code attached to the button calls the utility. If you were to click **Setup**, the **Windows Phone And Modem Options** dialog box would be displayed. (If you don't have a modem installed, the **Install New Modem** dialog box appears instead.)

14 Click **Cancel** to close the **AutoDialer** dialog box, and then click the **Calls** button to display this Calls form:

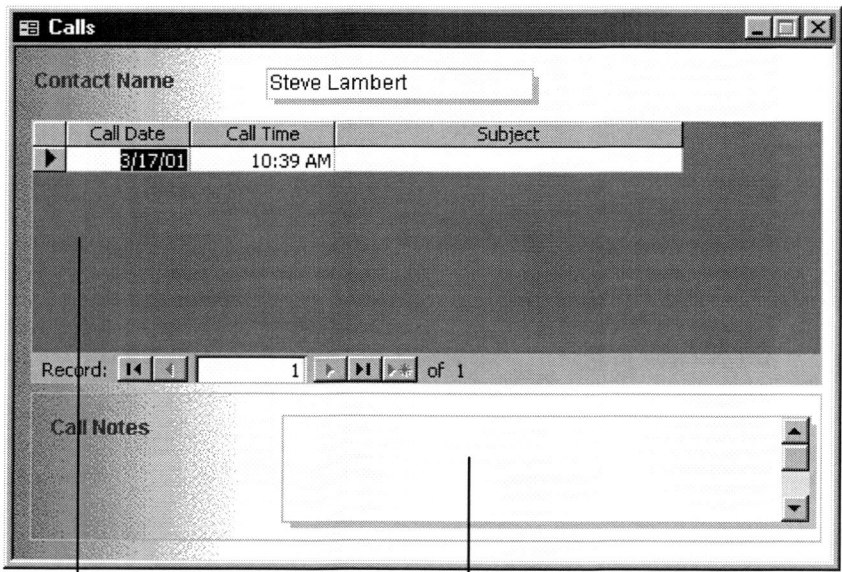

Call Listing subform   Call Details subform

This form includes the Call Listing subform, which lists any previous calls you have recorded, and the Call Details subform, which displays details of the selected call. You can record information about communications (phone calls, e-mail exchanges, and so on) that you've had with this contact.

15 Click in the **Subject** cell of the new record, and enter **Order information** as the subject.

Access adds a **New Record** line, where the **Call Date** and **Call Time** fields default to the current date and time, as shown here:

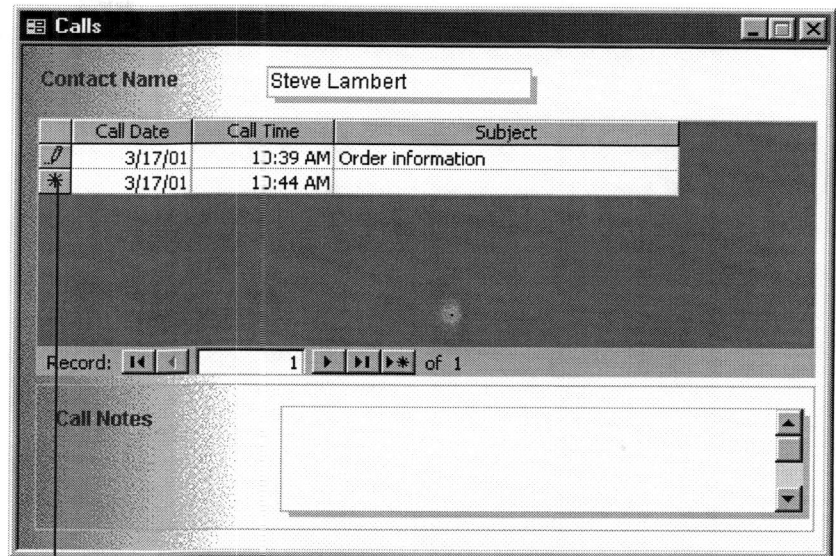

New Record line

16 Click in the **Call Notes** box, and type a short note.

17 Click the **Close** button to close the Calls form, and then click **Close** again to close the Contacts form.

18 Click **Preview Reports** to display the Reports Switchboard window.

19 Preview the two short reports by clicking the button for each one, reading it, and then closing it.

When you preview the Weekly Call Summary report, the Report Date Range form is displayed to allow you to enter a range of dates for the report. If you accept the default range of the current week, the summary of the call you just added is included in the report.

20 Click **Return to Main Switchboard**, and then click the **Close** button to close the Main Switchboard window without closing the database.

21 Double-click the database window's title bar to restore the window, which looks like this:

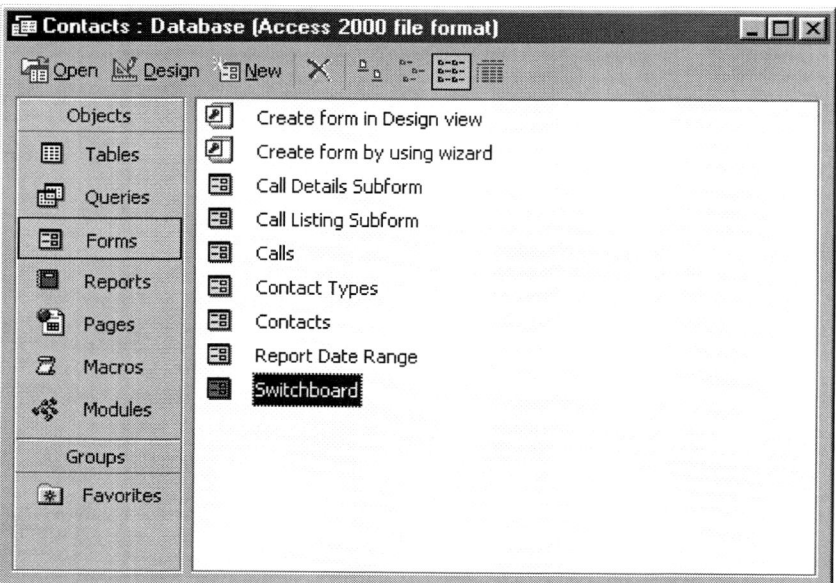

22 Explore all the tables, forms, and reports in the database by clicking each object type on the **Objects** bar and then opening the individual objects.

You won't be able to open the Report Date Range form directly, because it is designed to be opened by VBA code that supplies the information that the form needs.

23 Close the **Contacts** database.

Creating Tables the Simple Way

Ac2002-2-1

When you use the **Database Wizard** to create a contact management database, the database has all the **components** needed to store basic information about people. But suppose The Garden Company needs to store different types of information for different types of contacts. For example, it might want to maintain different types of information about employees, customers, and suppliers. In addition to the standard information - such as names, addresses, and phone numbers - the company might want to track these other kinds of information:

- Employee Social Security number, date of hire, marital status, deductions, and pay rate

- Customer order and account status

- Supplier contact, current order status, and discounts

The company could add a lot of extra fields to the Contacts table and then fill in just the ones it needs for each contact type, but cramming all this information into one table would soon get pretty messy. Instead, it should create a database with one table for each contact type: employee, customer, and supplier.

The **Database Wizard** doesn't offer exactly this combination of tables, so in this exercise, you will create a GardenCo database with an empty structure. You will then add several tables to the database using the **Table Wizard**. The working folder for this exercise is *SBS\Access\CreateDB\CreatingDB*. Follow these steps:

New

1 Click the **New** button on the toolbar to display the **New File** task pane.

2 In the **New** section of the task pane, click **Blank Database**.

3 Browse to the working folder for this exercise, type **GardenCo** as the name of the new database, and click **Create**.

Access displays a database window that contains no tables, queries, forms, or other database objects. (You can confirm that the database is empty by clicking each of the object types on the **Objects** bar.)

New

4 Click the **New** button on the database window's toolbar to display the **New Table** dialog box.

tip

Instead of clicking the **New** button, you can click the **New Object** button's down arrow, and then click **Table**; or you can click **Tables** on the **Objects** bar, and then double-click **Create table by using wizard**; or you can click **Table** on the **Insert** menu

5 Double-click **Table Wizard** to display the wizard's first page, shown here:

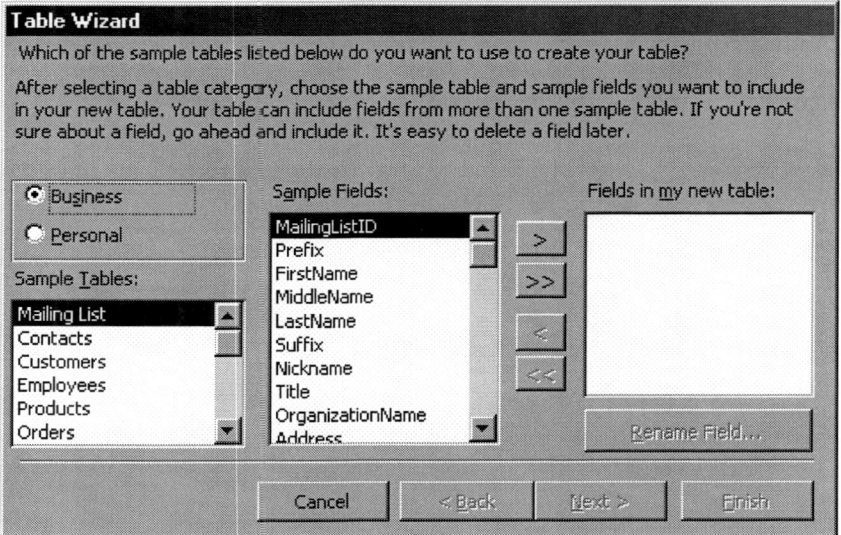

You can display a list of either business tables or personal tables. Although these categories are generally oriented toward business or personal use, depending on the nature of your business or preferences, you might find the sample table you want in either list.

6 Take a few minutes to browse through the business list, and then check the **Personal** button to see those sample tables.

Each category contains a list of sample tables. When you click an item in the **Sample Tables** list, the **Sample Fields** list to the right displays all the fields available for that table. (You can add more fields after creating the table if you need them.) Selecting an item in the **Sample Fields** list and then clicking the > button moves the selected field to the **Fields in my new table** list. Clicking the >> button moves *all* sample fields to the **Fields in my new table** list. The < and << buttons remove one or all fields from your new table list.

7   With the **Business** category selected, select **Customers** in the **Sample Tables** list.

8   Click the >> button to copy all the fields to the **Fields in my new table** list, and then click **Next** to move to the next page of the wizard.

On this page you can provide a name for your new table and specify whether the wizard should set a **primary key** for the table. A primary key consists of one or more fields that differentiate one record from another.

9   Leave **Customers** as the table name, click **No, I'll set the primary key**, and then click **Next**.

The wizard suggests **CustomerID** as the field that will uniquely identify records, and asks what type of data the field will contain.

10 Click **Numbers and/or letters I enter when I add new records**, and then click **Next** to move to the last page of the wizard.

You can select one of the three option buttons on this page to determine whether the table should open in Design view or in Datasheet view, or whether a wizard-generated form should open so that you can enter data.

11 Accept the default selection, **Enter data directly into the table**, and click **Finish** to create and open the Customers table.

12 Scroll horizontally through the table to view all the fields created by the wizard based on your selections on its first page. Then close the table.

The Customers table now appears in the database window.

13 Start the **Table Wizard** again, this time by double-clicking **Create table by using wizard** in the database window.

14 Select **Employees** in the **Sample Tables** list, and move only the following fields to the **Fields in my new table** list, by selecting each field in the **Sample Fields** list and clicking the ➤ button:

EmployeeID
FirstName
LastName
Title
Address
City
StateOrProvince
PostalCode
HomePhone
Birthdate
DateHired
Photograph
Notes

15   In the **Fields in my new table** list, select **StateOrProvince**, click **Rename Field**, change the name of the field to **State**, and click **OK**.

16   Click the **Next** button twice to move two pages forward, naming the table **Employees** and allowing Access to create a primary key.

Because one table already exists in the database, the wizard attempts to establish a relationship between the tables and displays a new page.

17   You will be able to establish relationships later, so skip over this page by clicking **Next**.

18   Click **Finish**, and then close the **Employees** table.

19   Repeat steps 13 through 18 to create a **Suppliers** table that includes all the fields provided. Click **Finish** to accept all the suggestions and defaults.

20   Close the **Suppliers** table.

Three tables are now listed in the **Tables** pane of the database window.

21   Close the database.

Refining How Data Is Displayed

Ac2002-1-2
Ac2002-2-4

You can use sample tables and fields to create your own tables.

When you use the **Table Wizard** to create tables and populate them with the fields you specify, it sets a variety of **properties** for each field. These properties determine what data be entered in a field and how the data will look on the screen.

The field properties set by Access are a good starting place, and most of them are probably fine as they are. However, suppose some of the properties don't meet your needs. You can change some of them without affecting the data stored in the table; others might affect the data, so it pays to be cautious about making drastic changes until you have some experience working with Access.

GardenCo

In this exercise, you will review and edit a few of the property settings for one of the tables in the GardenCo database located in the working folder for this exercise, *SBS\Access\CreateDB\Refining*. Follow these steps:

1   Open the **GardenCo** database located in the working folder.

2   In the database window, double-click **Employees** in the **Tables** pane to open the table in Datasheet view, as shown on the next page.

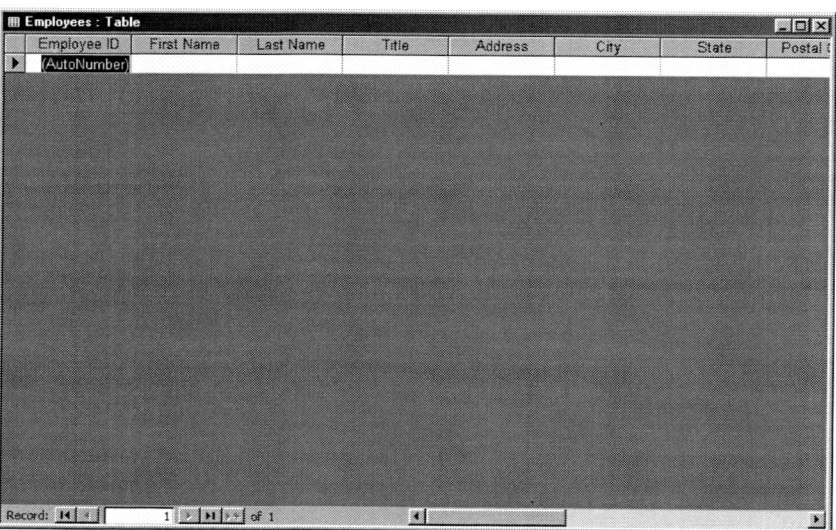

Your table window might be a different size than this one. Notice that any field name that is composed of two words has a space between the words, whereas the name you specified in the wizard had no space. Remember this when you are looking at the table in Design view later.

tip

As with other Microsoft Office XP applications, you can change the size of the window by moving the pointer to a corner and, when the pointer becomes a double-headed arrow, dragging to expand or reduce the size of the window.

View

3   Click the **View** button on the toolbar to display the table in Design view, like this:

Primary key

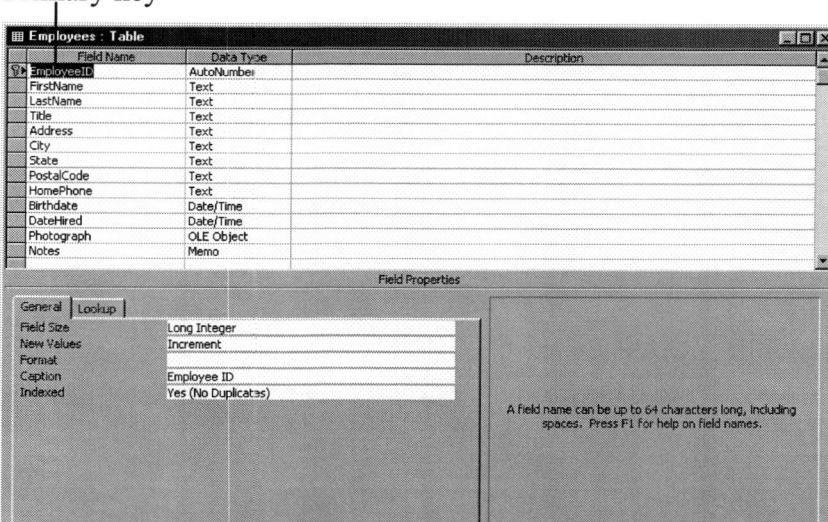

In Design view, the top portion of the window contains a list of the table's fields. The **Field Name** column contains the names you specified when you created the table. Notice that there are no spaces in the names. The **Data Type** column specifies the type of data that the field can contain. The **Description** column can contain a description of the field.

The Primary Key is set automatically when you create a table using the wizard and the default settings are not affected.

Notice the **Primary Key** icon to the left of the EmployeeID field. The value in the primary key field is used to uniquely identify each record; that is, no two records can have the same value in this field. You can take responsibility for entering this value, or you can let Access help you with this chore. When the data type of a field is set to **AutoNumber**, Access fills this field in every new record with the next available number.

tip

If you no longer want the table to have a primary key, select the field designated as the primary key in the top portion of the window, and click **Primary Key** on the **Edit** menu. If you want to assign a different field as the primary key, select that field, and click **Primary Key** on the **Edit** menu.

4   Click in the **Data Type** cell for the **EmployeeID** field-the one with **AutoNumber** in it- and then click the down arrow that appears.

The cell expands to show a list of all possible **data types**. Each data type cell contains this list, allowing you to set the appropriate data type for each field. The data type setting restricts data entry to that specific type. If you try to enter data that is incompatible with that type, Access rejects it.

tip

For a description of all the data types, search for the *data type* topic in Access online Help.

5 Press the ⌈ Esc ⌋ key to close the list without changing the data type.

6 Click in each box in the **Field Properties** section at the bottom of the table window.

The number of properties in the **Field Properties** section varies with each data type. For example, the **AutoNumber** data type has five properties, four of which have drop down lists from which you can select settings. As you click each property, a description of that property appears in the area on the right, as shown on the next page.

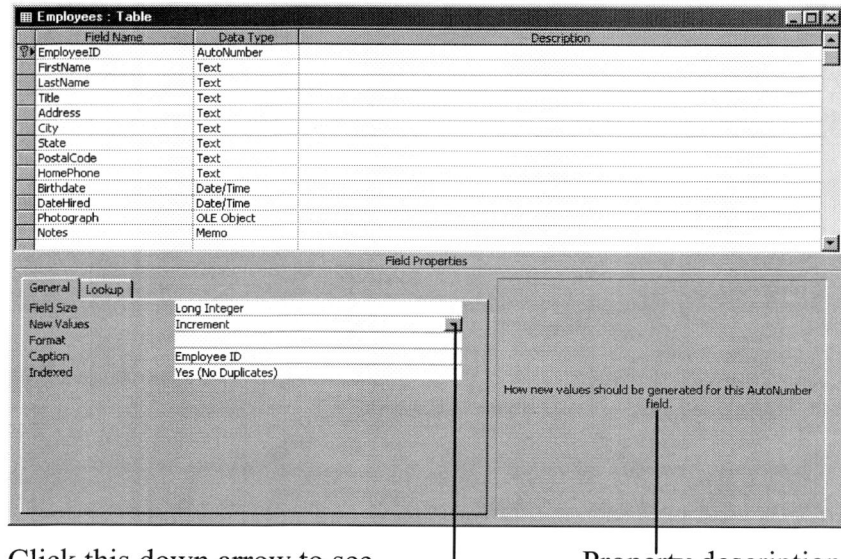

Click this down arrow to see property options   Property description

The **Field Size** property determines the size and type of value that can be entered in the field. For example, if this property is set to **Long Integer**, the field will accept entries from -2,147,483,648 to 2,147,483,647. If the data type is **AutoNumber**, entries in this field will start with 1, so you could conceivably have over two billion employees before you outgrew this table.

The **Increment** setting for the **New Values** property specifies that Access should use the next available sequential number. The alternative (which you can see by expanding the list for this cell) is **Random**.

The **Format** property determines how data from the field is displayed on the screen and in print; it does not control how it is stored. Some data types have predefined formats, and you can also create custom formats.

Remember that when you displayed the table in Datasheet view, some of the field names had spaces in them? The way the field names are displayed in Datasheet view is controlled by the **Caption** property. If there is an entry for this property, it is used in place of the actual field name.

The **Yes (No Duplicates)** setting for the **Indexed** property indicates that the information in this field will be indexed for faster searching, and that duplicate values are not allowed. For the primary key field, this property is automatically set to **Yes (No Duplicates)**, but a field can also be indexed without being a primary key.

tip

For more information about a particular property, click in its box, and press F1 to see the pertinent Access online Help topic.

7   With the **EmployeeID** field still selected (as indicated by the arrow in the **row selector**), click in the **Format** box, and enter three zeros (**000**).

The ID number generated by Access will now be displayed as three digits. If the number isn't three digits long, it will be padded on the left with zeros.

8   Click the **Photograph** field, and change its data type from **OLE Object** to **Text**.

The **Table Wizard** included the **Photograph** field in this table and set this field's data type to **OLE Object** so that you can store a graphic in the field. But you will be storing the file name of a graphic, not the graphic itself, so **Text** is a more appropriate data type.

9   Click in the **HomePhone** field to display these properties:

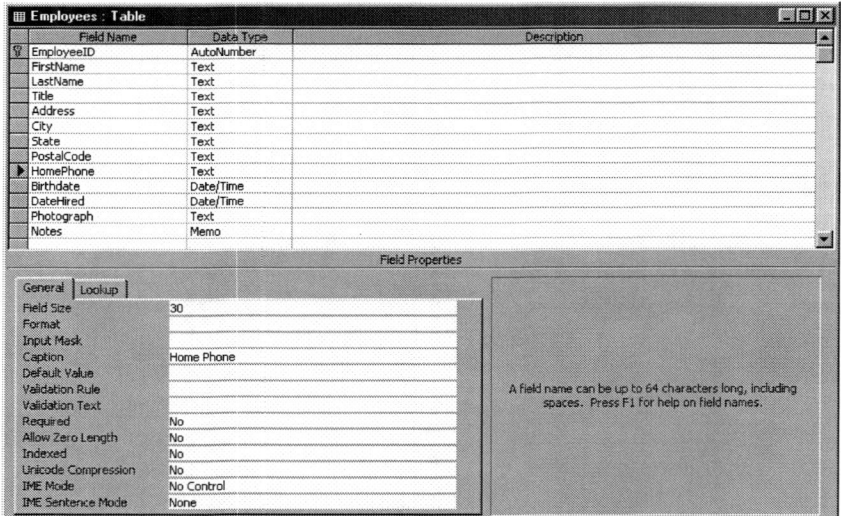

The data type for **HomePhone** is **Text**, even though the data will be a string of numbers. Because this type of entry can also contain parentheses, dashes, and spaces and is not the type of number that you would use in a calculation, **Text** is the appropriate data type.

Looking at the **Field Properties** section for this field, you can see that fields with this data type have more properties than fields with the **AutoNumber** data type.

The **Field Size** property for a field with the **Text** data type determines the number of characters that can be entered in the field. If you attempt to enter too many characters, Access displays a warning message, and you won't be able to leave the field until you reduce the number of characters to this many or fewer.

The **Caption** property is set to **Home Phone**. This name will be used at the top of the field's column in Datasheet view. The wizard supplies these descriptive names, but you can change them.

10 Click in the **DateHired** field to display the properties shown here:

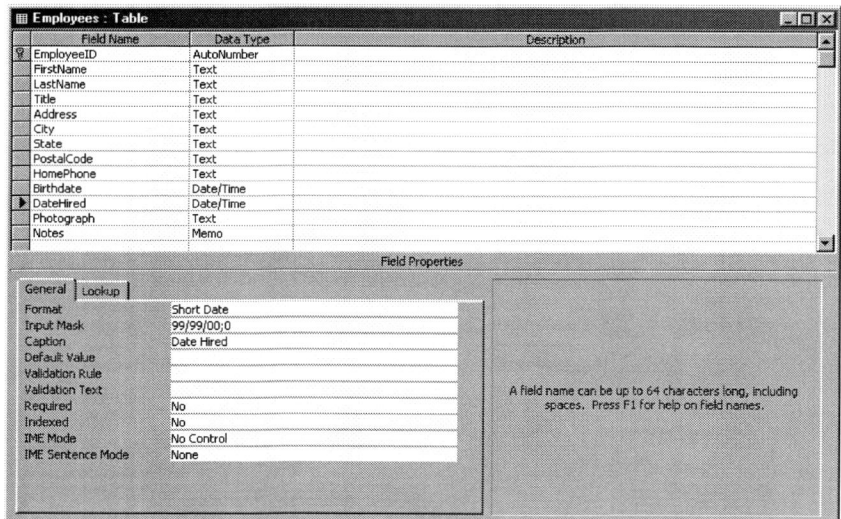

The **Format** property for this field is set to **Short Date**, which looks like this: 4/21/01. If a valid date is entered in just about any standard format, such as 21 April 01, this property displays the date as 4/21/01.

important

Exercises in this book that use the short date format assume that the year display is set to two digits (M/d/yy) in the **Regional Settings Properties** dialog box in Microsoft Windows 98, or the **Regional Options** dialog box in Microsoft Windows 2000. You can check this on your computer by opening Control Panel (click **Start**, move the pointer over **Settings**, and click **Control Panel**) and then double-clicking **Regional Settings** or **Regional Options**, as appropriate. In either case, the setting is found on the **Date** tab.

This field also has its **Input Mask** property set to **99/99/00;0**. An **input mask** controls how data looks when you enter it and the format in which it is stored. Each 9 represents an optional numeral, and each 0 represents a required one. When you move to this field to enter a date in Datasheet view, you will see a mask that looks like this: __/__/__. The mask indicates that the date must be entered in the 4/21/01 format, but as soon as you press [Enter] to move to the next field, the date will change to whatever format is specified by the **Format** property.

Another interesting property is **Validation Rule**. None of the wizard-generated tables use **validation rules**, because the rules are too specific to the data being entered to anticipate, but let's take a quick look at how they work.

11 Click in the **Validation Rule** box, and enter **<Now()**. Then click in the **Validation Text** box, and enter **"Date entered must be today or earlier."**

This rule states that the date entered must be before (less than) the current instant in time, as determined by the system clock of the computer where the database is stored. If you enter a date in the future, Access will not accept it and will display the validation text in an alert box.

important

The **Format**, **Input Mask**, and **Validation Rule** properties seem like great ways to be sure that only valid information is entered in your tables. But if you aren't careful, you can make data entry difficult and frustrating. Test your properties carefully before releasing your database for others to use.

View

12 Click the **View** button to return to Datasheet view, clicking **Yes** when prompted to save the table.

tip

When you try to switch from Design view to Datasheet view after making changes (and sometimes even if you haven't made any changes), you are presented with an alert box stating that you must save the table. If you click **No**, you remain in Design view. If you click **Yes**, Access saves your changes and switches to Datasheet view. If you want to switch views without saving changes that you have made inadvertently, click **No**, and then click the table's **Close** button. When Access displays another alert box, click **No** to close the table without saving any changes.

13 Enter a future date in both the **Birthdate** and **DateHired** fields.

The **Birthdate** field, which has no validation rule, accepts any date, but the **DateHired** field won't accept a date beyond the one set on your computer.

14 Click **OK** to close the alert box, change the **DateHired** value to a date in the past, and click the **Close** button to close the Employees table.

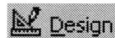

15 In the database window, select **Suppliers**, and click the **Design** button to open the table in Design view.

16 Double-click the **StateOrProvince** field name to select it, and change it to **State**. Then click the **Caption** property in the **Field Properties** section, and change it to **State**, too.

17 Delete the **Country/Region**, **PaymentTerms**, **EmailAddress**, and **Notes** fields by clicking in the row selector and pressing the ⌈Del⌋ key.

tip

Access alerts you that deleting the **EmailAddress** field requires deleting the field and all its indexes. Click **Yes**. (You will see this alert again in step 19; click **Yes** each time to delete the fields.)

18 Click the **Close** button to close the Suppliers table, clicking **Yes** to save your changes.

19 Open the **Customers** table in Design view, and delete the following fields: **CompanyName**, **CompanyOrDepartment**, **ContactTitle**, **Extension**, **FaxNumber**, **EmailAddress**, and **Notes**.

20 Click in the **CustomerID** field, and change the **Field Size** property to **5**.

21 Change these fields and their captions: *ContactFirstName* to **FirstName** and **First Name**, *ContactLastName* to **LastName** and **Last Name**, *BillingAddress* to **Address**, *StateOrProvince* to **Region**, and *Country/Region* to **Country**.

22 Click the **Close** button to close the Customers table, clicking **Yes** to save it.

23 Close the **GardenCo** database.

Manipulating Table Columns and Rows

Ac2002-1-4

When you refine a table's structure by adding fields and changing field properties in Design view, you are affecting the data that is stored in the table. But sometimes you will want to adjust the table itself to get a better view of the data. If you want to look up a phone number, for example, but the names and phone numbers are several columns apart, you will have to scroll the table window to get the information you need. You might want to rearrange columns or hide a few columns to be able to see the fields you are interested in at the same time.

You can manipulate the columns and rows of an Access table without in any way affecting the underlying data. You can size both rows and columns, and you can also hide, move, and freeze columns. You can save your table formatting so that the table will look the same the next time you open it, or you can discard your table adjustments without saving them.

GardenCo

In this exercise, you will open a table and manipulate its columns and rows. To make the value of table formatting more apparent, you will work with a version of the GardenCo database that has several tables containing many records. The working folder for this exercise is *SBS\Access\CreateDB\Manipulate*. Follow these steps:

1 Open the **GardenCo** database located in the working folder.

2 Click **Tables** on the **Objects** bar.

3 Double-click the **Customers** table to open it in Datasheet view.

4 Drag the vertical bar at the right edge of the **Address** column header to the left until the column is about a half inch wide.

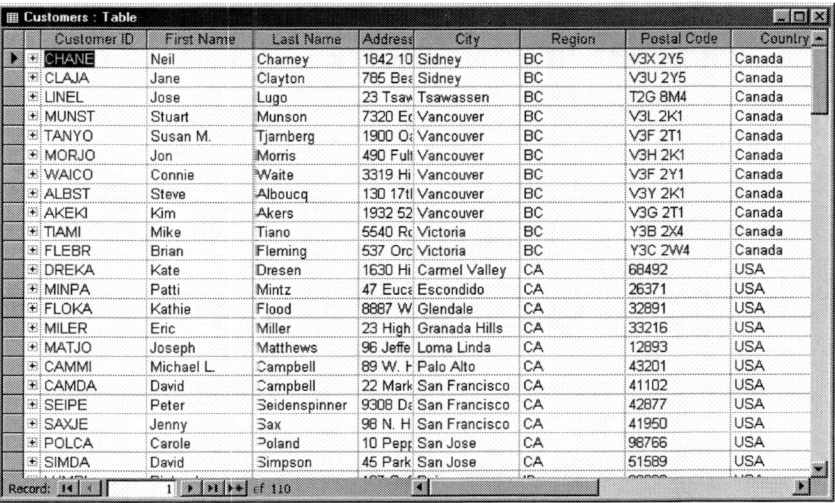

The column is now too narrow to display the entire address.

5 Point to the vertical bar between the **Address** and **City** column headers, and double- click.

The column to the left of the vertical bar is now the minimum width that will display all the text in that field in all records. This technique is particularly useful in a large table where you can't easily determine the length of a field's longest entry.

6 On the left side of the datasheet, drag the horizontal bar between any two record selectors downward.

As you can see here, the height of all rows in the table increases:

7 On the **Format** menu, click **Row Height** to display the **Row Height** dialog box.

8 Select the **Standard Height** check box, and then click **OK**.

The height of all rows is returned to the default setting. (You can also set the rows to any other height in this dialog box.)

9 Click in the **First Name** column, and then click **Hide Columns** on the **Format** menu.

The First Name column disappears, and the columns to its right shift to the left. If you select several columns before clicking **Hide Columns**, they all disappear.

tip

You can select adjacent columns by clicking in the header of one, holding down the ⟨ Shift ⟩ key, and then clicking in the header of another. The two columns and any columns in between are selected.

10 To restore the hidden field, click **Unhide Columns** on the **Format** menu to display this dialog box:

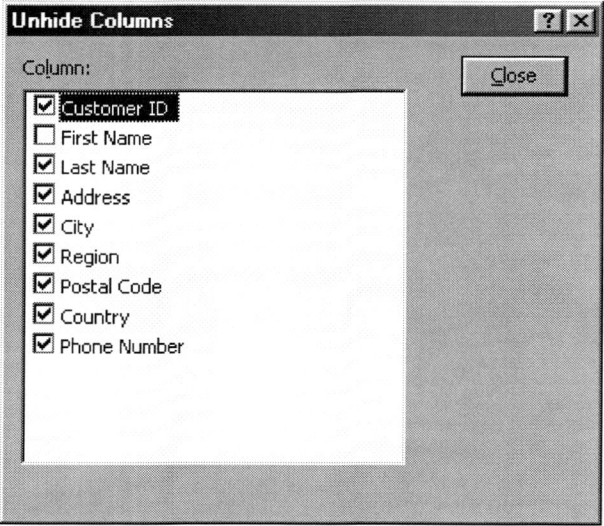

11 Select the **First Name** check box, and then click **Close**.

Access redisplays the First Name column.

12 Drag the right side of the database window to the left to reduce its size so that you cannot see all fields in the table.

13 Point to the **Customer ID** column header, hold down the mouse button, and drag through the **First Name** and **Last Name** column headers. Then with the three columns selected, click **Freeze Columns** on the **Format** menu.

Now as you scroll the window horizontally to view columns that are off the screen to the right, the first three columns will remain in view.

14 On the **Format** menu, click **Unfreeze All Columns** to restore the columns to their normal condition.

15 Close the table without saving your changes, and then close the **GardenCo** database.

Quick Quizzes

● What is a wizard?

● What are field properties?

● What is the primary key?

● What is an AutoNumber field?

LESSON 3: Getting Information Into and Out of a Database

After completing this chapter, you will be able to:

✔ *Import information from various programs*

✔ *Import information from other Access databases*

✔ *Export information to other programs*

Not many people enjoy typing information in a database, so one of your goals when designing a **relational database** is to structure the tables in such a way that the same information never has to be entered more than once. If, for example, you are designing a database to track customer orders, you don't want sales clerks to have to type the name of the customer in each order. Unless you are running a mortuary, you will probably have repeat customers. So you need a customer table to hold all the pertinent information about each customer, and you can then simply reference a customer ID in each order. If information about a customer changes, you have to update it in only one place in the database: the customer table. In this way, the only item of customer information in the order records (the ID) remains accurate. An added benefit of this system is that you reduce the confusion that can result from typos and from having the same information appear in different formats throughout the database.

Good database design saves keystrokes while entering new information and maintaining the database, but even more time and effort can be saved in another way. As a Microsoft Office XP application, Microsoft Access can easily share information with the other applications in the Office suite. But it also makes it easy to populate a database by **importing** information in numerous other formats. If the information that you intend to store in an Access database has already been entered into almost any other electronic document, it is quite likely that you can move it into Access without retyping it.

If your information is still being actively maintained in another application and you want to bring it into Access to analyze it, create reports, or easily export it to another format, you should consider **linking** your Access database to the existing information in its original application rather than importing the information. When you link to data in another application, you can view and edit it in both applications, and what you see in Access is always up to date.

Many companies that store accounting, manufacturing, marketing, sales, and other information on their computers have discovered the advantages of sharing this information within the company through an **intranet**, or with the rest of the world through the Internet. With Access, you can speed up this process by **exporting** the information stored in a database as Hypertext Markup Language (HTML) and Extensible Markup Language (XML) pages.

In this chapter, you'll import information stored in various formats into the GardenCo database. You'll also export some of their data to several standard formats. After all this importing and exporting, you will experiment with viewing and updating information in another application by linking to it. You will be working with GardenCo database files and several other sample files that are stored in the following subfolders of the *SBS\Access\Importing* folder: *ImportExcel*, *ImportDText*, *ImportFText*, *ImportAccess*, *ImportDbase*, *ImportHTML*, *ImportXML*, *Export*, *Link*, and *OfficeLink*.

Importing Information from Excel

Ac2002-8-1

Creating a database by importing data is a way of speeding up data input.

An Excel worksheet is an item which can be easily adapted and converted into a database table.

GardenCo
Customers

Access works well with Microsoft Excel. You can import entire **worksheets** or a **named range** from a worksheet into either a new table (one that is created during the import) or an existing table. You can also import specific fields from a worksheet or range.

Excel is a good intermediate format to use when importing information that isn't set up quite right. For example, if you want to add or remove fields, combine or split fields, or use complex math functions to manipulate data before importing it into Access, Excel is a great place to do it.

In this exercise, you will import information about The Garden Company's customers, which is stored in an Excel worksheet, into the Customers table in the GardenCo database. The working folder for this exercise is *SBS\Access\Importing\ImportExcel*. Follow these steps:

1   Open the **GardenCo** database located in the working folder.

2   On the **File** menu, point to **Get External Data**, and then click **Import**.

3   In the **Files of type** list, click **Microsoft Excel**.

4   Browse to the *SBS\Access\Importing\ImportExcel* folder, click **Customers**, and then click **Import**.

     Access displays the first page of the **Import Spreadsheet Wizard**, which is shown here:

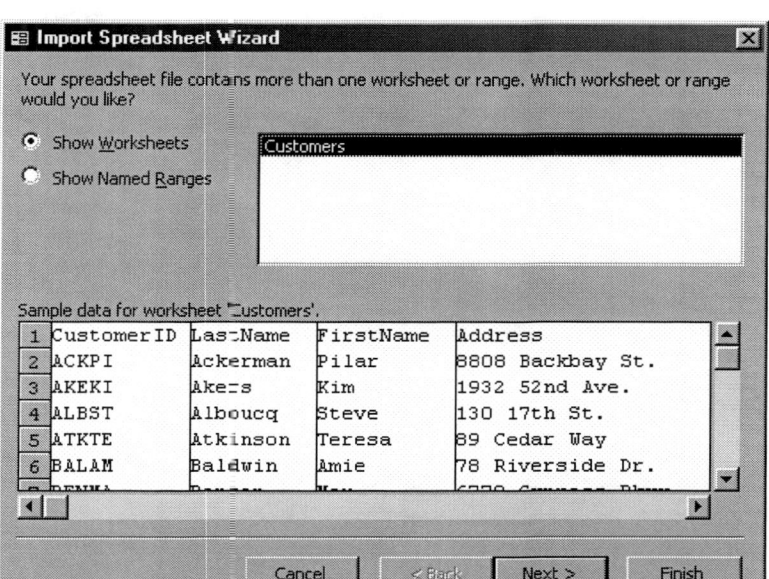

On this page, you can browse the contents of any worksheets or named ranges in the spreadsheet you just selected. You can scroll horizontally and vertically to view the worksheet's columns and rows, which are d splayed in the lower pane.

5   With **Customers** selected in the list of worksheets, click **Next** to display this page of the wizard:

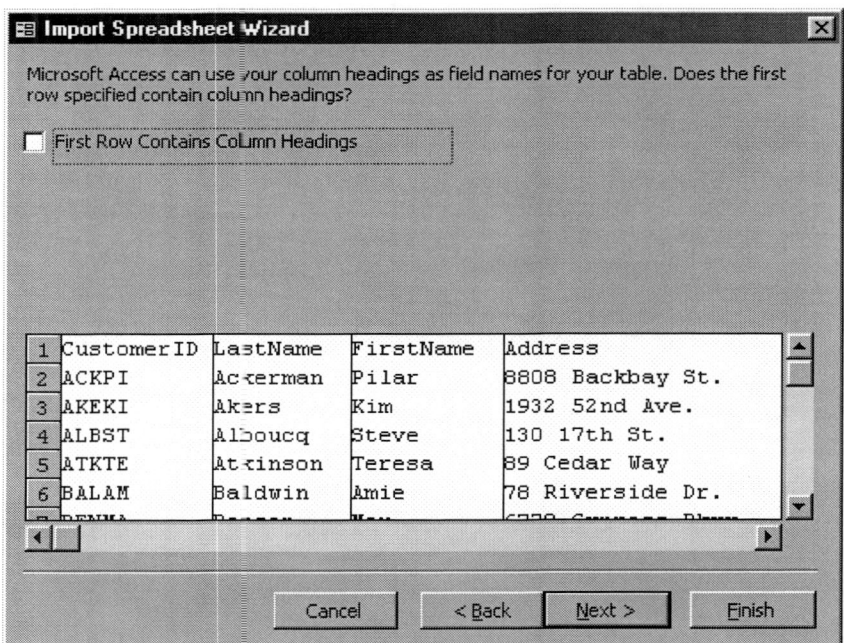

6   Select the **First Row Contains Column Headings** check box, and click **Next**.

The background for the top row changes to grey, and when you scroll up and down, the top row no longer scrolls.

7   Click **In an Existing Table**, select the **Customers** table from the adjacent drop-down list, and click **Next**.

important

When importing into an existing table, all the field names and data types must match exactly; otherwise, Access can't import the file and displays an error. If the structure matches but data in a field is too large or has some other minor problem, Access might import the record containing the field into an ImportError table, rather than into the desired one. You can fix the problem there and then copy and paste the record into the correct table.

8   Click **Finish** to import the file.

Access informs you that the file was imported.

9   Click **OK** to close the message box, and then open the **Customers** table to confirm that Access imported the customer list.

10   Close the **Customers** table, and then close the database.

Importing Information from a Delimited Text File

Ac2002-8-1

Importing data from delimited text files is a way of converting files created by word processors into database format. The most important factor is that the format of the original file must be compatible. That is, every record must end with a "Return" and the fields must be separated by a semi-colon or by another special character.

GardenCo
Employees

Text files are the common denominator of documents. Almost every application that works with words and numbers can generate some kind of a text file, in addition to files in its **native format**. Access can import tabular data (tables and lists) from text files if the data has been stored in a recognizable format. The most common formats are delimited and fixed width.

In a **delimited text file**, each record ends in a carriage return, and each field is separated from the next by a comma or some other special character, called a **delimiter**. If a field contains one of these special characters, you must enclose the entire field in quotation marks. (Some people enclose all fields in quotation marks to avoid having to locate and enclose the special cases.)

In this exercise, you will import information about The Garden Company's employees, which is stored in a **comma-delimited text file**, into the Employees table in the GardenCo database. The working folder for this exercise is *SBS\Access\Importing \ImportDText*. Follow these steps:

1   Open the **GardenCo** database located in the working folder.

2   On the **File** menu, point to **Get External Data**, and then click **Import**.

3   In the **Files of type** list, click **Text Files**.

tip

Text files typically have an extension of *.txt*. However, some programs save delimited text files with a *.csv* or *.tab* extension. You will also occasionally see text files with an extension of *.asc* (for **ASCII**). Fixed-width files are sometimes stored with an extension of *.prn* (for *printer*), but Access doesn't recognize this extension, so you will have to rename it to one it does recognize. All of the acceptable extensions are treated the same way by Access.

4   Browse to the *SBS\Access\Importing\ImportDText* folder, click
Employees, and then click **Import**.

Access displays the first page of the **Import Text Wizard**, shown
here:

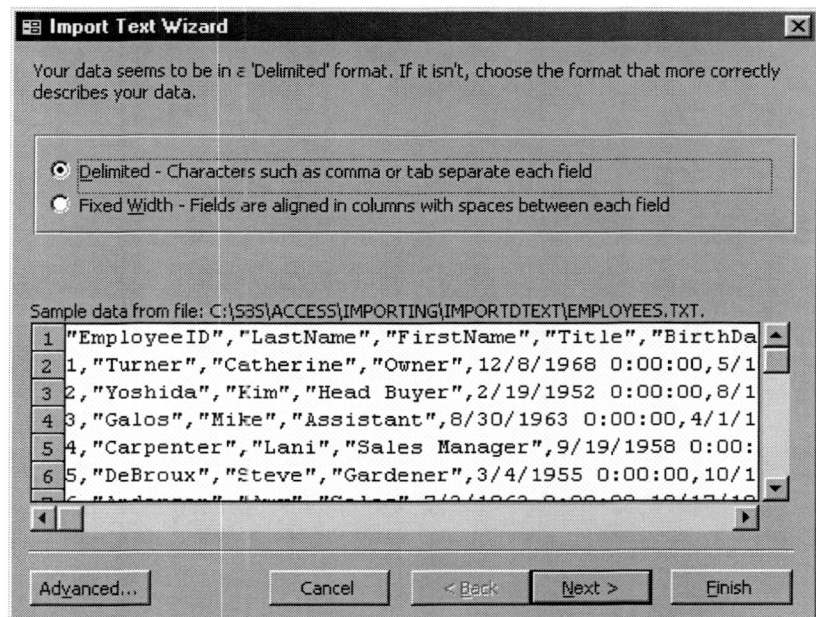

You can see that each field is enclosed in quotation marks, and
there is a comma between them. Access recognized that the
selected file is delimited and has selected that option.

5   Click the **Advanced** button to display the default import
specifications for this file.

You don't need to change anything in the **Employees Import
Specification** dialog box, but you can see that you could fine-tune
the import process here.

> ## tip
>
> If you want to import several files that deviate in some way from the default set-
> tings, you can specify the new settings and save them. Then as you open each of
> the other files, you can display this dialog box and click the **Specs** button to select
> and load the saved specifications.

6   Click **Cancel** to close the **Employees Import Specification** dialog
box, and then click **Next** to display this page of the wizard:

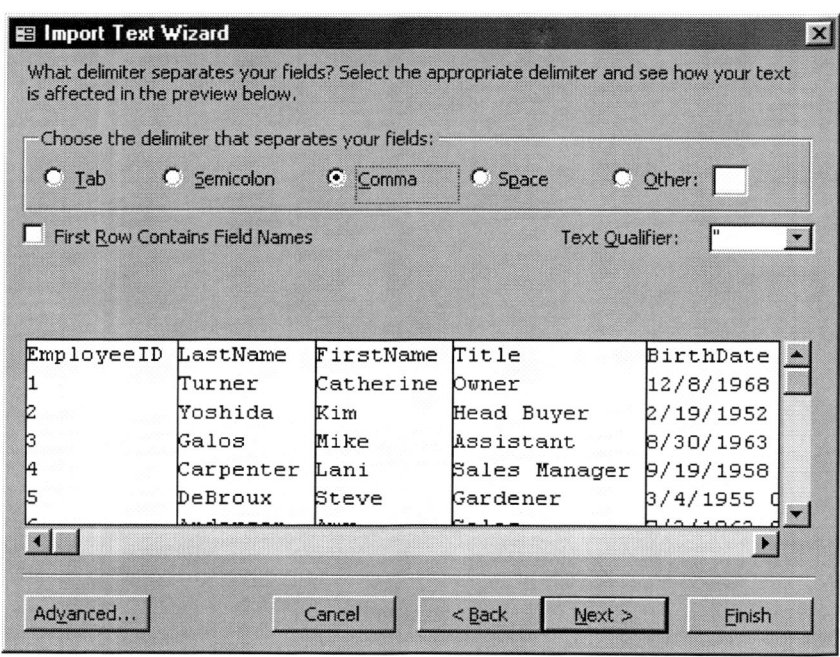

The wizard breaks the file into fields, based on its assumption that items are separated by commas. From the neat columns you see here, this assumption is obviously a good one. But if the columns are jumbled, you can choose a different delimiter from the options at the top of this page.

7   Select the **First Row Contains Field Names** check box, and then click **Next**.

The background of the first row becomes grey to indicate that these entries are field names.

8   Click **In an Existing Table**, select **Employees** from the drop-down list, and click **Next**.

9   Click **Finish** to import the text file into the Employees table.

A message informs you that the file was imported.

10   Click **OK** to close the message box, and then open the **Employees** table to confirm that Access imported nine records from the employees list.

11   Close the **Employees** table, and then close the database.

Importing Information from a Fixed-Width Text File

Ac2002-8-1

The only way to get the data of many older applications into Access is to export the data to a **fixed-width text file** and then import that file into Access. In a fixed-width text file, the same field in every record contains exactly the same number of characters. If the actual data doesn't fill a field, the field is padded with spaces so that the starting point of the data in the next field is the same number of characters from the beginning of every record. For example, if the first field contains 12 characters, the second field always starts 13 characters from the beginning of the record, even if the actual data in the first field is only 4 characters.

Fixed-width text files used to be difficult to import into databases, because you had to carefully count the number of characters in each field and then specify the field sizes in the database layout or the import program. If the text in any field were even one character off, all records from that point on would be jumbled. That is no longer a problem with Access, because the **Import Text Wizard** makes importing a fixed-width text file simple.

GardenCo Suppliers

In this exercise, you will import a fixed-width text file into the Suppliers table in the GardenCo database. The working folder for this exercise is *SBS\Access\Importing \ImportFText*. Follow these steps:

1   Open the **GardenCo** database located in the working folder.

2   On the **File menu**, point to **Get External Data**, and then click **Import**.

3   In the **Files of type** list, click **Text Files**.

4   In the working folder for this exercise, click **Suppliers**, and then click **Import** to display the first page of the **Import Text Wizard**, shown here:

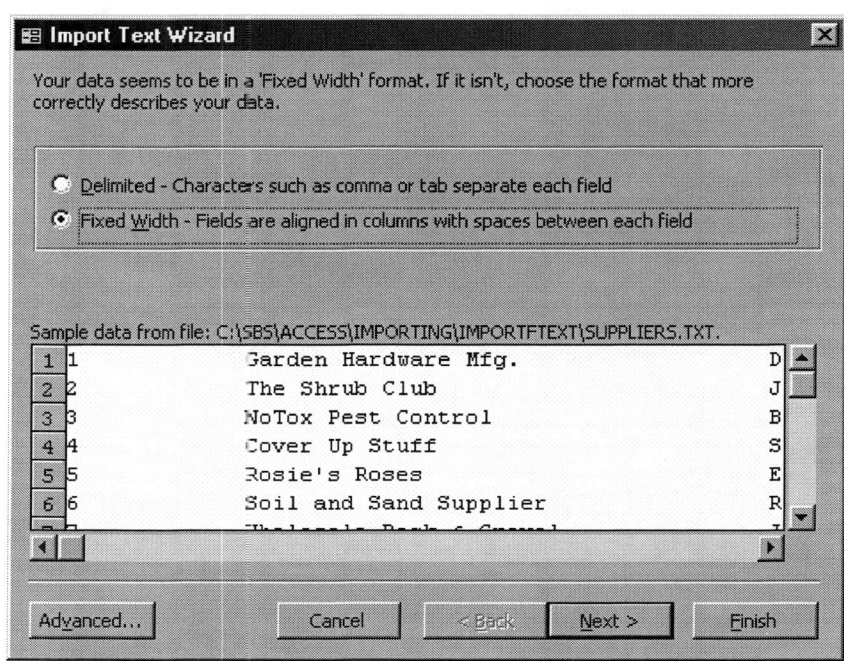

The wizard found that chunks of text seemed to line up, so it selected **Fixed Width** as the format.

5 Click **Next** to display the second page of the wizard, shown on the following page.

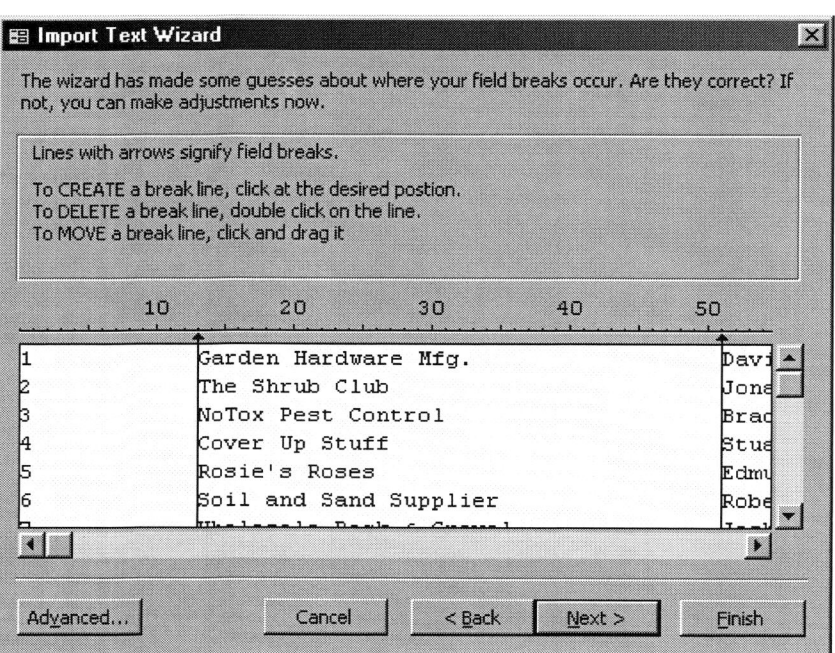

The wizard breaks the file into fields based on its assumption that a column of one or more spaces extending through all records marks the end of a field. If you take a casual glance at the fields, the wizard seems to have done its job well, but take a closer look.

6 Use the horizontal scroll bar to scroll through the fields until you get to the two fields that contain phone numbers, which are shown here:

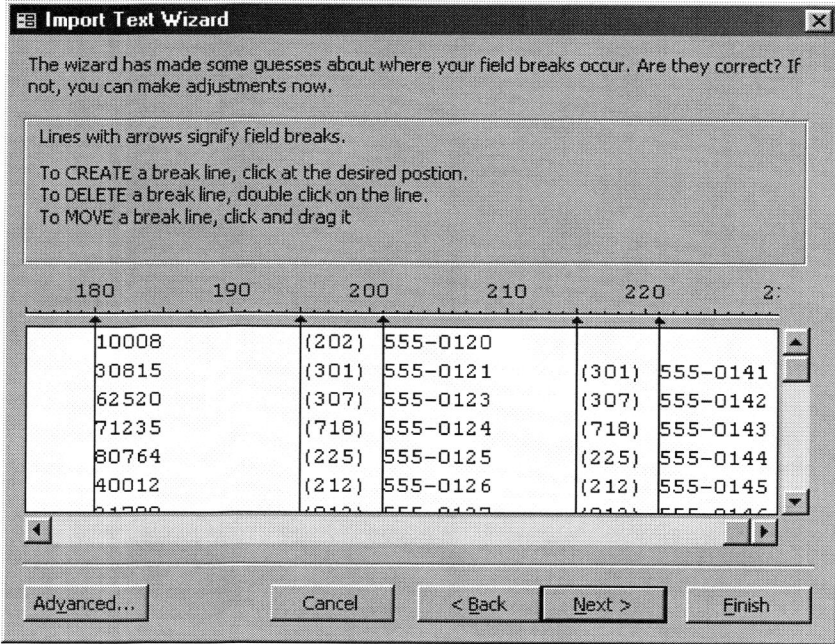

As you can see, the wizard broke each phone number into two fields because a column of spaces separates the area code from the number. Breaking the numbers this way would be fine if you wanted to store the area codes in separate fields, but you don't want to do that in this database.

7   Double-click the dividing line at column 201 to remove it. Then repeat this step for the dividing line at column 221, and click **Next**.

tip

If necessary, you can also add or move lines in the table. Simply follow the wizard's directions.

8   Click **In an Existing Table**, select **Suppliers** from the drop-down list, and then click **Next**.

9   Click **Finish** to import the text file into the Suppliers table.

Access informs you that the file was imported.

10   Click **OK** to close the message box, and then open the **Suppliers** table to confirm that Access imported 20 records from the suppliers list.

11   Close the **Suppliers** table, and then close the database.

Importing Information from an Access Database

Ac2002-8-1

Suppose you already have an Access database that includes tables of information about products and orders and another that includes contact information. Now you wish you had just one database so that all the information you use on a regular basis is in one place. You had to create the existing databases by hand and then type in all the data, and you don't relish the thought of having to retype anything. You can take advantage of this earlier work by importing the product and orders information into the contacts database, rather than recreating it all.

You can easily import one or more of the standard Access objects: tables, queries, forms, reports, pages, macros, and modules. When importing a table, you have the option of importing just the table definition (the structure that you see in Design view), or both the definition and the data. When importing a query, you can import it as a query or you can import the results of the query as a table.

When you import an Access object, the entire object is imported as an object of the same name in the active database. You don't have the option of importing selected fields or records. If the active database already has an object of the same name, Access imports the object with a number added to the end of its name.

tip

If you need only some of the fields or records from a table in another database, you can create a query in the other database to select just the information you need, and then import the results of the query as a table. Alternatively, you can import the table and then either edit it in Design view or use queries to clean it up.

GardenCo Products

In this exercise, you will import a couple of tables from a Products database into the GardenCo database. The working folder for this exercise is *SBS\Access\Importing \ImportAccess*. Follow these steps:

1 Open the **GardenCo** database located in the working folder.

2 On the **File** menu, point to **Get External Data**, and then click **Import**.

3 In the **Files of type** list, make sure **Microsoft Access** is selected.

4 Browse to the *SBS\Access\Importing\ImportAccess* folder, click **Products**, and then click **Import** to open the **Import Objects** dialog box.

As you might guess from looking at the tabs across the top of this dialog box, you can import any type of Access object from this database.

5 Click the **Options** button to expand the dialog box to display these import options:

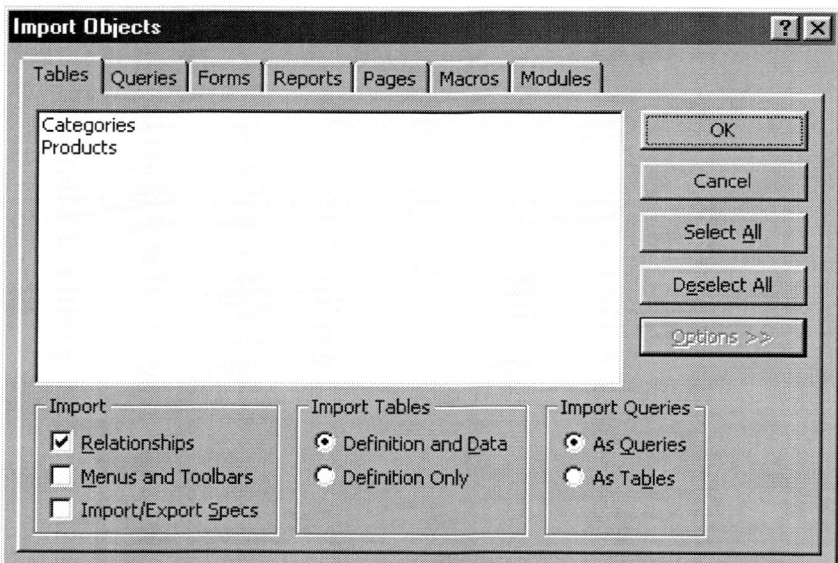

The default options are fine for the current task, but if it were necessary, you could use these options to refine the import process.

6 Click **Select All** to select the two tables listed.

You can also click individual tables one at a time to select them.

7 Click **OK** to import the tables.

8 Open the new **Categories** and **Products** tables to confirm that records were imported. Then close them.

9 Close the database.

Importing Information from Other Databases

Ac2002-1-1

Importing information from databases other than Access is usually an all-or-nothing situation, and quite often, what you get isn't in the exact format you need. You might find, for example, that **transaction records** include redundant information, such as the name of the product or purchaser, in every record. Or information about people might include the full name and address in one field, when you would like separate fields for the first name, last name, street address, and so on. You can choose to import information as it is and manipulate it in Access, or you can move it into some other program, such as Excel or Word, and manipulate it there before importing it into Access.

Access can import data from the following versions of dBASE, Lotus 1-2-3, and Paradox:

Program	Versions
dBASE	III, IV, and 5
Lotus 1-2-3	WK1, WK3, WJ2
Paradox	3, 4, 5, 7-8

GardenCo Shippers

In this exercise, you will import information from a dBASE file into the Shippers table in the GardenCo database. The working folder for this exercise is *SBS\Access \Importing\ImportDbase*. Follow these steps:

1 Open the **GardenCo** database located in the working folder.

2 On the **File** menu, point to **Get External Data**, and then click **Import** to open the **Import** dialog box.

3 In the **Files of type** list, click **dBASE 5**.

4 In the *SBS\Access\Importing\ImportDbase* folder, click **Shippers.dbf**, and then click **Import**.

After a few seconds of processing, Access lets you know that the file was imported. There are no options to select; whatever was in the file was imported.

5 Click **OK** to close the message box, close the **Import** dialog box, and then open the **Shippers** table to confirm that five records were imported properly.

6 Close the table and the database.

Importing Information from an HTML File

Ac2002-8-1

You might be familiar with the **Hypertext Markup Language (HTML)**, which is used to create Web pages. HTML uses **tags** to control the appearance and alignment of text when it is displayed in a Web browser. To display a table on a Web page, the table's elements – rows and cells – are enclosed in appropriate **HTML tags**. For example, a simple HTML table might look like this:

.
.
.

```
<table>
<tr>
  <td>LastName</td><td>FirstName</td>
</tr>
<tr>
  <td>Anderson</td><td>Amy</td>
<tr>
</table>
```

.
.
.

Of course, a lot of other tags and text would appear above and below this little table, and few tables are this simple. But you can get the general idea. With an HTML document, it is the <table>, <tr> (table row), and <td> (table data) tags that make the data look like a table when viewed in a Web browser.

All Office XP programs can save a document in HTML format, and to a limited extent, they can read or import a document saved in HTML format by another program. If you attempt to import an HTML document into Access, it will **parse** the document and identify anything that looks like structured data. You can then look at what Access has found and decide whether or not to import it.

important

If you want to import data into an existing table but the structure of the data isn't the same as the table structure, it is often easier to import the data into Excel, massage it there, and then import it into Access.

GardenCo
NewCust

In this exercise, you will import new customer information that is stored in an HTML document into the Customers table in the GardenCo database. The working folder for this exercise is *SBS\Access\Importing\ImportHTML*. Follow these steps:

1   Open the **GardenCo** database located in the working folder.

2   Open the **Customers** table, and notice that it contains 107 records. Close the table.

3   On the **File** menu, point to **Get External Data,** and then click **Import**.

4   In the **Files of type** list, click **HTML Documents**.

5   Browse to the *SBS Access\Importing\ImportHTML* folder, click **NewCust,** and then click **Import** to display the first page of the **Import HTML Wizard,** shown here:

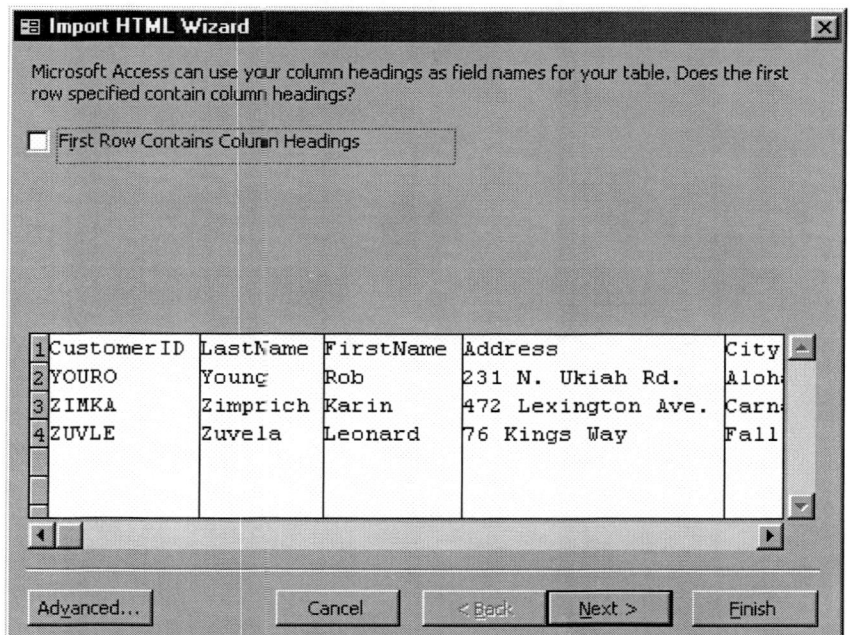

The wizard has found the table in the NewCust file and displays its contents, divided into rows and columns. If the file contains multiple tables or lists, the wizard lists them here, and you can select the one you want to import.

6   Select the **First Row Contains Column Headings** check box.

The background of the first row becomes grey to indicate that the entries in this row are field names.

7   Click the **Advanced** button to display the **Import Specification** dialog box, shown here:

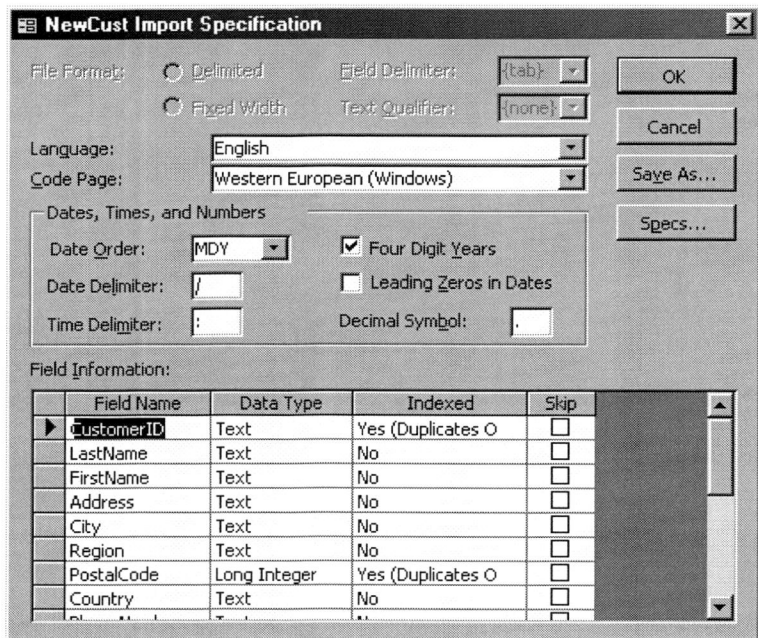

In the **Field Information** section, the data type of the **PostalCode** field is set to **Long Integer** because, in the file being imported, this field contains what appear to be large numbers. You don't need to manipulate these numbers mathematically, and you might want to change them to the ZIP+4 Code format or to a foreign code. Additionally, you are importing this information to the Customers table, which already considers postal codes to be text, so you need to change this setting.

8   Click in the **Data Type** cell for **PostalCode**, and then click **Text** in the drop-down list.

9   Click **OK**, and then click **Next** to display the next page of the wizard.

10 Click **In an Existing Table**, select **Customers** from the drop-down list, and then click **Next**.

11 Click **Finish** to import the new customers into the Customers table.

12 In the message box that appears, click **OK** to close it, and then open the **Customers** table.

The table now contains 110 records.

13 Close the **Customers** table and the database.

Exporting Information to Other Applications

Ac2002-8-2
Ac2002e-7-2

You can export Access database objects in a variety of formats. The specific formats available depend on the object you are trying to export. Tables, for example, can be exported in pretty much the same formats in which they can be imported. Macros, on the other hand, can be exported only to another Access database.

The following table lists the export formats available for each object:

Object	Export Formats
Table	Access, dBASE, Excel, FoxPro, HTML, Lotus 1-2-3, Paradox, Text, Active Server Pages (ASP), Microsoft Internet Information Server (IIS), Rich Text Format (RTF), Word Merge, XML, Open Database Connectivity (ODBC)
Query	Access, dBASE, Excel, HTML, Lotus 1-2-3, Paradox, Text, ASP, IIS, RTF, Word Merge, XML, ODBC
Form	Access, Excel, HTML, Text, ASP, IIS, RTF, XML
Report	Access, Excel, HTML, Text, RTF, Snapshot, XML
Page	Access, Data Access Page (DAP)
Macro	Access
Module	Access, Text

Tables and queries can be exported to most versions of the listed formats. Forms and reports are more limited, but even so, exporting to the formats you are most likely to use is pretty straightforward. The ones that get a little tricky are Active Server Pages (ASP), Microsoft Internet Information Server (IIS), and Open Database Connectivity (ODBC).

GardenCo

In this exercise, you will export the Suppliers table from the GardenCo database in a format that can be used by Excel. Then you'll export the Customers table to an XML document. The working folder for this exercise is *SBS\Access\Importing\Export*.

tip

To complete this exercise, you will need to have Excel 97 or later installed on your computer.

Follow these steps:

1   Open the **GardenCo** database located in the working folder.

2   In the database window, click the **Suppliers** table.

3   On the **File** menu, click **Export** to display the **Export Table `Suppliers' To** dialog box.

4   With the working folder for this exercise active, check that **Suppliers** is the name in the **File name** box.

5   Select **Microsoft Excel 97-2002** in the **Save as type** list.

6   Click **Export**.

Access exports the table and closes the dialog box.

7   Start Microsoft Windows Explorer, browse to the *SBS\Access\Importing \Export* folder, and double-click **Suppliers** to open it in Excel.

The new worksheet looks like this:

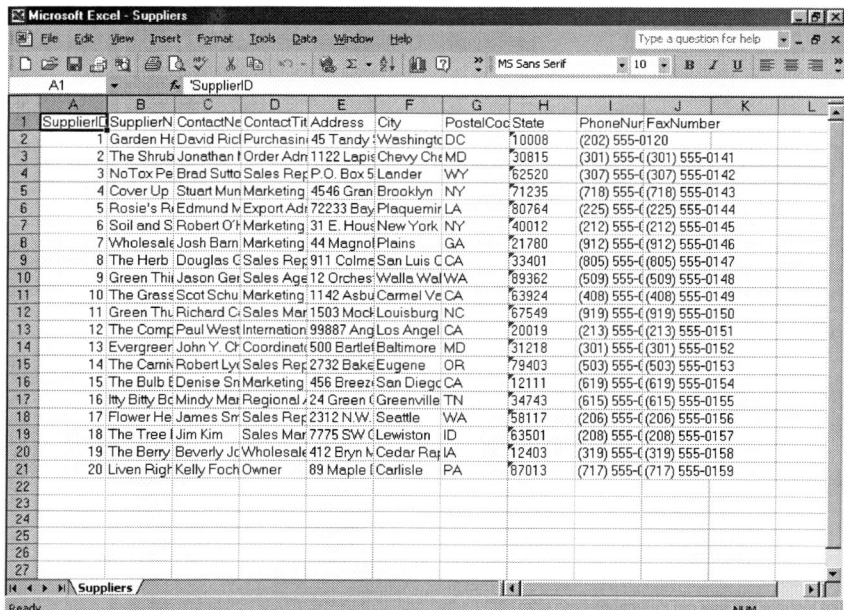

8   Quit Excel, and minimize Windows Explorer.

9   Click the title bar of the database window to activate it, and with the Suppliers table still selected, click **Export** on the **File** menu.

10   In the *SBS\Access\Importing\Export* folder, select **XML Documents** in the **Save as type** box, accept **Suppliers** as the file name, and click the **Export** button to open the **Export XML** dialog box.

11   Make sure both **Data (XML)** and **Schema of the data** are selected, and then click **OK**.

12   Switch to Windows Explorer, and notice that Access exported the Suppliers table as both an *.xml* and an *.xsd* file.

tip

You can combine the data and schema in one file by clicking the **Advanced** button, clicking the **Schema** tab, and then selecting the appropriate option.

13   Repeat steps 9 and 10 and try exporting the Suppliers table in various other formats by changing the options in the **Save As Type** box. Then view the exported files to see the results.

tip

If you export to an HTML file, you can view the table in a browser such as Microsoft Internet Explorer. To see the tags that define the structure of the table, either view the source in the browser or open the file in a text editor.

14   Close the database, and close Windows Explorer.

Quick Quizzes

●   What is a relational database?

●   What is a fixed width text file?

●   What does html mean?

●   What are XML files for?

LESSON 4: Simplifying Data Entry with Forms

After completing this chapter, you will be able to:

✓ *Create a form using a wizard*

✓ *Refine the properties of a form*

✓ *Add controls that help enter data*

✓ *Create a form using AutoForm*

✓ *Create a form based on more than one table*

A database that contains the day-to-day records of an active company is useful only if it can be kept up to date and if particular items of information can be found quickly. Although Microsoft Access is fairly easy to use, entering, editing, and retrieving information in Datasheet view is not a task you would want to assign to someone who's not familiar with Access. Not only would these tasks be tedious and inefficient, but working in Datasheet view leaves far too much room for error, especially if details of complex transactions have to be entered into several related tables. The solution to this problem, and the first step in the conversion of this database to a database application, is to create and use forms.

A form is an organized and formatted view of some or all of the fields from one or more tables or queries. Forms work interactively with the tables in a database. You use **controls** on the form to enter new information, to edit or remove existing information, or to locate information. Like printed forms, Access forms can include **label controls** that tell users what type of information they are expected to enter, as well as **text box controls** in which they can enter the information. Unlike printed forms, Access forms can also include a variety of other controls, such as **option buttons** and **command buttons**, that transform Access forms into something very much like a Microsoft Windows dialog box or one page of a wizard.

tip

Some forms are used to navigate among the features and functions of a database application and have little or no connection with its actual data. A **switchboard** is an example of this type of form.

As with other Access objects, you can create forms by hand or with the help of a wizard. Navigational and housekeeping forms, such as switchboards, are best created by hand in Design view. Forms that are based on tables, on the other hand, should always be created with a wizard and then refined by hand-not because it is difficult to drag the necessary text box controls onto a form, but because there is simply no point in doing it by hand.

For this chapter, you will create some forms to hide the complexity of the GardenCo database from the people who will be entering and working with its information. First you will discover how easy it is to let the **Form Wizard** create forms that you can then modify to suit your needs. You'll learn about the controls you can place on a form, and the properties that control its function and appearance. After you have created a form containing controls, you will learn how to tell Access what to do when a user performs some action in a control, such as clicking or entering text. You will also take a quick look at subforms (forms within a form). You will be working with the GardenCo database files and other sample files that are stored in the following subfolders of the *SBS\Access\Forms* folder: *FormByWiz*, *Properties*, *Layout*, *Controls*, *Events*, *AutoForm*, and *Subform*.

Creating a Form Using a Wizard

Ac2002-4-1

Before you begin creating a form, you need to know what table it will be based on and have an idea of how the form will be used. Having made these decisions, you can use the **Form Wizard** to help create the basic form. Remember though, that like almost any other object in Access, after the form is created you can always go into Design view to customize the form if it does not quite meet your needs.

GardenCo

In this exercise, you'll create a form that will be used to add new customer records to the Customers table of The Garden Company's database. The working folder for this exercise is *SBS\Access\Forms\FormByWiz*. Follow these steps:

1   Open the **GardenCo** database located in the working folder.

2   On the **Objects** bar, click **Forms**.

3   Double-click **Create form by using wizard** to start the **Form Wizard**, whose first page looks like this:

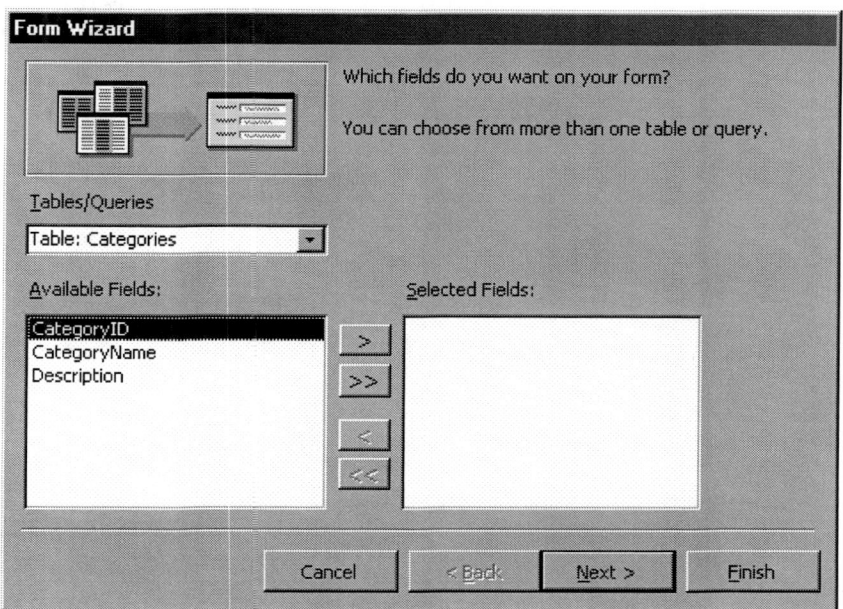

4   In the **Tables/Queries** drop-down list, click **Table: Customers** to display the fields from that table in the **Available Fields** list.

5   Click the **>>** button to move all the fields from the Customers table to the **Selected Fields** list, and then click **Next**.

You use the second page of the **Form Wizard** to select the layout of the fields on the new form. When you click an option on the right side of the page, the preview area on the left side shows what the form layout will look like with that option applied.

6   Select **Columnar**, and then click **Next**.

In this page, you can click a style option to see how the selected style will look when applied to the form.

7   Select the **Sumi Painting** style from the list, and click **Next**.

8   Because this form is based on the Customers table, Access suggests *Customers* as the form's title. Accept this suggestion, leave the **Open the form to view or enter information** option selected, and click **Finish**.

The new Customers form opens, displaying the first customer record in the Customers table, like this:

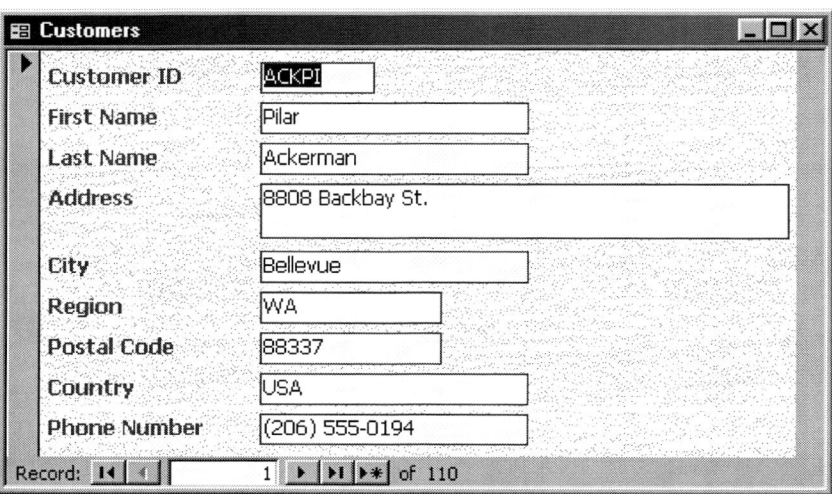

9 Use the navigation controls at the bottom of the form to scroll through a few of the records.

10 Close the form and the database.

Refining Form Properties

Ac2002-4-2

You can only change control properties by selecting them when you are in Design view. For example, you can apply the same background colour to several labels by selecting them together. Select the controls by dragging with the mouse, or, select all the controls by using the keyboard combination:

Ctrl + A , and then choose the colour to apply.

GardenCo tgc_bkgrnd

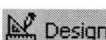 Design

As with tables, you can work with forms in multiple views. The two most common views are Form view, which you use to view or enter data, and Design view, which you use to add controls to the form or change the form's properties or layout.

When you use the **Form Wizard** to create a form in a column format, every field you select from the underlying table is represented by a text box control and its associated label control. A form like this one, which is used to enter or view the information stored in a specific table, is linked, or **bound**, to that table. Each text box - the box where data is entered or viewed - is bound to a specific field in the table. The table is the **record source**, and the field is the **control source**. Each control has a number of properties, such as font, font size, alignment, fill colour, and border. The wizard assigns default values for these properties, but you can change them to improve the form's appearance.

In this exercise, you will edit the properties of the Customers form so that it suits the needs of the people who will be using it on a daily basis. The working folder for this exercise is *SBS\Access\Forms\Properties*. Follow these steps:

1 Open the **GardenCo** database located in the working folder.

2 With **Forms** selected on the **Objects** bar, select **Customers** in the list of forms, and click the **Design** button.

This form opens in Design view, like this:

Label control   Text box control   Toolbox

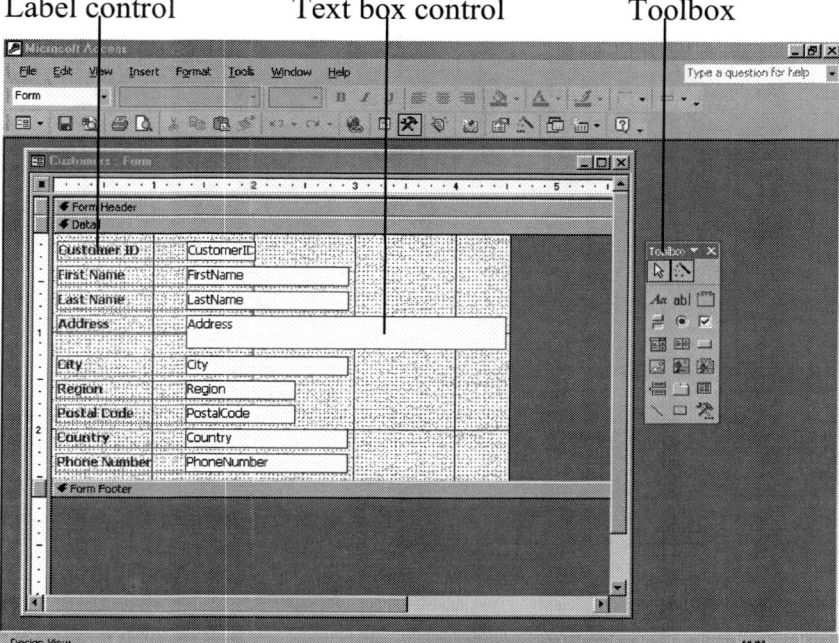

When a form is created, some of its properties are inherited from the table on which it is based. In this case, the names assigned to the text boxes (*FirstName*, *LastName*, and so on) are the field names from the Customers table, and the labels to the left of each text box reflect the **Caption** property of each field. The size of each text box is determined by the **Field Size** property.

tip

After a form has been created, its properties are not bound to their source. Changing the table's field properties has no impact on the corresponding form property, and vice versa.

3   Change the font of the **Customer ID** label by clicking the label and clicking **Microsoft Sans Serif** in the **Font** list on the Formatting toolbar. (If you don't see **Microsoft Sans Serif**, click **MS Sans Serif**.)

4   With the label still selected, click **8** in the **Font Size** list to make the font slightly smaller.

5   Right-click the **CustomerID** text box (not its label), and click **Properties** on the shortcut menu to display this **Properties** dialog box for the **CustomerID** text box:

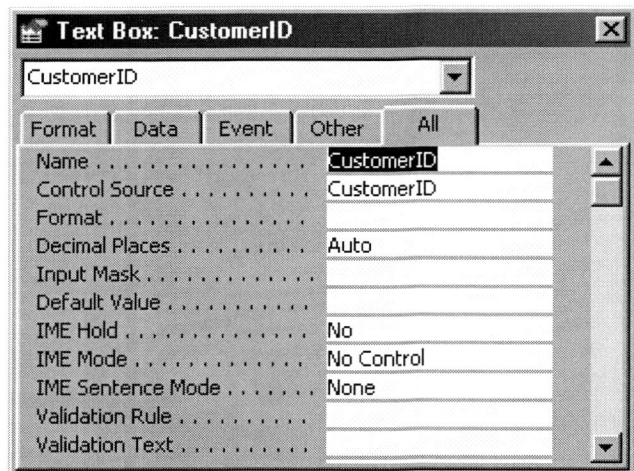

All the settings available on the toolbar are also available (with other settings) in a **Properties** dialog box that is associated with each control. You can use this dialog box to display the properties of any object on the form, including the form itself: simply select the object from the drop-down list at the top of the dialog box.

You can display related types of properties by clicking the appropriate tab: **Format, Data, Event,** or **Other.** Or you can display all the properties by clicking the **All** tab.

6 Click the **Format** tab, scroll to the **Font Name** property, and change it to **Microsoft Sans Serif (or MS Sans Serif).** Then set **Font Size** to **8,** and set **Font Weight** to **Bold.**

On the form behind the dialog box, you can see how these changes affect the *CustomerID* text in the text box.

tip

When you are working in Design view with the **Properties** dialog box open, you can drag the dialog box by its title bar to the side of the screen so that you can see the changes you're making to the form.

7 Click **FirstName_Label** in the drop-down list at the top of the **Properties** dialog box to select the label to the left of the **FirstName** text box.

8 Repeat step 6 to change the font settings for this control.

These different ways of selecting a control and changing its properties provide some flexibility and convenience, but you can see that it would be a bit tedious to apply any of them to a few dozen controls on a form. The next two steps provide a faster method.

9 Press Ctrl + A to select all the controls in the **Detail** section of the form.

tip

You can also select all of the controls on a form by clicking **Select All** on the **Edit** menu, or by dragging a rectangle over some portion of all the controls.

Small black handles appear around all the controls to indicate that they are selected. The title bar of the **Properties** dialog box now displays *Multiple selection*, and the **Objects** list is blank. Only the **Format** settings that have the same settings for all the selected controls are displayed. Because the changes you made in the previous steps are not shared by all the selected controls, the **FontName**, **Font Size**, and **Font Weight** settings are now blank.

10 To apply the settings to all the selected controls, set the **Font Name**, **Font Size**, and **Font Weight** as you did in step 6.

11 With all controls still selected, click **Back Style** on the **Format** tab, and set it to **Normal.**

The background of the labels will no longer be transparent.

12 Click **Back Color**, and then click the button at the right end of the box to display this **Color** dialog box:

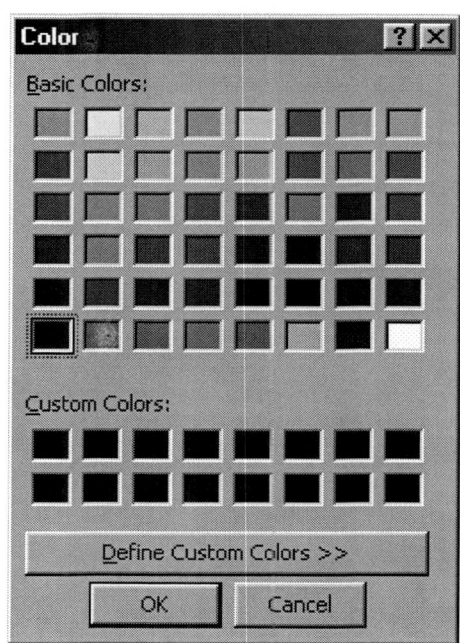

13 Click pale yellow, and click **OK.**

The background of all the controls changes to pale yellow.

tip

If you don't see a colour you want to use, click **Define Custom Colors**, work with the various settings until you have specified the desired colour, and then click **Add to Custom Colors**.

14 Set **Special Effect** to **Shadowed**, and set **Border Color** to a shade of green.

You can either click the button and make a selection, or type a colour value such as **32768** in the **BorderColor** box.

15 Click the **Detail** section to deselect all the controls. Your form should now look something like this:

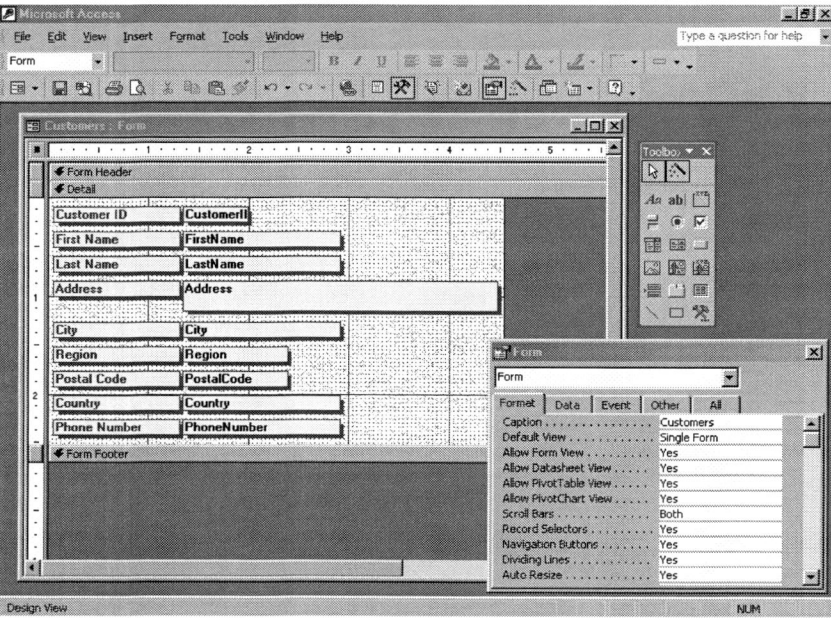

16 Click the label to the left of **FirstName**, and in the **Properties** dialog box, change the caption to **Name**.

17 Repeat step 16 to change *Phone Number* to **Phone**.

tip

You can edit the **Caption** property of a label or the **Control Source** property of a text box by selecting it, clicking its text, and then editing the text as you would in any other Windows application. However, take care when editing the **Control Source** property, which defines where the content of the text box comes from.

18 Remove the label to the left of **LastName** by clicking it and then pressing the ⎡Del⎤ key.

19 Select all the labels, but not their corresponding text boxes, by holding down the ⎡Shift⎤ key as you click each of them. Then in the **Properties** dialog box, set the **Text Align** property to **Right**.

20 On the **Format** menu, point to **Size**, and then click **To Fit** to size the labels to fit their contents, as shown here:

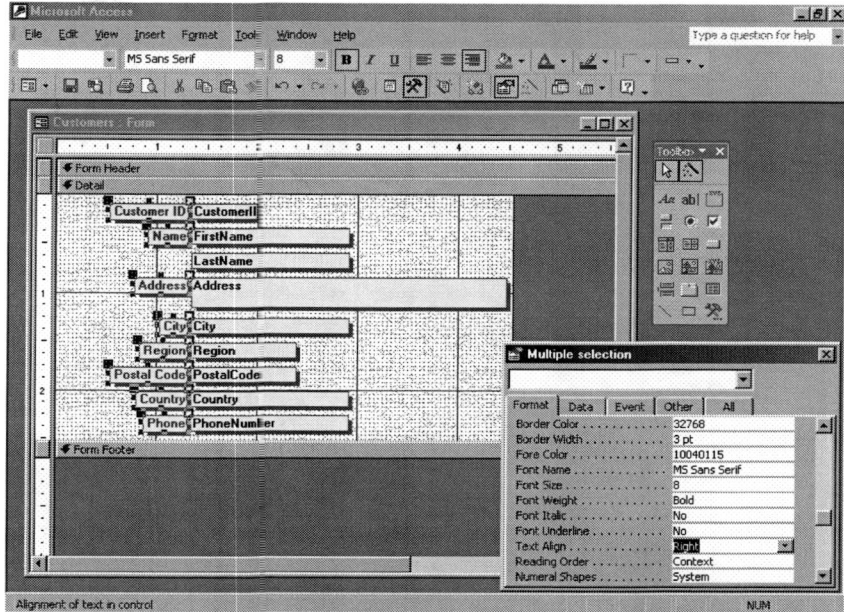

tip

The order in which you make formatting changes, such as the ones above, can have an impact on the results. If you don't see the expected results, click the **Undo** button or press $\boxed{\text{Ctrl}} + \boxed{Z}$ to step back through your changes, and then try again.

21 Now select all the text boxes but not their corresponding labels, and in the **Properties** dialog box, change the **Left** setting to **1.5"** to insert a little space between the labels and the text boxes.

22 Change **Font Weight** to **Normal**, and then click anywhere outside the controls to deselect them.

23 To change the background to one that better represents The Garden Company, select **Form** from the drop-down list of objects at the top of the **Properties** dialog box, click the **Picture** property-which shows *(bitmap)*-and then click the button to open the **Insert Picture** dialog box.

24 Browse to the *SBS\Access\Forms\Properties* folder, change the **Files of type** setting to **Graphics Interchange Format**, and double-click **tgc_bkgrnd**.

The form's background changes, and the path to the graphic used for the new background is displayed in the **Picture** property, as shown on the next page.

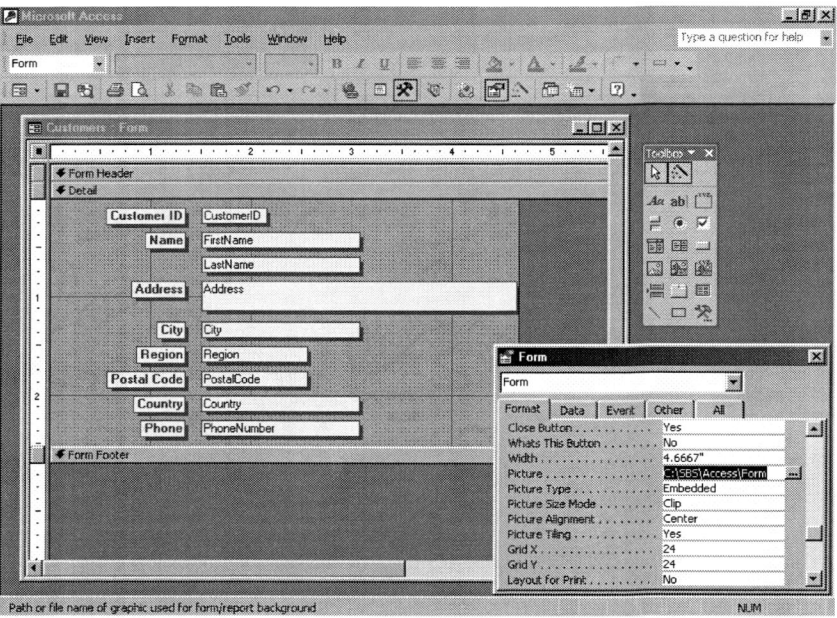

Save

25   Click the **Save** button to save the design of your Customers form.

26   Close the form and the database.

Adding Controls to a Form

Ac2002-4-2

Every form has three basic sections: **Form Header**, **Detail**, and **Form Footer**. When you use a wizard to create a form, the wizard adds a set of controls for each field that you select from the underlying table to the **Detail** section and leaves the **Form Header** and **Form Footer** sections blank. Because these sections are empty, Access collapses them, but you can size all the sections by dragging their **selectors**. Although labels and text box controls are perhaps the most common controls found on forms, you can also enhance your forms with many other types of controls. For example, you can add groups of option buttons, check boxes, and list boxes to present people with choices instead of making them type entries in text boxes.

More Controls

To give your form a professional look you can insert control buttons.

The most popular controls are stored in the toolbox. Clicking the **More Controls** button displays a list of all the other controls that Access has discovered on your computer. The controls displayed when you click the **More Controls** button are not necessarily associated with Access or even with another Microsoft Office application. The list includes every control that any application has installed and registered on your computer.

important

Some controls, such as the Calendar Control, can be very useful. Others might do nothing when you add them to a form, or might do something unexpected and not entirely pleasant. If you feel like experimenting, don't do so in a database that is important to you.

GardenCo
tgc_logo2

In this exercise, you will use the Customers form from the GardenCo database to add a graphic and a caption to the **Form Header** section. You will also replace the Country text box control in the **Detail** section with a combo box control. The working folder for this exercise is *SBS\Access\Forms\Controls*. Follow these steps:

1   Open the **GardenCo** database located in the working folder.

2   Open the **Customers** form in Design view.

3   Point to the horizontal line between the **Form Header** section selector and the **Detail** section selector and, when the pointer changes to a double arrow, drag the **Detail** section selector down about I inch.

The form now looks like this:

Form selector

Form Header
section selector

Details section
header

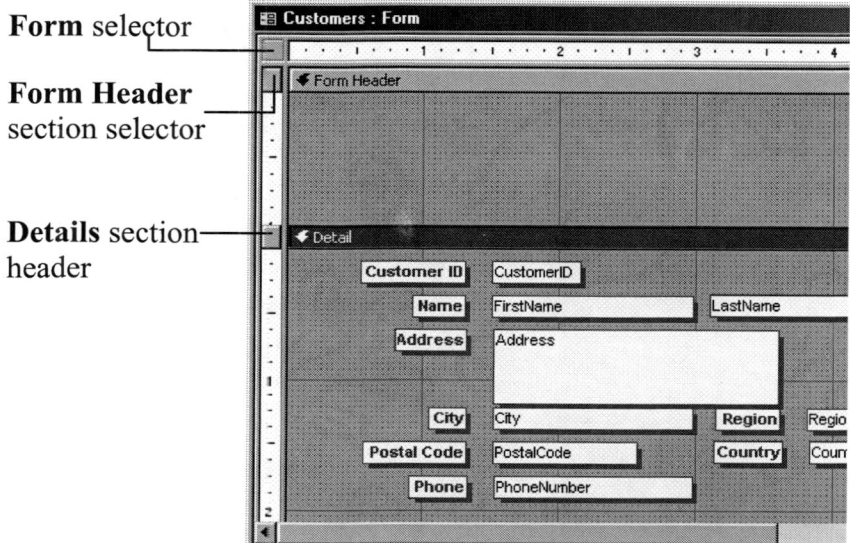

Toolbox

4   If the toolbox isn't displayed, click the **Toolbox** button on the toolbar.

You can also check the **Toolbox** command on the **View** menu. To keep the toolbox open but out of the way, you can dock it along one edge of the screen.

5   To get an idea of what controls are available, move the pointer over the buttons in the toolbox, pausing just long enough to display each button's ScreenTip.

Image

6   Click the **Image** control in the toolbox, and then drag a rectangle about I inch high and 3 inches wide at the left end of the **Form Header** section.

When you release the mouse button, Access displays the **Insert Picture** dialog box, where you can select an image to insert in the control.

7   Make sure that the *SBS\Access\Forms\Controls* folder is selected and that **Graphics Interchange Format** is the **Files of type** setting. Then double-click **tgc_logo2**.

The Garden Company logo appears inside the image control, like this:

tip

If the control isn't large enough, the image is cropped. You can enlarge the control to display the entire image. (You might also have to enlarge the **Form Header** section.)

Label

8   To add a caption to the header, click the **Label** control in the toolbox, and then drag another rectangle in the header section.

Access inserts a label control containing the insertion point, ready for you to enter a caption.

9   Type the caption **Customers**, and press ⌷ Enter ⌷.

The Customers label takes on the formatting of the other labels.

10   With the **Customers** label selected, press the ⌷ F4 ⌷ key to display the **Properties** dialog box.

11   Change **Font Size** to **18**, and change **Text Align** to **Center**. Then close the **Properties** dialog box.

12   On the **Format** menu, point to **Size**, and then click **To Fit**.

13   Adjust the size and position of the two controls you added until they look something like this:

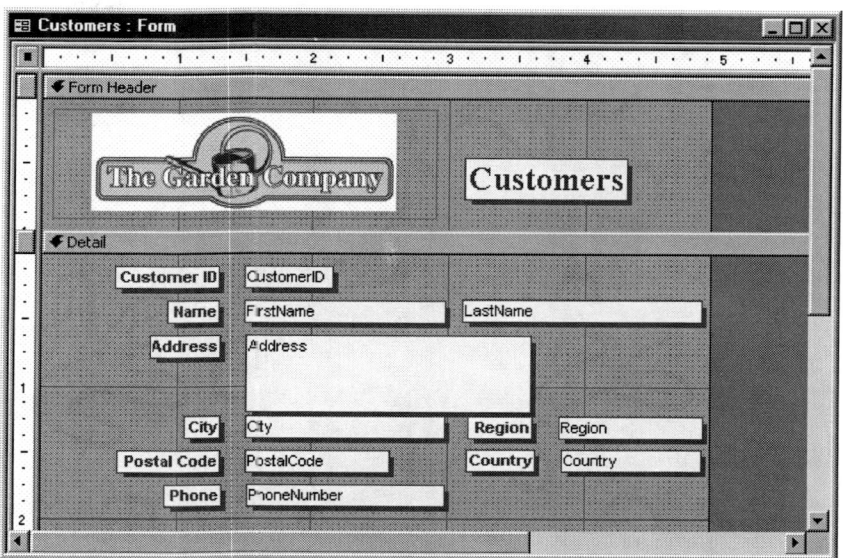

Control Wizards

14 If the **Control Wizards** button is active in the toolbox (has a border around it), click it to deselect it.

Deselecting this button enables you to create a control with all the default settings without having to work through the wizard's pages.

Combo Box

15 Insert a combo box in the **Details** section by clicking the **Combo Box** control in the toolbox and then dragging a rectangle just below the current **Country** text box.

When you release the mouse, Access displays a combo box control, which is **unbound** (not attached to a field in the Customers table).

Format Painter

16 Copy the formatting of the **Country** text box to the new combo box control by clicking the **Country** text box, clicking the **Format Painter** button on the toolbar, and then clicking the combo box control.

Both the combo box control and its label take on the new formatting.

17 Select the combo box again, and then display the **Properties** dialog box.

18 Click the **Data** tab, set **Control Source** to **Country**, and then type the following in the **Row Source** box:

SELECT DISTINCT Customers.Country FROM Customers;

(Note that there is no space between *Customers* and *Country*; there is only a period.)

This line is a query that extracts one example of every country in the Country field of the Customers table and displays the results as a list when you click the box's arrow.

The **Properties** dialog box now looks like this (you'll have to widen it to display the whole query):

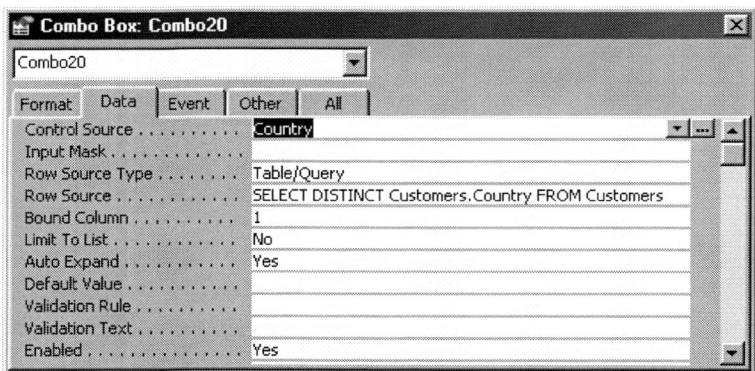

tip

If you need to add a new customer from a country that is not on the list, you can type the new country in the combo box. After the record is added to the database, that country shows up when the combo box list is displayed.

19 If necessary, set the **Row Source Type** to **Table/Query**.

20 Click the label to the left of the combo box, click the dialog box's **Format** tab, change the caption to **Country**, and close the dialog box.

21 Delete the original **Country** text box and its label, and move the new combo box and label into their place, resizing them as needed.

View

22 Click the **View** button to see your form, which looks similar to this:

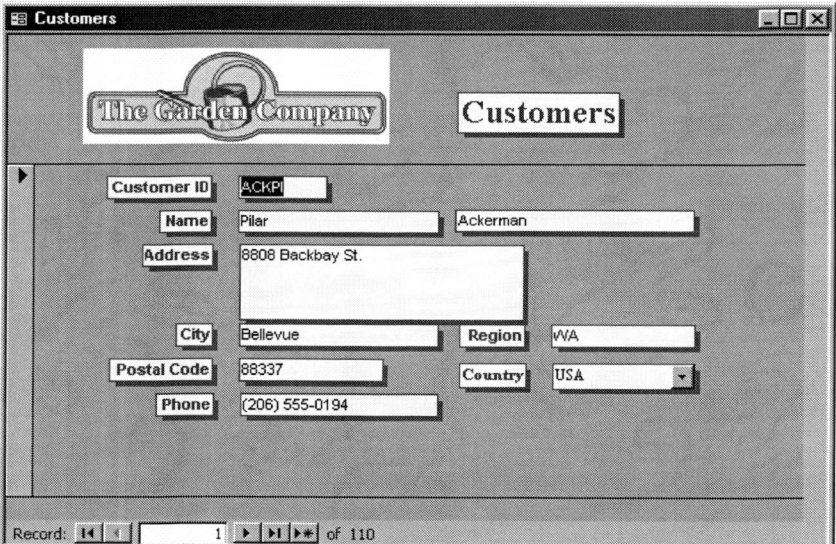

23 Scroll through a couple of records, and display the combo box's list to see how you can select a country.

24 You don't need the **record selector** - the grey bar along the left edge of the form-so return to Design view, and display the **Properties** dialog box for the entire form by checking the **Form** selector and pressing [F4]. Then on the **Format** tab, change **Record Selectors** to **No**. While you're at it, change **Scroll Bars** to **Neither**. Then close the **Properties** dialog box.

25 Save the form's new design, and switch to Form view for a final look.

26 Close the form and the database.

Creating a Form Using an AutoForm

Ac2002-4-1

GardenCo

Although a form doesn't have to include all the fields from a table, when it is used as the primary method of creating new records, it usually does include all of them. The quickest way to create a form that includes all the fields from one table is to use an **AutoForm**. And as with the forms created by a wizard, you can easily customize these forms.

In this exercise, you will create an AutoForm that displays information about each of the products carried by The Garden Company. The working folder for this exercise is *SBS\Access\Forms\AutoForm*. Follow these steps:

1 Open the **GardenCo** database located in the working folder.

2 On the **Objects** bar, click **Forms**.

3 On the database window's toolbar, click the **New** button to display this **New Form** dialog box, which lists all the ways you can create a form:

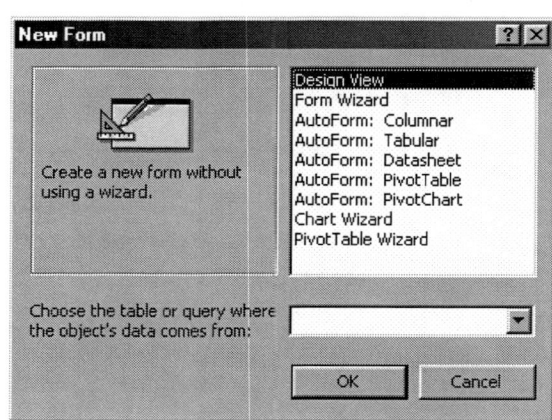

4 Click **AutoForm: Columnar** in the list of choices, select the **Categories** table from the drop-down list at the bottom of the dialog box, and then click **OK**.

The dialog box closes, and after a moment a new Categories form is displayed in Form view.

Save

5   Click the **Save** button, accept the default name of *Categories* in the **Save As** dialog box, and click **OK** to view your form, which looks like this:

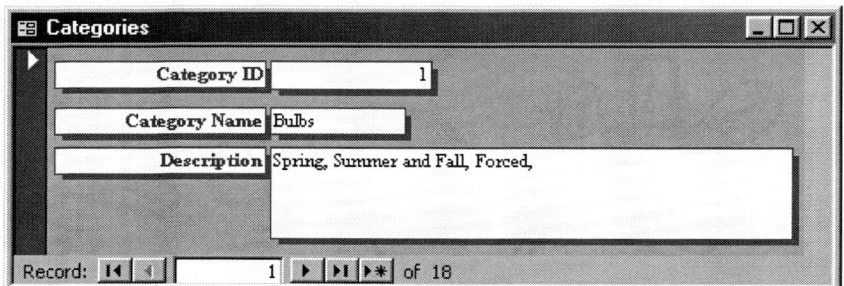

tip

When AutoForm creates a form, Access applies the background style you selected the last time you used the **Form Wizard** (or the default style, if you haven't used the wizard). If your form doesn't look like this one, switch to Design view, and on the **Format** menu, click **AutoFormat**. You can then select **The Garden Company** style from the list displayed.

6   This form looks pretty good as it is, but switch to Design view so that you can make a few minor changes.

7   Delete the word *Category* from the **Category Name** label.

8   The **CategoryID** value is provided by Access and should never be changed, so you need to disable that text box control. Click and, if necessary, press F4 to display the control's **Properties** dialog box.

9   On the **Data** tab, change **Enabled** to **No**, and close the dialog box.

10 Switch to Form view, and scroll through a few categories. Try to edit entries in the **Category ID** field to confirm that you can't.

11 You don't need the record selector for the form, so return to Design view, and display the form's **Properties** dialog box by clicking the **Form** selector and pressing F4 . Then on the **Format** tab, change **Scroll Bars** to **Neither** and **Record Selectors** to **No**.

12 Save and close the **Categories** form.

13 Close the database.

Adding a Subform to a Form

Ac2002-61-1
Ac2002e-2-3
Ac2002e-5-1
Ac2002e-5-2

A form can display information (fields) from one or more tables or queries. If you want to display fields from several tables or queries on one form, you have to give some thought to the **relationships** that must exist between those objects.

In Access, a relationship is an association between common fields in two tables, and it allows you to relate the information in one table to the information in another table. For example, in the GardenCo database a relationship can be established between the Categories table and the Products table because both tables have a CategoryID field. Each product is in only one category, but each category can contain many products, so this type of relationship - the most common - is known as a **one-to-many relationship**.

As you create forms and queries, Access might recognize some relationships between the fields in the underlying tables. However, it probably won't recognize all of them without a little help from you.

GardenCo

In this exercise, you will first define the relationship between the Categories and Products tables in the GardenCo database. You will then add a **subform** to a form. For each category displayed on the main form, this subform will display all the products in that category. The working folder for this exercise is *SBS\Access\Forms \Subform*. Follow these steps:

1 Open the **GardenCo** database located in the working folder.

Relationships

2 On the Access toolbar, click the **Relationships** button to open the Relationships window.

Show Table

3 If the **Show Table** dialog box isn't displayed, click the **Show Table** button on the toolbar. Then double-click **Categories** and **Products** in the list displayed. Close the **Show Table** dialog box to view the Relationships window, which looks like this:

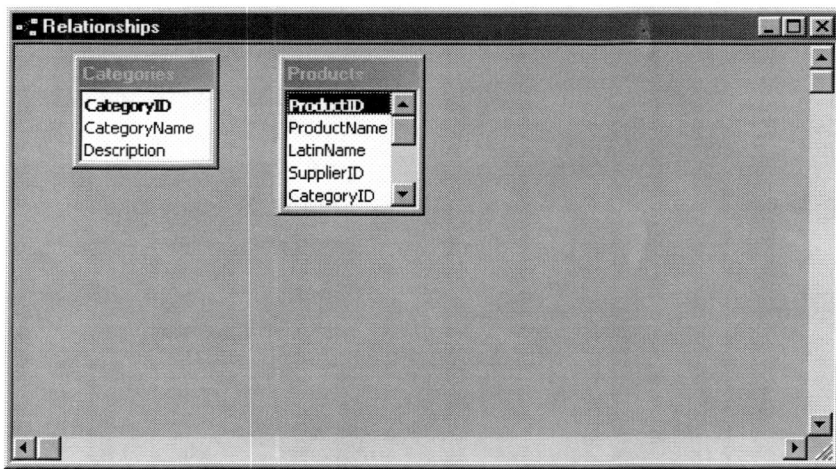

4 Point to **CategoryID** in one table, and drag it on top of **CategoryID** in the other table.

Access displays the **Edit Relationships** dialog box, which lists the fields you have chosen to relate and offers several options, as shown here:

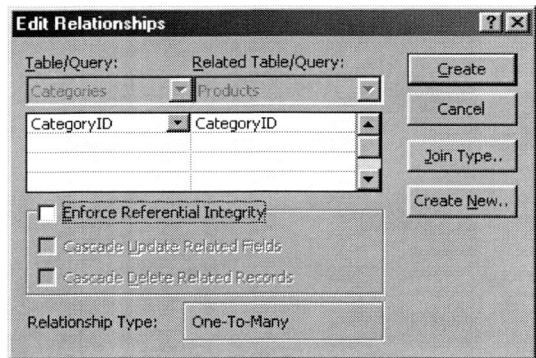

Other Types of Relationships

In addition to one-to-many relationships, you can create **one-to-one relationships** and **many-to-many relationships**, but they are not as common.

In a one-to-one relationship, each record in one table can have one and only one related record in the other table. This type of relationship isn't commonly used because it is easier to put all the fields in one table. However, you might use two related tables instead of one to break up a table with many fields, or to track information that applies to only some of the records in the first table.

A many-to-many relationship is really two one-to-many relationships tied together through a third table. For example, the GardenCo database contains Products, Orders, and Order Details tables. The Products table has one record for each product sold by The Garden Company, and each product has a unique ProductID. The Orders table has one record for each order placed with The Garden Company, and each record in it has a unique OrderID. However, the Orders table doesn't specify which products were included in each order; that information is in the Order Details table, which is the table in the middle that ties the other two tables together. Products and Orders each have a one-to-many relationship with Order Details. Products and Orders therefore have a many-to-many relationship with each other. In plain language, this means that every product can appear in many orders, and every order can include many products.

5   Select the **Enforce Referential Integrity** check box, select the other two check boxes, and then click **Create**.

tip

Access uses a system of rules called **referential integrity** to ensure that relationships between records in related tables are valid, and that you don't accidentally delete or change related data. When the **Cascade Update Related Fields** check box is selected, changing a primary key value in the primary table automatically updates the matching value in all related records. When the **Cascade Delete Related Records** check box is selected, deleting a record in the primary table deletes any related records in the related table.

Access draws a line representing the one-to-many relationship between the **CategoryID** fields in each of the tables, as shown here:

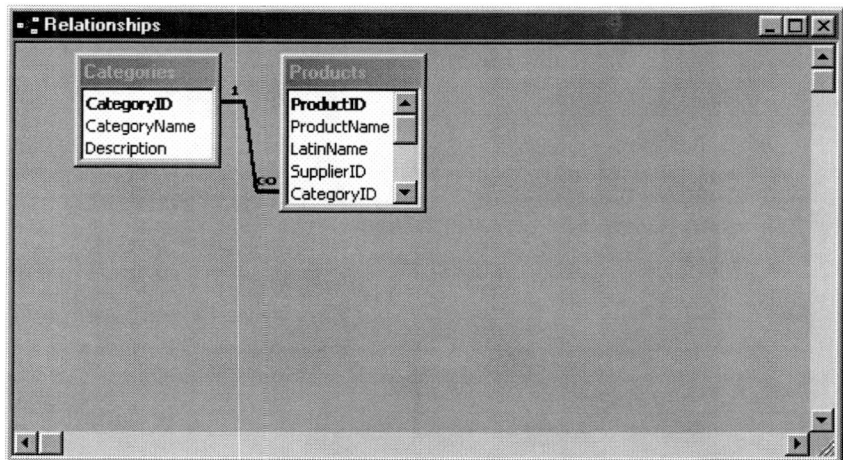

tip

You can edit or delete a relationship by right-clicking the line and clicking the appropriate command on the shortcut menu.

6 Close the Relationships window, clicking **Yes** when prompted to save the window's layout.

7 Open the **Categories** form in Design view.

Toolbox

8 Enlarge the Form window, and drag the **Form Footer** section selector down about 1 inch to give yourself some room to work.

9 If the toolbox isn't displayed, click the **Toolbox** button.

Control Wizards

10 Make sure the **Control Wizards** button in the toolbox is active (has a border around it).

11 Click the **Subform/Subreport** button, and drag a rectangle in the lower portion of the **Details** section.

Subform/Subreport

A white object appears on the form, and the first page of the **Subform Wizard** opens.

12 Leave **Use existing Tables and Queries** selected, and click **Next**.

13 In the **Tables/Queries** list, click **Table: Products**.

14 Add the **ProductName, CategoryID, QuantityPerUnit, UnitPrice,** and **UnitsInStock** fields to the **Selected Fields** list by clicking each one and then clicking the > button. Then click **Next** to display the third page of the wizard:

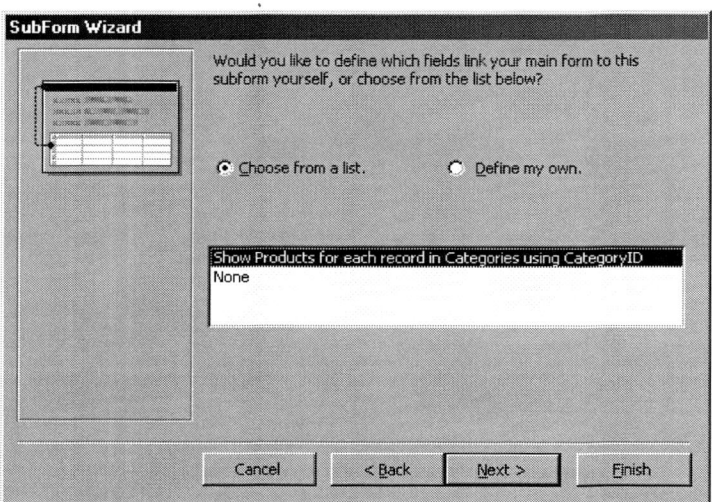

Because the Category ID field in the subform is related to the Category ID field in the main form, the wizard selects **Show Products for each record in Categories using CategoryID** as the **Choose from a list** option.

tip

If the wizard can't figure out which fields are related, it selects the **Define my own** option and displays list boxes in which you can specify the fields to be related.

15 Click **Next** to accept the default selection, and then click **Finish** to accept the default name for the subform and complete the process.

Access displays the Categories form in Design view, with an embedded Products subform. The size and location of the subform is determined by the original rectangle you dragged on the form.

16 Adjust the size and location of the objects on your form so that it resembles this one:

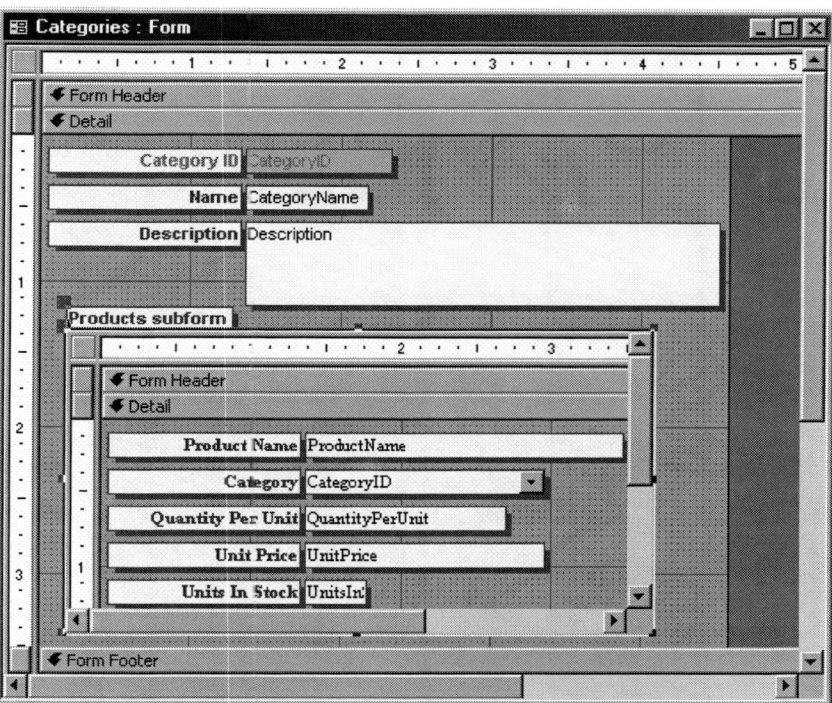

17   Notice the layout of the subform, and then click **View** to switch to Form view, where the form looks like the one shown on the next page.

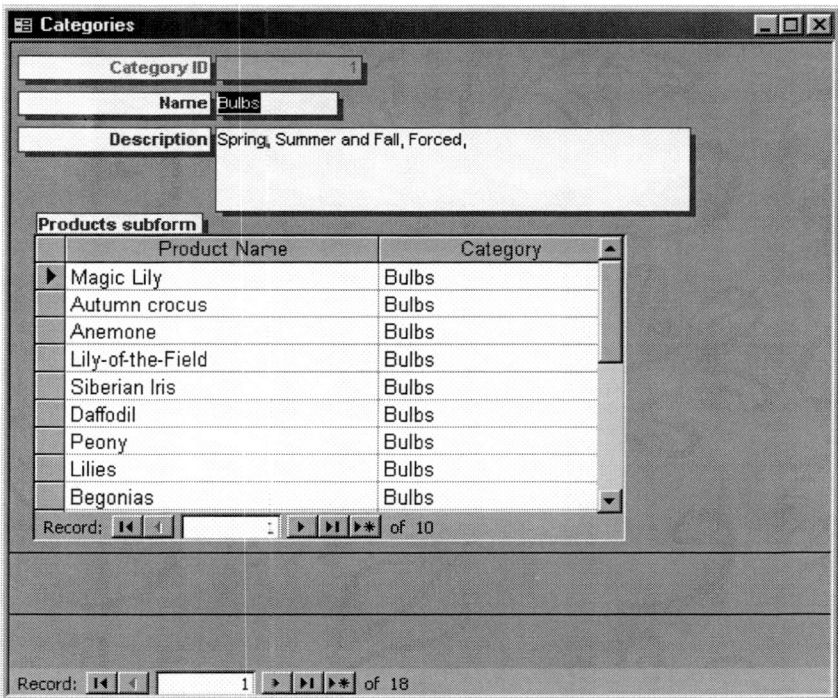

The format of the subform has totally changed. In Design view, it looks like a simple form, but in Form view, it looks like a datasheet.

18   Switch back to Design view, make any necessary size adjustments, and if necessary, open the **Properties** dialog box.

19   Click the **Form** selector in the upper left corner of the subform twice.

The first click selects the Products subform control, and the second click selects the form. A small black square appears on the selector.

20 On the **Format** tab of the **Properties** dialog box, change both **Record Selectors** and **Navigation Buttons** to **No**.

While on this tab, notice the **Default View** property, which is set to **Datasheet**. You might want to return to this property and try the other options after finishing this exercise.

21 Switch back to Form view, and drag the dividers between column headers until you can see all the fields. Here are the results:

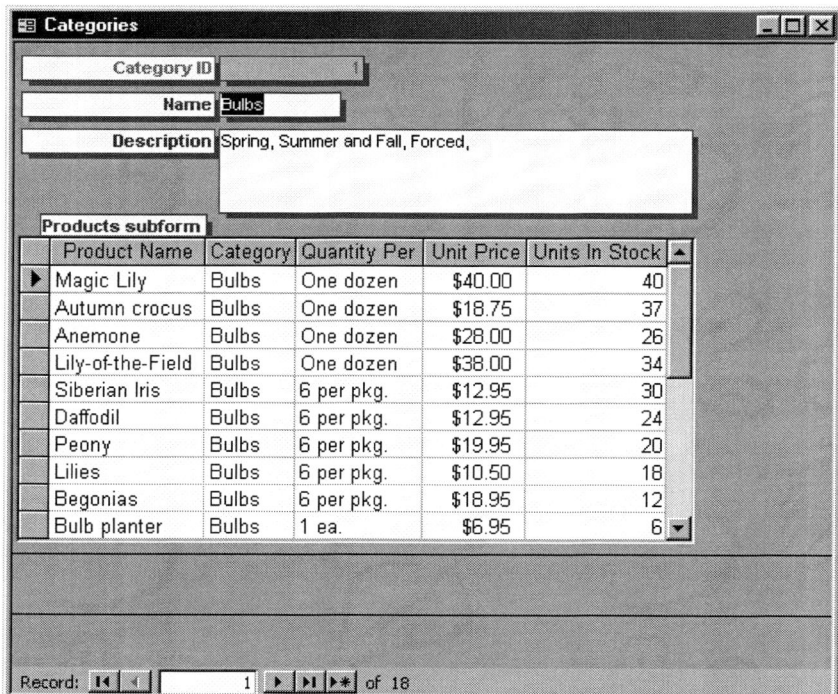

> **tip**
>
> You can quickly adjust the width of columns to fit their data by double-clicking the double arrow between column headings.

First Record

22 Click the navigation buttons to scroll through several categories. When you are through, click the **First Record** button to return to the first category (Bulbs).

As each category is displayed at the top of the form, the products in that category are listed in the datasheet in the subform.

23 Click the category name to the right of the first product.

The arrow at the right end of the box indicates that this is a combo box.

24 Click the arrow to display the list of categories, and change the category to **Cacti**.

Next Record

25 Click the **Next Record** navigation button to move to the next category (Cacti).

You can see that the first product is now included in this category.

26   Display the list of categories, and then restore the first product to the **Bulbs** category.

27   You don't want people to be able to change a product's category, so return to Design view. Then, in the subform, click the **CategoryID** text box control, and press ⌷Del⌷.

important

You included the **CategoryID** field when the wizard created this subform because it is the field that relates the Categories and Products tables. The underlying Products table uses a combo box to display the name of the category instead of its ID number, so that combo box also appears on the subform.

28   Save the form, switch back to Form view, and then adjust the width of the subform columns and the size of the Form window until your form looks like this one:

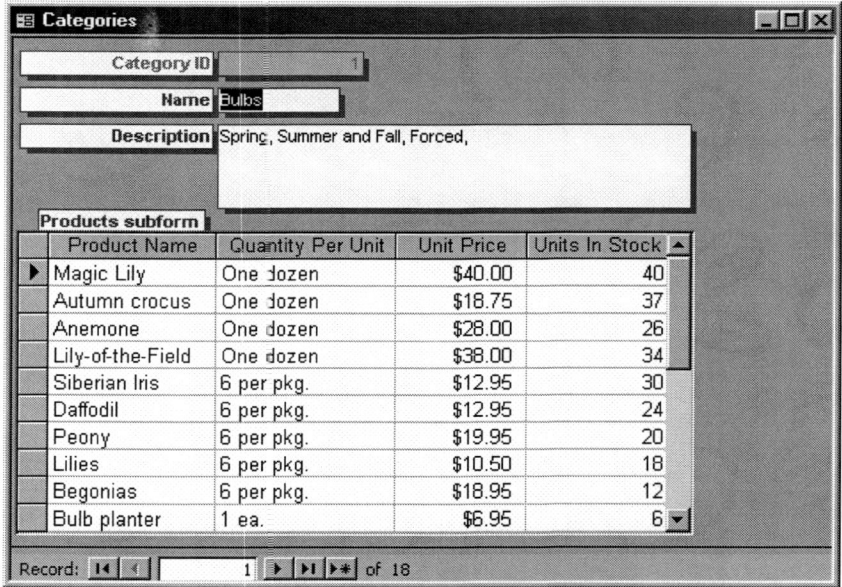

29   Close the **Categories** form, saving your changes to both the form and the subform.

30   Close the database.

31   If you are not continuing on to the next chapter, quit Access.

Creating a Form and Subform with a Wizard

If you know, when you create a form, that you are going to add a subform, you can do the whole job with the **Form Wizard**, like this:

1   On the **Objects** bar, click **Forms**, and then click the **New** button on the database window's toolbar.

2   Click **Form Wizard**, select the form's base table from the list at the bottom of the page, and then click **OK**.

3 Verify that the table you selected is shown in the **Table/Queries** list, and then click the ⟩⟩ button to include all the fields in the new form.

4 Drop down the **Tables/Queries** list, and select the subform's base table.

5 Double-click the desired fields to add them to the list of selected fields, and then click **Next**.

6 Accept the default options, and click **Next**.

7 Accept the default **Datasheet** option, and click **Next**.

8 Click **Finish** to create the form and subform.

You can then clean up the form to suit your needs, just as you did in the previous exercise.

Quick Quizzes

● What is a form?

● What is the control source?

● What is a relationship?

● How do you create a command button?

LESSON 5: Locating Specific Information

After completing this chapter, you will be able to:

✓ *Sort information on one or more fields*

✓ *Filter information in various ways*

✓ *Create queries that find information in one or more tables*

A database is a repository for information. It may hold a few records in one table or thousands of records in many related tables. No matter how much information is stored in a database, it is useful only if you can locate the information you need when you need it. In a small database you can find information simply by scrolling through a table until you spot what you are looking for. But as a database grows in size and complexity, locating specific information becomes more difficult.

Microsoft Access provides a variety of tools you can use to organize the display of information in a database and to locate specific items of information. Using these tools, you can focus on just part of the information by quickly sorting a table based on any field (or combination of fields), or you can filter the table so that information containing some combination of characters is displayed (or excluded from the display). With a little more effort, you can create queries to display specific fields from specific records from one or more tables. You can even save these queries so that you can use them over and over again.

A query can do more than simply return a list of records from a table. You can use functions in a query that perform calculations on the information in the table to produce the sum, average, count, and other mathematical values.

In this chapter, you will learn how to pinpoint precisely the information you need in a database using sorting and filtering tools, and queries. You will be working with the GardenCo database files that are stored in the following subfolders of the *SBS\Access\Queries* folder: *Sort*, *FilterDS*, *FilterForm*, *AdvFilter*, *QueryDS*, *QueryWiz*, and *Aggregate*.

Sorting Information

Ac2002-5-3

The order varies according to the field chosen as the criteria; in fact you can order data according to name or date of birth etc

Information stored in a table can be sorted in either ascending or descending order, based on the values in one or more fields in the table. You could, for example, sort a customer table alphabetically based first on the last name of each customer and then on the first name. Such a sort would result in this type of list, which resembles those found in telephone books:

Last	First
Smith	Denise
Smith	James
Smith	Jeff
Thompson	Ann
Thompson	Steve

Occasionally you might need to sort a table to group all entries of one type together. For example, to qualify for a discount on postage, The Garden Company might want to sort customer records on the postal code field to group the codes before printing mailing labels.

GardenCo

In this exercise, you will learn several ways to sort the information in a datasheet or a form. The working folder for this exercise is *SBS\Access\Queries\Sort*. Follow these steps:

1 Open the **GardenCo** database located in the working folder.

2 Open the **Customers** table in Datasheet view.

Sort Ascending

3 To sort by Region, click anywhere in the **Region** column, and then click the **Sort Ascending** button.

tip

You can also use the **Sort Ascending** or **Sort Descending** commands on the **Records** menu; or you can right-click the column in the datasheet and click either command on the shortcut menu.

The records are rearranged in order of region.

Sort Descending

4 To reverse the sort order, while still in the **Region** column, click the **Sort Descending** button.

The records for Washington State (WA) are now at the top of your list. In both sorts, the region was sorted alphabetically, but the City field was left in a seemingly random order, when what you really want to see is the records arranged by city within each region.

How Access Sorts

The concept of sorting seems pretty intuitive, but sometimes your computer's approach to such a concept is not so intuitive. Sorting numbers is a case in point. In Access, numbers can be treated as text or as numerals. Because of the spaces, hyphens, and punctuation typically used in street addresses, postal codes, and telephone numbers, the numbers in these fields are usually treated as text, and sorting them follows the logic applied to sorting all text. Numbers in a price or quantity field, on the other hand, are typically treated as numerals. When Access sorts text, it sorts first on the first character in the selected field in every record, then on the next character, then on the next, and so on, until it runs out of characters. When Access sorts numbers, it treats the contents of each field as a single value, and sorts the records based on that value. This tactic can result in seemingly strange sort orders. For example, sorting the list in the first column of the following table as text produces the list in the second column. Sorting the same list as numerals produces the list in the third column.

Original	Sort as Text	Sort as Number
1	1	1
1234	11	2
23	12	3
3	1234	4
11	2	5
22	22	11
12	23	12
4	3	22
2	4	23
5	5	1234

If a field with the Text data type contains numbers, you can sort the field numerically by padding the numbers with leading zeros so that all entries are the same length. For example, 001, 011, and 101 are sorted correctly even if the numbers are defined as text.

tip

Access can sort on more than one field, but it sorts consecutively from left to right. So the fields you want to sort must be adjacent, and they must be arranged in the order in which you want to sort them.

5   To move the **Region** field to the left of the **City** field, click its header to select the column, and then drag the column to the left until a dark line appears between **Address** and **City**.

6   Because **Region** is already selected, hold down the $\boxed{\text{Shift}}$ key and click the **City** header to extend the selection so that both the **Region** and **City** columns are selected.

7   Click the **Sort Ascending** button to arrange the records with the regions in ascending order and the city names also in ascending order within each region (or in this case, each state).

tip

You can sort records while viewing them in a form. Simply click the box of the field on which you want to base the sort, and then click one of the **Sort** buttons. However, you can't sort on multiple fields in Form view.

8   The order of the columns in the Customers table doesn't really matter, but go ahead and move the **Region** column back to where it was.

9   Save and close the **Customers** table.

10   Close the database.

Filtering Information in a Table

Ac2002-5-4

Sorting the information in a table organizes it in a logical manner, but you still have the entire table to deal with. If your goal is to locate all records containing information in one or more fields that match a particular pattern, one of the available **Filter** commands will satisfy your needs. For example, you could quickly create a filter to locate every customer of The Garden Company who lives in Seattle. Or you could find everyone who placed an order on January 13. Or you could locate all customers who live outside of the United States.

You can apply simple filters while viewing information in a table or a form. These filters are applied to the contents of a selected field, but you can apply another filter to the results of the first one to further refine your search.

tip

The **Filter** commands you will use in this exercise are available by pointing to **Filter** on the **Records** menu; by clicking buttons on the toolbar; and on the shortcut menu. However, not all **Filter** commands are available in each of these places.

GardenCo

In this exercise, you will practice several methods of filtering information in a table. The working folder for this exercise is *SBS\Access\Queries\FilterDS*. Follow these steps:

1   Open the **GardenCo** database located in the working folder.

2   Open the **Customers** table in Datasheet view.

Filter by Selection

3   Click any instance of **Sidney** in the **City** field, and then click the **Filter By Selection** button.

The number of customers displayed in the table changes from 110 to 2 because only two customers live in Sidney.

important

When you filter a table, the records that don't match the filter aren't removed from the table, they are simply not displayed.

Remove Filter

4   Click the **Remove Filter** button to redisplay the rest of the customers.

5   What if you want a list of all customers who live anywhere that has a postal code starting with *V3F*? Find an example of this type of postal code in the table, select the characters **V3F**, and then click the **Filter By Selection** button again.

Only the two records with postal codes starting with *V3F* are now visible.

6   Click **Remove Filter**.

7   What if this table is enormous and you aren't sure if it contains even one *V3F*? Right- click any postal code, click **Filter For** on the shortcut menu, type **V3F*** in the cell, and press [Enter] to see the same results.

The asterisk (*) is a wildcard that tells Access to search for any entry in the postal code field that starts with *V3F*.

8   To find out how many customers live outside the United States, remove the current filter, right-click the **Country** field in any USA record, and click **Filter Excluding Selection** on the shortcut menu.

You see all customers from other countries (in this case, only Canada).

Wildcards

When you don't know or aren't sure of a character or set of characters, you can use **wildcard characters** as placeholders for those unknown characters in your search criteria. The most common wildcards are:

Character	Description	Example
*	Match any number of characters.	*Lname = Co** returns Colman and Conroy
?	Match any single alphabetic character.	*Fname = eri?* returns Eric and Erik

Character	Description	Example
#	Match any single numeric character.	*ID = 1## * returns any ID from 100 through 199

9 To experiment with one more filtering technique, remove the filter, save and close the **Customers** table, and open the **Orders** table in Datasheet view.

10 To find all orders taken by Michael Emanuel on January 23, right-click **Emanuel, Michael** in the **Employee** field, and click **Filter By Selection** on the shortcut menu.

11 Right-click **1/23/01** (or the equivalent date) in the **OrderDate** field, and again click **Filter By Selection** on the shortcut menu.

You now have a list of Michael's orders on the 23rd. You could continue to refine this list by filtering on another field, or you could sort the results by clicking in a field and then clicking one of the **Sort** buttons.

tip

After you have located just the information you want and have organized it appropriately, you can display the results in a form or report. Simply click the **New Object** button on the toolbar, and follow the directions.

12 Remove the filters by clicking the **Remove Filter** button.

13 Save and close the **Orders** table.

14 Close the database.

tip

You can use the **Filter** commands to filter the information in a table when you are viewing it in a form. The **Filter For** command is often useful with forms because you don't have to be able to see the desired selection.

Filtering By Form

Ac2002-5-4

The **Filter By Form** command provides a quick and easy way to filter a table based on the information in several fields. If you open a table and then click the **Filter By Form** button, what you see looks like a simple datasheet. However, each of the blank cells is a combo box with a scrollable drop-down list of all the entries in that field, like this:

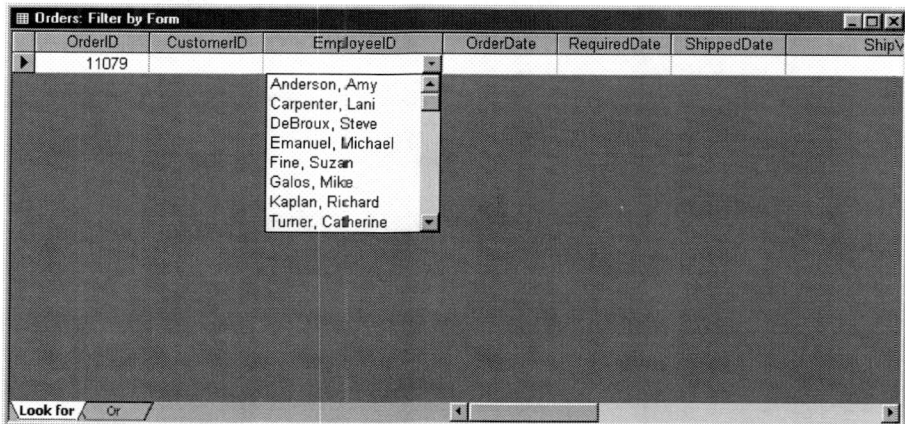

You can make a selection from the list and click the **Apply Filter** button to display only the records containing your selection.

Using **Filter By Form** on a table that has only a few fields, such as this one, is easy. But using it on a table that has a few dozen fields gets a bit cumbersome. Then it's easier to use **Filter By Form** in the form version of the table. If you open a form and then click **Filter By Form**, you see an empty form. Clicking in any box and then clicking its down arrow displays a list of all the entries in the field, as shown here:

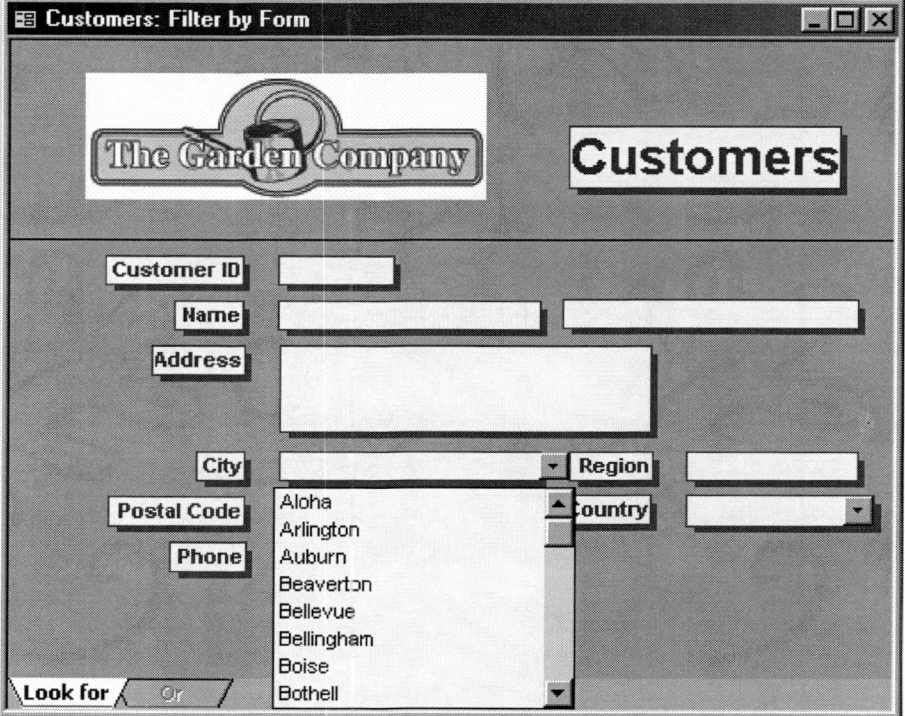

If you make a selection and click the **Apply Filter** button, clicking the **Next Record** navigation button displays the first record that meets your selection criteria, then the next, and so on.

tip

Filter By Form offers the same features and techniques whether you are using it in a form or a table. Because defining the filter is sometimes easier in a form and viewing the results is sometimes easier in a table, you might consider using **AutoForm** to quickly create a form for a table. You can then use the form with **Filter By Form** rather than the table, and then switch to Datasheet view to look at the results.

GardenCo

In this exercise, you will try to track down a customer whose last name you have forgotten. You're pretty sure the name starts with *S* and the customer is from California or Washington, so you're going to use **Filter By Form** to try and locate the customer's record. The working folder for this exercise is *SBS\Access\Queries\FilterForm*. Follow these steps:

1   Open the **GardenCo** database located in the working folder.

2   Click **Forms** on the **Objects** bar, and double-click **Components** to open the Customers form in Form view.

Filter by Form

3   Click the **Filter By Form** button on the toolbar.

The Customers form, which displays the information from one record, is replaced by its Filter By Form version, which has a blank box for each field and the **Look for** and **Or** tabs at the bottom.

4   Click the second **Name** box, type s*, and press [Enter] to tell Access to display all last names starting with *S*.

Access converts your entry to the proper format, or **syntax**, for this type of expression: *Like "s*"*.

5   Click the **Region** box, and select **CA** from the drop-down list.

Apply Filter

6   Click the **Apply Filter** button to see only the customers living in California whose last names begin with *S*.

Access replaces the filter window with the regular Customers form, and the navigation bar at the bottom of the form indicates that three filtered records are available.

7   Click the **Filter By Form** button to switch back to the filter.

Your filter criteria are still displayed. When you enter filter criteria using any method, they are saved as a form property and are available until replaced by other criteria.

8   To add the customers from another state, click the **Or** tab.

This tab has the same blank cells as the **Look for** tab. You can switch back and forth between the two tabs to confirm that your criteria haven't been cleared.

tip

When you display the **Or** tab, a second **Or** tab appears so that you can include a third state if you want.

9   Type **s*** in the **LastName** box, type or select **WA** in the **Region** box, and then click the **Apply Filter** button.

You can scroll through the filtered Customers form to view the six matched records.

10   Close the **Customers** form, and then close the database.

Locating Information That Matches Multiple Criteria

Ac2002-5-3
Ac2002-5-4
Ac2002e-3-2

Filter By Selection, **Filter For <input>**, and **Filter By Form** are quick and easy ways to hone in on the information you need, as long as your filter criteria are fairly simple. But suppose The Garden Company needs to locate all the orders shipped to Midwest states between specific dates by either of two shippers. When you need to search a single table for records that meet multiple criteria or that require complex expressions as criteria, you can use the **Advanced Filter/Sort** command.

When using **Filter by Selection** and **Filter for** you must be on the field which contains the filter item and then apply the desired filter.

You work with the **Advanced Filter/Sort** command in the design grid shown here:

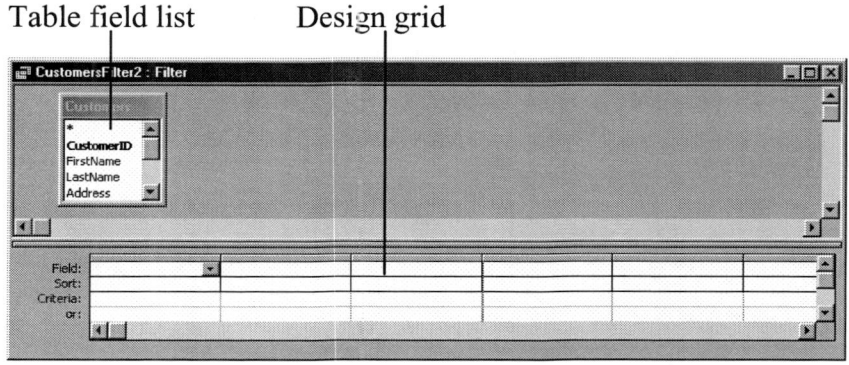

You can use this **design grid** to work with only one table.

tip

If you create a simple query in the filter window that you think you might like to use again, you can save it as a query. Either click **Save As Query** on the **File** menu; click the **Save As Query** button on the toolbar; or right-click in the filter window, and then click **Save As Query** on the shortcut menu.

GardenCo

In this exercise, you will create a filter to locate customers in two states by using the **Advanced Filter/Sort** command. After locating the customers, you will experiment a bit with the design grid to get a better understanding of its filtering capabilities. The working folder for this exercise is *SBS\Access\Queries\AdvFilter*. Follow these steps:

1   Open the **GardenCo** database located in the working folder.

2   Click **Tables** on the **Objects** bar, and double-click **Customers** to open the Customers table in Datasheet view.

3 On the **Records** menu, point to **Filter**, and then click **Advanced Filter/Sort**.

Access opens the filter window with the **Customers** field list in the top area.

4 If the design grid is not blank, click **Clear Grid** on the **Edit** menu.

5 Double-click **LastName** to copy it to the **Field** cell in the first column of the design grid.

6 Click in the **Criteria** cell under **LastName**, type **s***, and press Enter .

Access changes the criterion to *"Like "s*".*

7 Scroll to the bottom of the **Customers** field list, and double-click **Region** to copy it to the next available column of the design grid.

8 Click in the **Criteria** cell under **Region**, type **ca or wa**, and press Enter .

The design grid looks like this:

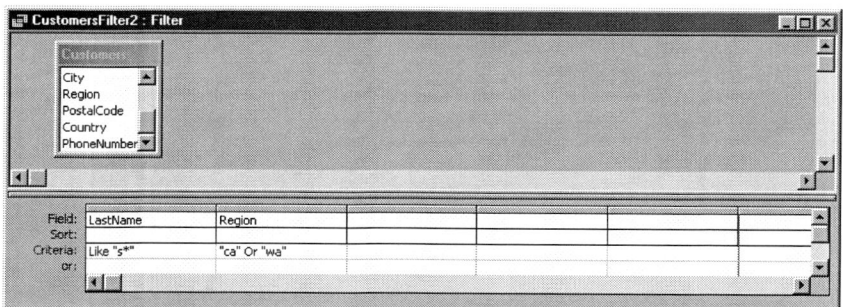

Your entry has changed to *"ca" Or "wa".* The filter will now match customers with a last name beginning with *s* who live in California or Washington.

9 On the **Filter** menu, click **Apply Filter/Sort** to view these records that match the criteria:

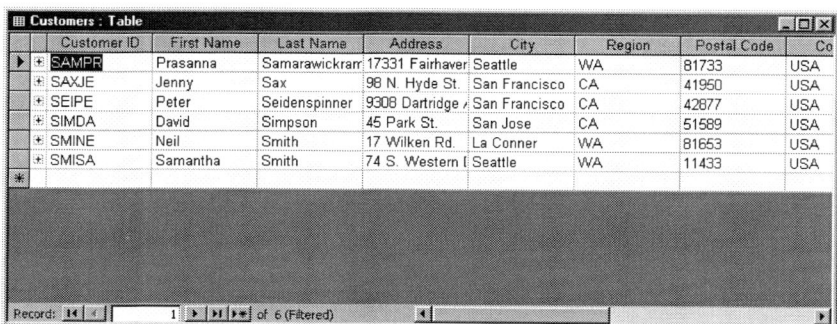

You can keep an eye on both the filter window and the table window if you reduce both in size.

10 On the **Records** menu, click **Filter** and then **Advanced Filter/Sort** to return to the filter window.

11 Click in the **or** cell in the **LastName** column, type **b***, and press [Enter]. The design grid now looks like this:

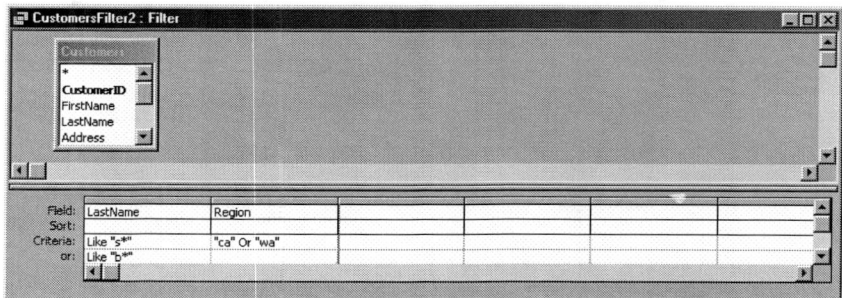

12 On the **Filter** menu, click **Apply Filter/Sort**.

The result includes records for all customers with a last name that begins with *s* or *b*, but some of the *b* names live in Montana and Oregon. If you look again at the design grid, you can see that the filter is formed by combining the fields in the **Criteria** row with the *And* operator, combining the fields in the **or** row with the *And* operator, and then using the *Or* operator to combine the two rows. So the filter is searching for customers with names beginning with *s* who live in California or Washington, or customers with names beginning with *b*, regardless of where they live.

13 Return to the filter window, type **ca or wa** in the **or** cell under **Region**, and press [Enter].

14 Apply the filter again to see only customers from California and Washington.

15 Close the **Customers** table, without saving your changes, and then close the database.

Expressions

The word **expressions**, as used in Access, is synonymous with *formulas*. An expression is a combination of **operators, constants, functions,** and **control properties** that evaluates to a single value. Access builds formulas using the format $a=b+c$, where a is the result and $=b+c$ is the expression. An expression can be used to assign properties to tables or forms, to determine values in fields or reports, as part of queries, and in many other places in Access.

The expressions you use in Access combine multiple **criteria** to define a set of conditions that a record must meet before Access will select it as the result of a filter or query. Multiple criteria are combined using logical, comparison, and arithmetic operators. Different types of expressions use different operators.

The most common **logical operators** are *And*, *Or*, and *Not*. When criteria are combined with the *And* operator, a record is selected only if it meets them all. When criteria are combined with the *Or* operator, a record is selected if it meets any one of them. The *Not* operator selects all records that don't match its criterion.

Common **comparison operators** include < (less than), > (greater than), and = (equal). These basic operators can be combined to form <= (less than or equal to), >= (greater than or equal to), and <> (not equal to). The *Like* operator is sometimes grouped with the comparison operators and is used to test whether or not text matches a pattern.

The common **arithmetic operators** are + (add), - (subtract), * (multiply), and / (divide), which are used with numerals. A related operator, & (a text form of +) is used to concatenate-or put together-two text strings.

Creating a Query in Design View

Ac2002-3-2
Ac2002-5-2

Sorting and filtering information is quick, easy, and useful. When you want to work with more than one table, however, you need to move beyond filters and into the realm of queries. The most common type of query selects records that meet specific conditions, but there are several other types, as follows:

The creation of a query in Design view allows you to choose the table or tables and the respective fields whose information you want to see. You can also set the query criteria or parameters directly in Design view.

■ A **select query** retrieves data from one or more tables and displays the results in a datasheet. You can also use a select query to group records and calculate sums, counts, averages, and other types of totals. You can work with the results of a select query in Datasheet view to update records in one or more related tables at the same time.

■ A **parameter query** prompts you for information to be used in the query-for example, a range of dates. This type of query is particularly useful if the query is the basis for a report that is run periodically.

■ A **crosstab query** calculates and restructures data for easier analysis. It can calculate a sum, average, count, or other type of total for data that is grouped by two types of information: one down the left side of the datasheet and one across the top. The cell at the junction of each row and column displays the results of the query's calculation.

■ An **action query** updates or makes changes to multiple records in one operation. It is essentially a select query that performs an action on the results of the selection process. Four types of actions are available: **delete queries**, which delete records from one or more tables; **update queries**, which make changes to records in one or more tables; **append queries**, which add records from one or more tables to the end of one or more other tables; and **make-table queries**, which create a new table from all or part of the data in one or more tables.

tip

Access also includes SQL queries, but you won't be working with this type of query in this book.

Filters and Sorts vs. Queries

The major differences between using filtering or sorting and using a query are:

- The **Filter** and **Sort** commands are usually faster to implement than queries.

- The **Filter** and **Sort** commands are not saved, or are saved only temporarily. A query can be saved permanently and run again at any time.

- The **Filter** and **Sort** commands are applied only to the table or form that is currently open. A query can be based on multiple tables and other queries, which don't have to be open.

You can create a query by hand or by using a wizard. Regardless of how you create the query, what you create is a statement that describes the conditions that must be met for records to be matched in one or more tables. When you run the query, the matching records appear in a datasheet in Datasheet view.

GardenCo

In this exercise, you will create an order entry form that salespeople can fill in as they take orders over the phone. The form will be based on a select query that combines information from the Order Details table and the Products table. The query will create a datasheet listing all products ordered with the unit price, quantity ordered, discount, and extended price. Because the extended price isn't stored in the database, you will calculate this amount directly in the query. The working folder for this exercise is *SBS\Access\Queries\QueryDes*. Follow the steps on the next page.

1 Open the **GardenCo** database located in the working folder.

2 On the **Objects** bar, click **Queries**.

3 Double-click **Create query in Design view**.

Access opens the query window in Design view and then opens the **Show Table** dialog box, like this:

Design grid   Table area

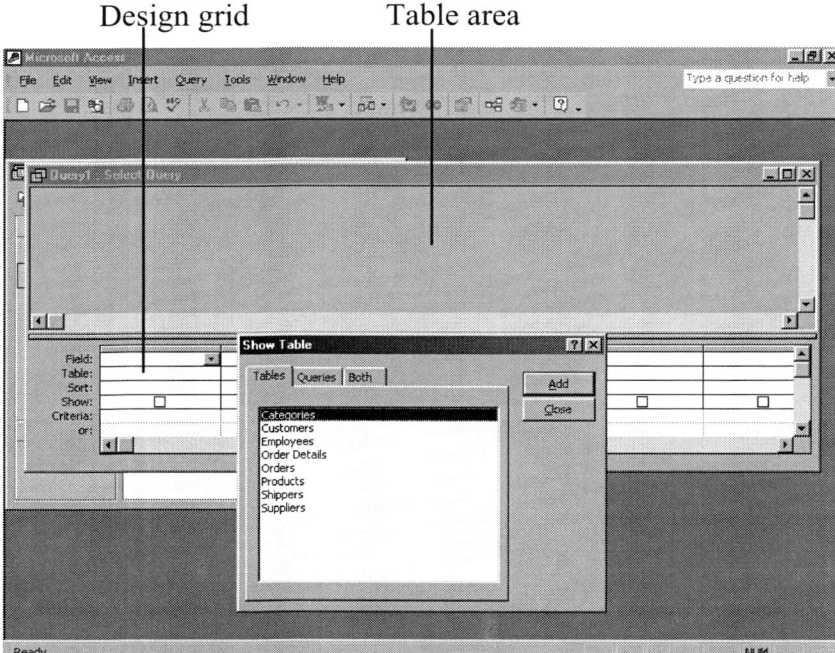

You use the **Show Table** dialog box to specify which tables and saved queries to include in the current query.

4   With the **Tables** tab active, double-click **Order Details** and **Products** to add both tables to the query window. Then close the dialog box.

Each table you added is represented in the top portion of the window by a small field list window with the name of the table - in this case, Order Details and Products - in its title bar, as shown here:

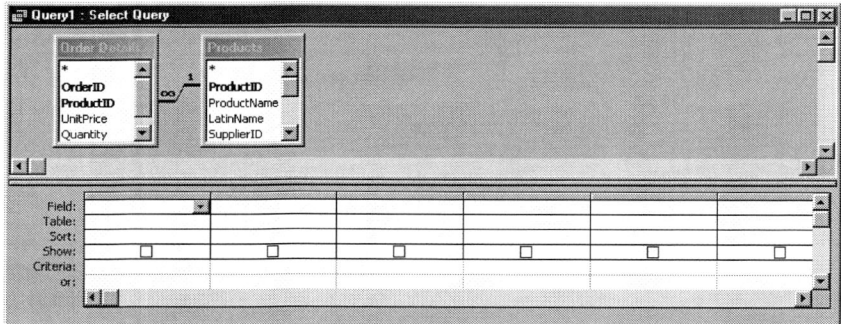

At the top of each list is an asterisk, which represents all the fields in the list. Primary key fields in each list are bold. The line from **ProductID** in the Order Details table to **ProductID** in the Products table indicates that these two fields are related.

tip

To add more tables to a query, reopen the **Show Tables** dialog box by right-clicking the top portion of the query window and clicking **Show Table** on the shortcut menu; or by clicking the **Show Tables** button on the toolbar.

The lower area of the query window is taken up by a design grid where you will build the query's criteria.

5 To include fields in the query, you drag them from the lists at the top of the window to consecutive columns in the design grid. Drag the following fields from the two lists:

From Table	Field
Order Details	OrderID
Products	ProductName
Order Details	UnitPrice
Order Details	Quantity
Order Details	Discount

tip

You can quickly copy a field to the next open column in the design grid by double-clicking the field. To copy all fields to the grid, double-click the title bar above the field list to select the entire list, and then drag the selection over the grid. When you release the mouse button, Access adds the fields to the columns in order. You can drag the asterisk to a column in the grid to include all the fields in the query, but you also have to drag individual fields to the grid if you want to sort on those fields or add conditions to them.

The query window now looks like the one shown on the next page.

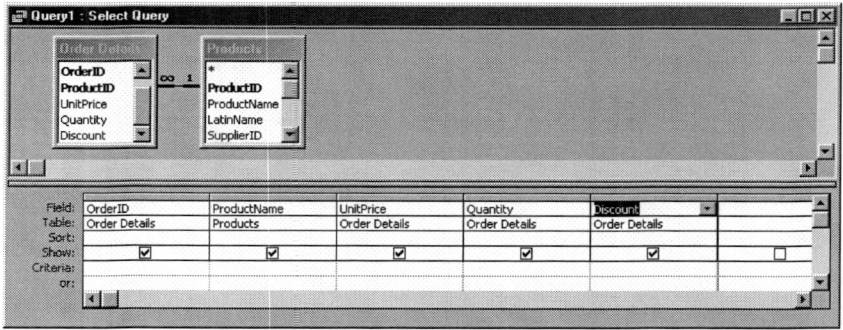

Run

6 Click the **Run** button to run the query and display the results in Datasheet view, like this:

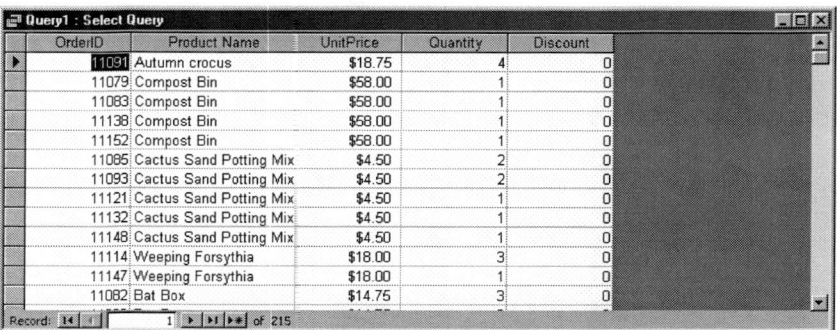

The results show that the query is working so far. There are two things left to do: sort the results on the **OrderID** field and add a field for calculating the extended price, which is the unit price times the quantity sold minus any discount.

View

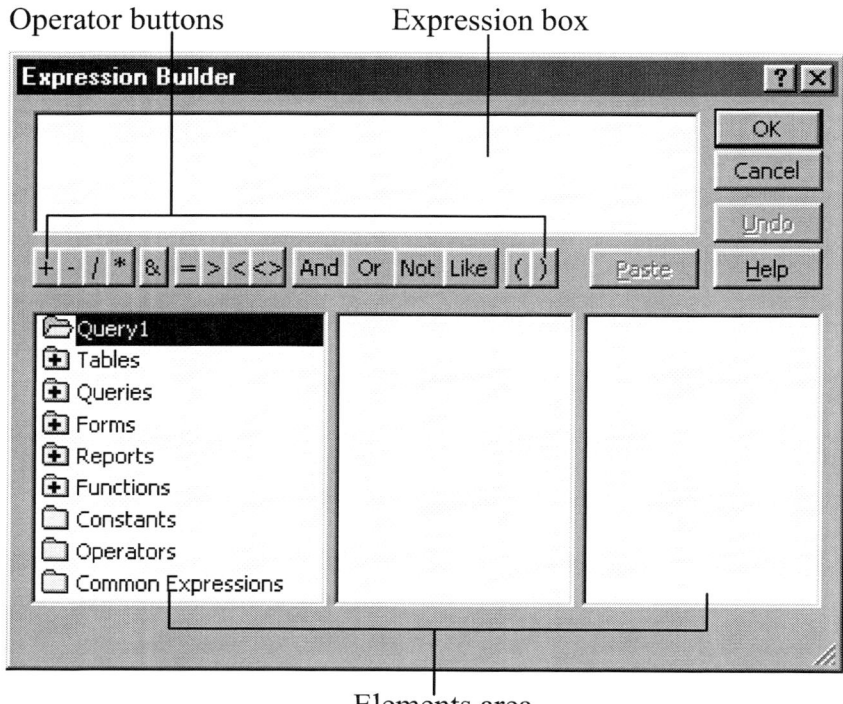

7   Click the **View** button to return to Design view.

The third row in the design grid is labelled *Sort*. If you click in the **Sort** cell in any column, you can specify whether to sort in ascending order, descending order, or not at all.

8   Click in the **Sort** cell in the **OrderID** column, click the down arrow, and click **Ascending**.

Neither of the tables includes an extended price field. There is no point in entering this information in a table, because you will use the Expression Builder to insert an expression in the design grid that computes this price from existing information.

9   Right-click the **Field** row of the first blank column in the design grid (the sixth column), and click **Build** on the shortcut menu.

The **Expression Builder** dialog box opens, as shown here:

Operator buttons   Expression box

Elements area

Here is the expression you will build:

<CCur([Order Details].[UnitPrice][Quantity]*(1-[Discount])/100)*100>*

The only part of this expression that you probably can't figure out is the CCur function, which converts the results of the math inside its parentheses to currency format.

10   Double-click the **Functions** folder in the first column of the elements area, and then click **Built-In Functions**.

The categories of built-in functions are displayed in the second column.

11 Click **Conversion** in the second column to limit the functions in the third column to those in that category. Then double-click **Ccur** in the third column.

The Expression Builder now looks like the one shown on the next page.

Expression Builder

When an expression is a valid filter or query option, you can usually either type the expression or use the Expression Builder to create it. You open the Expression Builder by either clicking **Build** on a shortcut menu or clicking the button (sometimes referred to as the **Build** button) at the right end of a box that can accept an expression.

The Expression Builder isn't a wizard; it doesn't lead you through the process of building an expression. But it does provide a hierarchical list of most of the elements that you can include in an expression. After looking at the list, you can either type your expression in the expression box, or you can select functions, operators, and other elements to copy them to the expression box, and then click **OK** to transfer them to the filter or query.

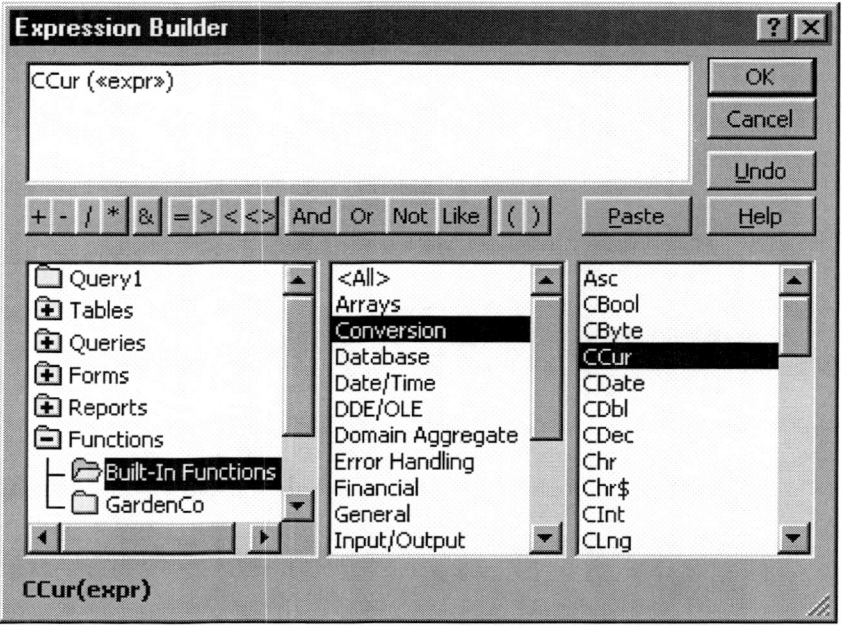

You've inserted the currency conversion function in the expression box. The <<*expr*>> inside the parentheses represents the other expressions that will eventually result in the number Access should convert to currency format.

12 Click <<**expr**>> to select it so that the next thing you enter will replace it.

13 The next element you want in the expression is the **UnitPrice** field from the Order Details table. Double-click **Tables**, click **Order Details**, and then double-click **UnitPrice**.

The Expression Builder now looks like this:

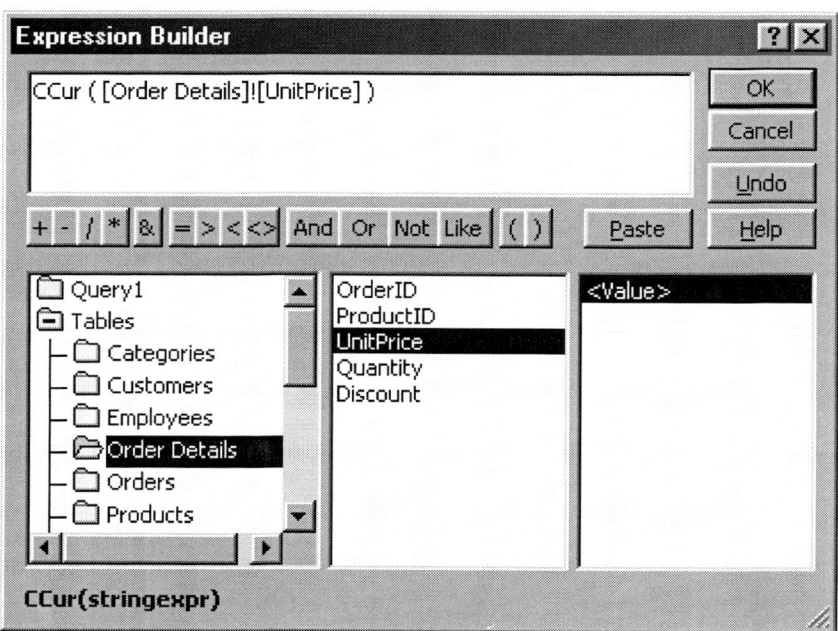

Your last action left the insertion point after UnitPrice, which is exactly where you want it.

14 Now you want to multiply the amount in the UnitPrice field by the amount in the Quantity field. Start by clicking the * (asterisk) button in the row of operator buttons below the expression box.

Access inserts the multiplication sign and another *<<expr>>* placeholder.

15 Click **<expr>>** to select it, and then insert the **Quantity** field by double- clicking it in the second column.

What you have entered so far multiplies the price by the number ordered, which results in the total cost for this item. However, The Garden Company offers discounts on certain items at different times of the year. The amount of the discount is entered by the sales clerk and stored in the Order Details table. In the table, the discount is expressed as the percentage to deduct-usually 10 to 20 percent. But it is easier to compute the percentage the customer will pay-usually 80 to 90 percent of the regular price-than it is to compute the discount and then subtract it from the total cost.

16 Type *(1-, then double-click **Discount**, and type).

The Expression Builder now looks like this (you will have to widen the window to see the whole expression):

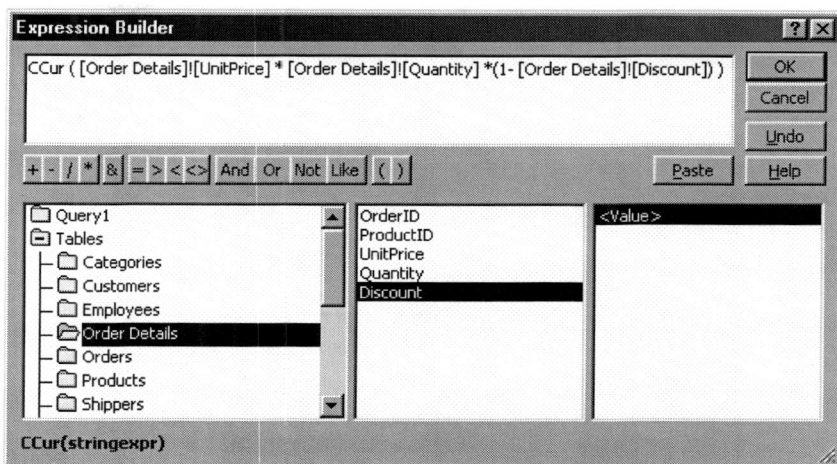

Remember that the discount is formatted in the datasheet as a percentage, but it is stored as a decimal number between 0 and 1. When you look at it you may see 10%, but what is actually stored in the database is 0.1. So if the discount is 10 percent, the result of *(1- Discount) is *.9. In other words, the formula multiplies the unit price by the quantity and then multiplies that result by 0.9.

17 Click **OK**.

Access closes the Expression Builder and copies the expression to the design grid.

18 Press ⎡ Enter ⎤ to move the insertion point out of the field, which completes the entry of the expression.

tip

You can quickly make a column in the design grid as wide as its contents by double-clicking the line in the grey selection bar that separates the column from the column to its right.

19 Access has given the expression the name *Expr1*. This name isn't particularly meaningful, so rename it by double-clicking **Expr1** and then typing **ExtendedPrice**.

20 Click the **View** button to see these results in Datasheet view:

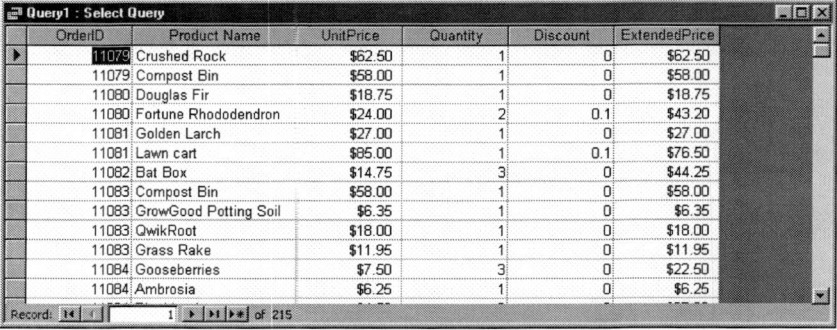

The orders are now sorted on the **OrderID** field, and the extended price is calculated in the last field.

21 Scroll down to see a few records with discounts.

If you check the math, you will see that the query calculates the extended price correctly.

22 Close the query window, and when prompted to save the query, click **Yes**. Type **Order Details Extended** to name the query, and click **OK** to close it.

23 Close the database.

Creating a Query with a Wizard

Ac2002-3-1
Ac2002e-3-3

The process used to create a simple select query with the **Query Wizard** is almost identical to that for creating a form with the **Form Wizard.** With the **Query Wizard**, you can add one or more fields from existing tables or queries to the new query.

For Access to work effectively with multiple tables, it must understand the relationships between the fields in those tables. You have to create these relationships before using the **Query Wizard**, by clicking the **Relationships** button and then dragging a field in one table over the identical field in another table.

GardenCo

In this exercise, you will use the **Query Wizard** to create a new query that combines information from the Customers and Orders tables to provide information about each order. These tables are related through their common CustomerID fields. (This relationship has already been established in the GardenCo database files used in this chapter.) The working folder for this exercise is *SBS\Access\Queries\QueryWiz*. Follow these steps:

1 Open the **GardenCo** database located in the working folder.

2 On the **Objects** bar, click **Queries**, and then double-click **Create query by using wizard**.

The first page of the **Simple Query Wizard** opens.

tip

You can also start the **Query Wizard** by clicking **Query** on the **Insert** menu or clicking the **New Object** button, and then double-clicking **Simple Query Wizard**.

3 Select **Table: Orders** from the **Tables/Queries** list.

4 Click the **>>** button to move all available fields to the **Selected Fields** list.

5 Select **Table: Customers** from the **Tables/Queries** list.

6 Double-click the **Address, City, Region, PostalCode**, and **Country** fields to move them to the **Selected Fields** list, and then click **Next**.

tip

If the relationship between two tables hasn't already been established, you will be prompted to define it and then start the wizard again.

7 Click **Next** again to accept the default option of showing details in the results of the query.

8 Change the query title to **Orders Qry**, leave the **Open the query to view information** option selected, and then click **Finish**.

Access runs the query and displays the results in Datasheet view. You can scroll through the results and see that information is displayed for all the orders.

View

9 Click the **View** button to view the query in Design view.

Notice that the **Show** box is, by default, checked for each of the fields used in the query. If you want to use a field in a query - for example, to sort on, to set criteria for, or in a calculation - but don't want to see the field in the results datasheet, you can clear its **Show** check box.

10 Clear the **Show** check box for **OrderID**, **CustomerID**, and **EmployeeID**, and then click the **View** button to switch back to Datasheet view.

The three fields have been removed from the results datasheet.

11 Click the **View** button to return to Design view.

This query returns all record in the Orders table. To have this query match the records for a range of dates, you will convert it to a parameter query, which asks for the date range each time you run it.

12 In the **OrderDate** column, click in the **Criteria** cell, and type the following:

Between [Type the beginning date:] And [Type the ending date:]

Run

13 Click the **Run** button to run the query.

Access displays this dialog box:

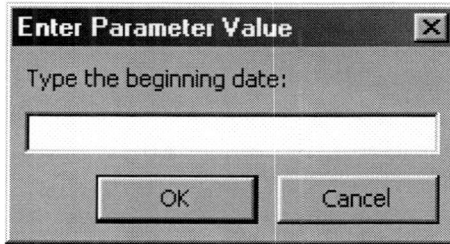

14 Type 1/1/01, and press ⌷ Enter ⌷.

15 In the second **Enter Parameter Value** dialog box, type 1/31/01, and press ⌷ Enter ⌷ again.

The datasheet is displayed again, this time listing only orders between the parameter dates.

16 Close the datasheet, clicking **Yes** to save the query.

17 Close the database.

Quick Quizzes

● How can you order information in a table?

● How does the Filter By Selection function work?

● What is a query with parameters?

● What is a criterion?

● What is an action query?

● What is multi-table query?

● What is a calculated field?

LESSON 6:

Keeping Your Information Accurate

After completing this chapter, you will be able to:

✓ *Restrict the information entered in a database using the data type*

✓ *Restrict the information entered in a database using various field properties*

✓ *Delete information from a table*

Depending on how much information you have and how organized you are, you might compare a database to an old shoebox or a file cabinet, into which you toss items such as photographs, bills, receipts, and a variety of other paperwork for later retrieval. However, neither a shoebox nor a file cabinet restricts what you can place in it (other than how much you can place in it) or imposes any order on its content. It is up to you to decide what you store there and to organize it properly so that you can find it when you next need it. And neither a shoebox nor a file cabinet helps you with the task of updating your information when it changes or becomes obsolete.

When you create a database with Microsoft Access, you can set properties that restrict what can be entered in it, thereby keeping the database organized and useful. For example, The Garden Company wouldn't want its employees to enter text into fields that should contain numbers, such as price fields. Similarly, they wouldn't want to encourage employees to enter a long text description of something when a simple "yes" or "no" answer would work best.

> The control properties which limit or validate data entry help to minimize the number of errors.

The field properties that control input are **Required, Allow Zero Length, Field Size, Input Mask,** and **Validation Rule.** The **Required** and **Allow Zero Length** properties are fairly obvious. If the **Required** property is set to **Yes,** the field can't be left blank. However, if **Allow Zero Length** is set to **Yes,** you can enter an empty **string** (two quotation marks with nothing in between), which looks like an empty field. The other properties are more complex, so you'll focus on them in the exercises in this chapter.

tip

Each property has many options. For more information about how to use properties, search for *field property* in Access online Help.

To ensure the ongoing accuracy of a database, you can create and run action queries that quickly update information or delete selected records from a table. For example, The Garden Company might decide to increase the price of all products in one category by some percentage, or to remove one entire product line. This type of updating is easy to do with an action query. Not only does using a query save time, but it also avoids human input errors.

The exercises in this chapter demonstrate how to use the data type and some of the field properties to restrict the data that can be entered in a table or form. It is difficult to experiment with field properties in a table that is already filled with information, because changing a field's data type or properties can destroy or alter the data. For that reason, the first few exercises in this chapter use a new database that you will create just for the purpose of experimenting with data types and properties. Then you will resume working with sample GardenCo database files located in the following subfolders of the *SBS\Access\Accurate* folder: *DataType, FieldSize, InputMask, ValRules, Lookup, QueryUp*, and *QueryDel*.

Using the Data Type to Restrict Data

Ac2002-5-1
Ac2002e-1-1

The **Data Type** setting restricts entries to a specific type of data: text, numbers, dates, and so on. If, for example, the **data type** is set to **Number** and you attempt to enter text, Access refuses the entry and displays a warning.

In this exercise, you will create a brand new database, you will add fields of the most common data types, and then you'll experiment to see how the **Data Type** setting and **Field Size** property can be used to restrict the data entered into a table. The working folder for this exercise is *SBS\Access\Accurate\DataType*. Follow these steps:

1   In the **New File** task pane, click **Blank Database** in the **New** section to display the **File New Database** dialog box.

If the **New File** task pane is not displayed, click the **New** button on the toolbar.

2   Type **Field Test** in the **File name** box, browse to the working folder for this exercise, and then click **Create**.

Access opens the database window for the new database.

3   Double-click **Create table in Design view**.

A blank Table window opens in Design view so that you can define the fields that categorize the information in the table. You will define five fields, one for each of the **Text, Number, Date/Time, Currency**, and **Yes/No** data types.

4   Click in the first **Field Name** cell, type **TextField**, and press
Tab to move to the **Data Type** cell.

5   The data type defaults to **Text**, which is the type you want. So press ⎡Tab⎤ twice to accept the default data type and move the insertion point to the next row.

6   Type **NumberField**, and press ⎡Tab⎤ to move to the **Data Type** cell.

7   Click the down arrow to expand the list of data types, click **Number**, and then press ⎡Tab⎤ twice.

8   Repeat steps 4 through 7 to add the following fields:

Field	Data Type
DateField	Date/Time
CurrencyField	Currency
BooleanField	Yes/No

tip

The data type referred to as **Yes/No** in Access is more commonly called **Boolean** (in honour of George Boole, an early mathematician and logistician). This data type can hold either of two mutually exclusive values, often expressed as *yes/no, 1/0, on/off,* or *true/false.*

Save

9   Click the **Save** button, type **Field Property Test** to name the table, and then click **OK**.

Access displays a dialog box recommending that you create a primary key.

10   You don't need a primary key for this exercise, so click **No**.

11   Click the row selector for **TextField** to select the first row.

Your table now looks like the one on the next page.

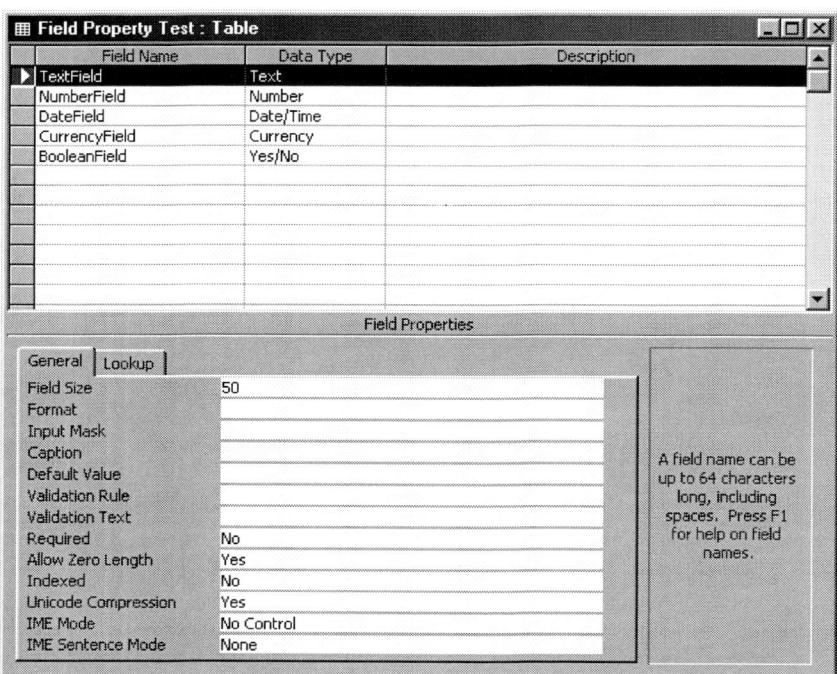

The properties for the selected field are displayed in the lower portion of the dialog box.

View

12 Click in each field and review its properties, and then click the **View** button to display the table in Datasheet view, as shown here:

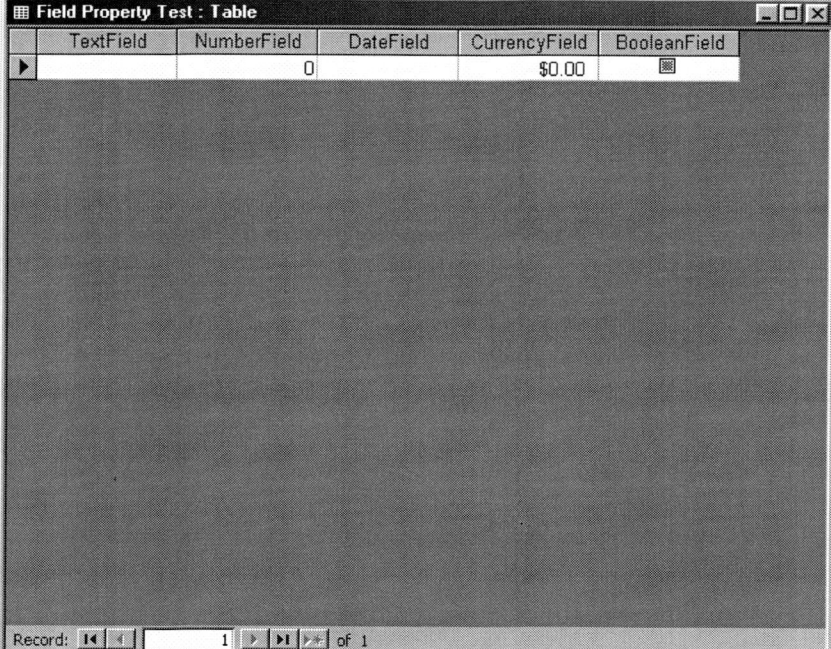

13 The insertion point should be in the first field. Type **This entry is 32 characters long**, and press $\boxed{\text{Tab}}$ to move to the next field.

14 Type **Five hundred**, and press $\boxed{\text{Tab}}$.

The data type for this field is **Number**. Access displays an alert box refusing your text entry.

15 Click **OK**, replace the text with the number **500**, and press `Tab`.

16 Type a number or text (anything but a date) in the date field, and press `Tab`. When Access refuses it, click **OK**, type **Jan 1**, and press `Tab`.

The date field accepts almost any entry that can be recognized as a date, and displays it in the default date format. Depending on the format on your computer, Jan 1 might be displayed as 1/1/2001 or 1/1/01.

tip

If you enter a month and day but no year in a date field, Access assumes the date is in the current year. If you enter a month, day, and two-digit year from 00 through 29, Access assumes the year is 2000 through 2029. If you enter a two- digit year that is greater than 29, Access assumes you mean 1930 through 1999.

17 Type any text or a date in the currency field, and press `Tab`. When Access refuses the entry, click **OK**, type **-45.3456** in the field, and press `Tab`.

Access stores the number you entered but displays ($45.35), the default format for displaying negative currency numbers.

tip

Access uses the regional settings in Microsoft Windows Control Panel to determine the display format for date, time, currency, and other numbers. If you intend to share database files with people in other countries, you might want to create custom formats to ensure that the correct currency symbol is always displayed with your values. Otherwise, the numbers won't change, but displaying them as dollars, pounds, marks, or lira will radically alter their value.

18 Try entering text or a number in the **Boolean** field. Then click anywhere in the field to toggle the check box between **Yes** (checked) and **No** (not checked), finishing with the field in the checked state.

This field won't accept anything you type; it only allows you to switch between two predefined values. Your datasheet now resembles the one shown on the next page.

⊞ Field Property Test : Table					_□×
	TextField	NumberField	DateField	CurrencyField	BooleanField
⏺ This entry is 32		500	1/1/01	($45.35)	☑
✳		0		$0.00	▦

Record: ◄ ◄ [1] ► ►I ►✳ of 1

tip

In Design view, you can use properties on the **Lookup** tab to display the Boolean field as a check box, text box, or combo box. You can also set the **Format** property on the **General** tab to use **True/False**, **Yes/No**, or **On/Off** as the displayed values in this field (though the stored values will always be -1 and 0).

19 Close the table, and then close the database.

Using an Input Mask to Restrict Data

Ac2002-2-2
Ac2002-2-4
Ac2002e-1-4

When you use **masks** in tables or forms, people entering information can see at a glance the format in which they should make entries and how long they should be. You can use the **InputMask** property to control how data is entered in text, number, date/time, and currency fields. This property has three sections, separated by semi-colons, like the mask for a telephone number shown here:

!\(000") "000\-0000;1;#

The first section contains characters that are used as placeholders for the information to be typed, as well as characters such as parentheses and hyphens. Together, all these characters control the appearance of the entry. The following list explains the purpose of the most common input mask characters:

Character	Description
0	Required digit (0 through 9).
9	Optional digit or space.

Character	Description
#	Optional digit or space; blank positions are converted to spaces; plus and minus signs are allowed.
L	Required letter (A through Z).
?	Optional letter (A through Z).
A	Required letter or digit.
A	Optional letter or digit.
&	Required character (any kind) or a space.
C	Optional character (any kind) or a space.
<	All characters that follow are converted to lowercase.
>	All characters that follow are converted to uppercase.
!	Characters typed into the mask fill it from left to right. You can include the exclamation point anywhere in the input mask.
\	Character that follows is displayed as a literal character.
Password	Creates a password entry box. Any character typed in the box is stored as the character but is displayed as an asterisk (*).

Any characters not included on this list are displayed as literal characters. If you want to use one of the special characters in this list as a literal character, precede it with the \ character.

The second and third sections of the input mask are optional. Including a 1 or leaving nothing in the second section tells Access to store only the characters entered; including a 0 tells it to store both the characters entered and the mask characters. The character in the third section is displayed in a new record as the placeholder for the characters to be typed. This placeholder defaults to an underscore if the section is omitted.

The input mask !\(000") "000\-0000;1;# creates this display in a field in both a table and a form:

(###) ###-####

In this case, you are restricting the entry to ten digits-no more and no less. Access stores just the digits entered, not the parentheses, space, and dash (though those characters could be displayed in your table, form, or report if you set the correct format property).

Field Test

In this exercise, you will use the **Input Mask Wizard** to apply a predefined telephone input mask to a text field, forcing entered numbers into the (206) 555-0001 format. You will then create a custom mask to force the first letter of an entry to be upper-case (a capital letter). The working folder for this exercise is *SBS\Access\Accurate \InputMask*. Follow these steps:

1   Open the **Field Test** database located in the working folder.

2   Open the **Field Property Test** table in Design view.

3   Type **PhoneField** in the first blank **Field Name** cell, and leave the data type set to **Text**.

4   Click the row selector to select the row, and then drag the new field to the top of the field list so that it will appear at the left end of the table.

5   Save the table design, and with **PhoneField** still selected, click **Input Mask** in the **Field Properties** section.

6   Click the button to the right of the cell to start the **Input Mask Wizard** and display the first page of the wizard, shown here:

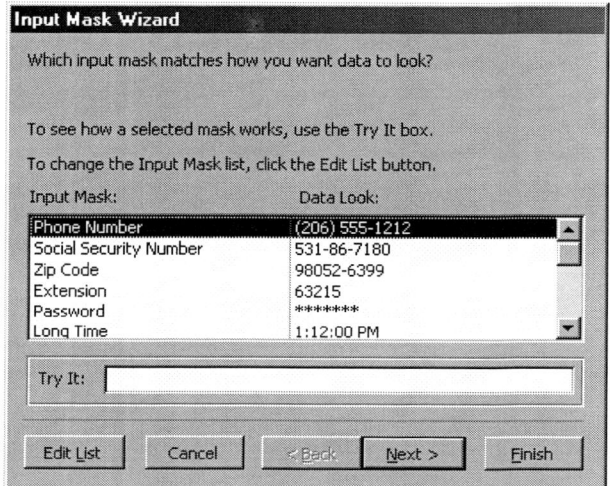

You can create an input mask by hand for text, number, date, or currency fields, or you can use this wizard to apply one of several standard masks for text and date fields.

7   With **Phone Number** selected in the **Input Mask** list, click **Next**.

The second page of the wizard displays the input mask and gives you the opportunity to change the placeholder character that will indicate what to type. The exclamation point causes Access to fill the mask from left to right with whatever is typed. The parentheses and hyphen are characters that Access will insert in the specified places. The 9s represent optional digits, and the 0s represent required digits, so you can enter a telephone number with or without an area code.

tip

Because Access fills the mask from left to right, you would have to press the

[→] key to move the insertion point past the first three placeholders to enter a telephone number without an area code.

8   Change *999* to **000** to require an area code, and then change the placeholder character to **#**.

The dialog box now looks like this:

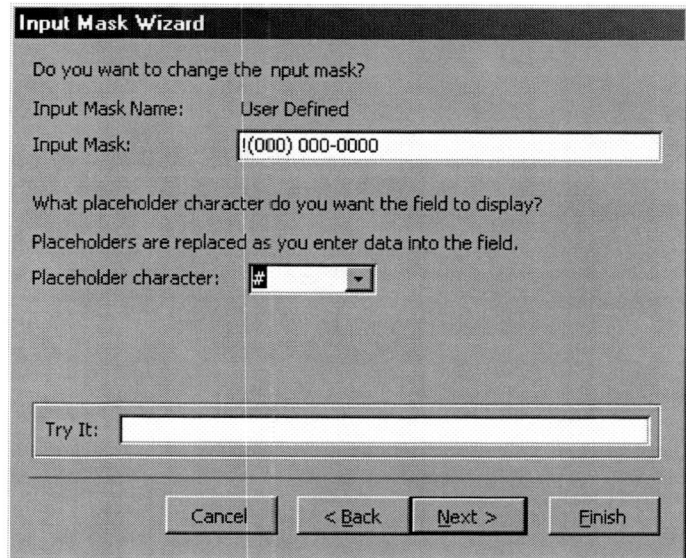

9   Click **Next**.

On the third page of the wizard, you specify whether you want to store the symbols with the data. If you store them, the data will always be displayed in tables, forms, and reports in this format. However, the symbols take up space, meaning that your database will be larger.

10   Leave the default selection - to store data without the symbols - and then click **Finish**.

Access closes the wizard and displays the edited mask as the **Input Mask** property, as shown on the next page.

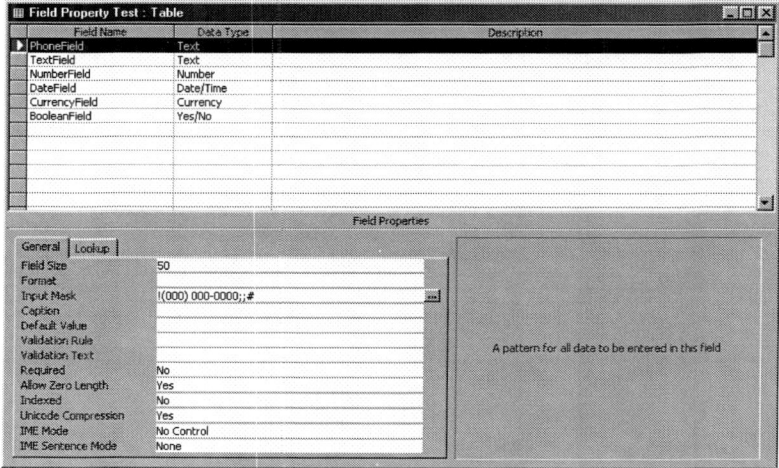

11 Press [Enter] to accept the mask.

Access changes the format of the mask to !\(000") "000\-0000;;#. Notice the two semicolons that separate the mask into its three sections. Since you told Access to store data without the symbols, nothing is displayed in the second section of the mask.

View

12 Save your changes, and click the **View** button to return to Datasheet view.

13 Press the [↓] key to move to the new record, and type a series of at least ten digits and some letters to see how the mask works.

Any letters you type are ignored. The first ten digits are formatted as a telephone number. If you type more than ten digits, they are also ignored. If you type fewer than ten digits and press [Tab] or [Enter], Access warns you that your entry doesn't match the input mask.

tip

An input mask can contain more than just the placeholders for the data to be entered. If, for example, you type **The number is** in front of the telephone number in the **Input Mask** property, the default entry for the field is *The number is (###) ###-####*. Then if you place the insertion point to the left of *The* and start typing numbers, the numbers replace the # placeholders, not the text. The **Field Size** setting is not applied to the characters in the mask, so if this setting is 15, the entry is not truncated even though the number of displayed characters (including spaces) is 28.

14 Return to Design view, and add a new field below **BooleanField**. Name it **LastName**. Leave the **Data Type** setting as the default **Text**.

15 Select the new field, click **Input Mask**, type **>L<??????????????????** (18 question marks), and press [Enter].

The > forces all following text to be uppercase. The *L* requires a letter. The < forces all following text to be lowercase. Each *?* allows any letter or no letter, and there is one fewer question mark than the maximum number of letters you want to allow in the field (19, including the leading capital letter). The **Field Size** setting must be greater than this maximum.

16 Save your changes, return to Datasheet view, type **smith** in the **LastName** field of one of the records, and press [Tab]. Try entering **SMITH**, and then **McDonald**.

As you can see, this type of mask has its limitations. But it can be useful in many situations.

17 Close the table, and then close the database.

Using Validation Rules to Restrict Data

Ac2002-6-2
Ac2002e-1-1

A **validation rule** is an **expression** that can precisely define the information that will be accepted in one or several fields in a record. You might use a validation rule on a field containing the date an employee was hired to prevent a date in the future from being entered. Or if you make deliveries to only certain local areas, you could use a validation rule on the phone field or ZIP code field to refuse entries from other areas.

You can type validation rules in by hand, or you can use the **Expression Builder** to create them. At the field level, Access uses the rule to test an entry when you attempt to leave the field. At the table level, Access can use the rule to test the content of several fields when you attempt to leave the record. If an entry doesn't satisfy the rule, Access rejects the entry and displays a message explaining why.

Field Test

In this exercise, you will create and test several field validation rules and one table validation rule. The working folder for this exercise is *SBS\Access\Accurate\ValRules*. Follow these steps:

1   Open the **Field Test** database located in the working folder.

2   Open the **Field Property Test** table in Design view.

3   To add a validation rule to **PhoneField** that will prevent the entry of an area code other than 206 or 425, start by selecting **PhoneField** and clicking in the **Validation Rule** box.

A button appears at the end of the **Validation Rule** box. You can click this button to use the Expression Builder to create an expression, or you can type an expression in the box.

4   Type the following in the **Validation Rule** box, and press ⟨ Enter ⟩:

Like "206*" Or Like "425*"

5   In the **Validation Text** box, type **Area code must be 206 or 425**.

You have set a rule for the first three digits typed in the **PhoneField** field and provided the text that Access should display if someone attempts to enter an invalid phone number.

6   Click in the **Caption** box, and type **Phone Number**.

The table window now looks like this:

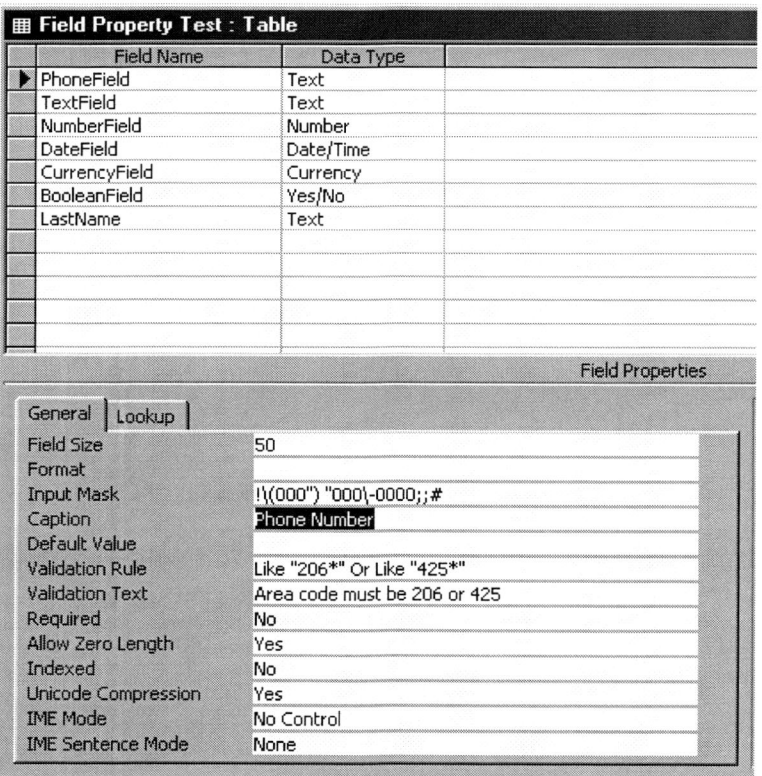

7 Save the table.

Access warns you that data integrity rules have changed. The table violates the new rule because it contains blank phone number fields.

8 Click **No** to close the message box without testing the data.

tip

You can test the validation rules in a table at any time by right-clicking the title bar of the table and clicking **Test Validation Rules** on the shortcut menu.

9 Return to Datasheet view, where the caption for the first field is now *Phone Number*.

10 Place the insertion point to the left of the first # of any **Phone Number** field, type **3605550009**, and press Enter.

tip

You can move the pointer to the left end of the **Phone Number** field and, when the pointer changes to a fat cross, click to select the entire field. The insertion point is then at the start of the area code when you begin typing.

The **Validation Rule** setting causes Access to display an alert box, warning you that the area code must be either 206 or 425.

11 Click **OK** to close the alert box, and type a new phone number with one of the allowed area codes.

12   Return to Design view, and add another date field. Type **Date2** as the field name, set the data type to **Date/Time**, and drag the new field to just below **DateField**.

13   Add a table validation rule to ensure that the second date is always later than the first one. Right-click the table window, and click **Properties** on the shortcut menu to open the **Table Properties** dialog box, shown here:

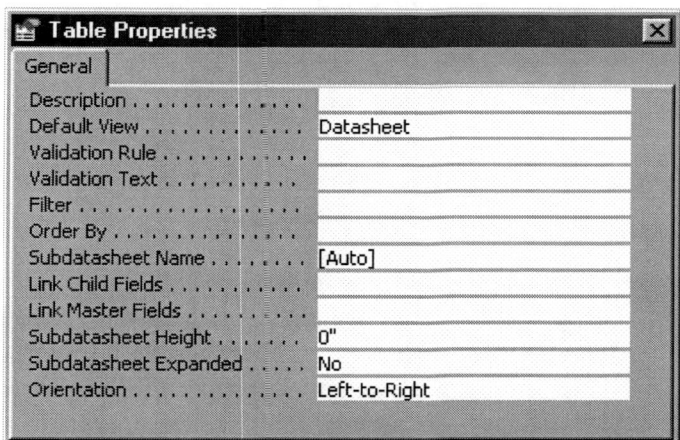

tip

This dialog box is not the one you see if you right-click the table in the database window and click **Properties**. The only point in common between the two is the **Description** property, which you can enter in either dialog box.

14   Click in the **Validation Rule** box, type **[DateField]<[Date2]**, and press ⎡ Enter ⎤.

15   Type **Date2 must be later than DateField**, and close the dialog box.

16   Save the table (click **No** to close the data-integrity alert box), and return to Datasheet view.

17   In any record, type **6/1/01** in **DateField** and **5/1/01** in **Date2**, and then click in another record.

Access displays the **Validation Text** setting from the **Table Properties** dialog box, reminding you that **Date2** must be later than **DateField**.

18   Click **OK**, change **Date2** to **6/2/2001**, and click in another record.

19   Close the table and the database.

Using a Lookup List to Restrict Data

Ac2002-2-3
Ac2002e-1-3

It is interesting how many different ways people can come up with to enter the same items of information in a database. Asked to enter the name of their home state, for example, residents of the state of Washington will type *Washington*, *Wash*, or *WA*, plus various typos and misspellings. If you ask a dozen sales clerks to enter the name of a specific product, customer, and shipper in an invoice, the probability that all of them will type the same thing is not very high. In cases like this, where the number of correct choices is limited (to actual product name, actual customer, and actual shipper), providing the option to choose the correct answer from a list will improve your database's consistency.

Creating a customized lookup list facilitates data input for that field.

Minor inconsistencies in the way data is entered might not be really important to someone who later reads the information and makes decisions. Most people know that *Arizona* and *AZ* refer to the same state. But a computer is very literal, and if you tell it to create a list so that you can send catalogues to everyone living in *AZ*, the computer won't include anyone whose state is listed in the database as *Arizona*.

You can limit the options for entering information in a database in several ways:

- For only two options, you can use a Boolean field represented by a check box. A check in the box indicates one choice, and no check indicates the other choice.

- For several mutually exclusive options on a form, you can use **option buttons** to gather the required information.

- For more than a few options, a **combo box** is a good way to go. When you click the down arrow at the end of a combo box, a list of choices is displayed. Depending on the properties associated with the combo box, if you don't see the option you want, you might be able to type something else, adding your entry to the list of possible options displayed in the future.

- For a short list of choices that won't change often, you can have the combo box look up the options in a list that you provide. Although you can create a lookup list by hand, it is a lot easier to use the **Lookup Wizard** to do it.

Field Test

In this exercise, you will use the **Lookup Wizard** to create a list of months from which the user can choose. You might use something like this to gather credit card information. The working folder for this exercise is *SBS\Access\Accurate\Lookup*. Follow these steps:

A lookup list can be created by typing in the values personally or by looking them up in an existing table or query.

1   Open the **Field Test** database located in the working folder.

2   Open the **Field Property Test** table in Design view.

3   Add a new field below **LastName**. Name it **Month**, and set the data type to **Lookup Wizard**.

The first page of the **Lookup Wizard** is displayed:

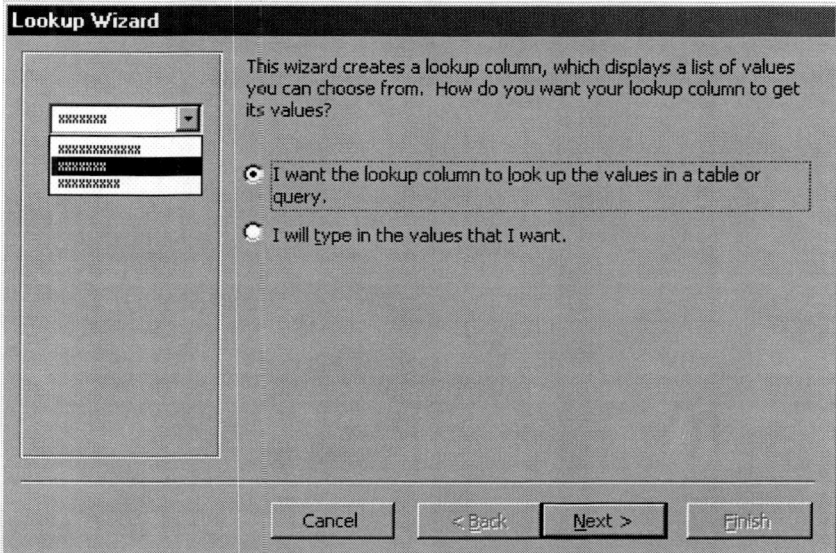

You can use this wizard to create a combo box that provides the entry for a text field. The combo box list can come from a table or query, or you can type the list in the wizard.

tip

If a field has a lot of potential entries, or if they will change often, you can link them to a table. (You might have to create a table expressly for this purpose.) If the field has only a few items and they won't change, typing the list in the wizard is easier.

4   Click **I will type in the values that I want**, and then click **Next**.

A combo box typically has only one column, but it can have more. On this page, you can set the number of columns and then enter the text that should appear in each one. If you specify more than one column, you also have to specify which column's text should be entered in the field when a selection is made from the list.

5   Leave the number of columns set to 1, and click in the **Col1** box.

6   Enter the 12 months of the year, pressing ⌈Tab⌋ to create new rows as you need them. Then click **Next**.

7   Accept the *Month* default label, and click **Finish**.

8   Click the **Lookup** tab in the **Field Properties** section to view the **Lookup** information for the **Month** field, which looks as shown on the next page.

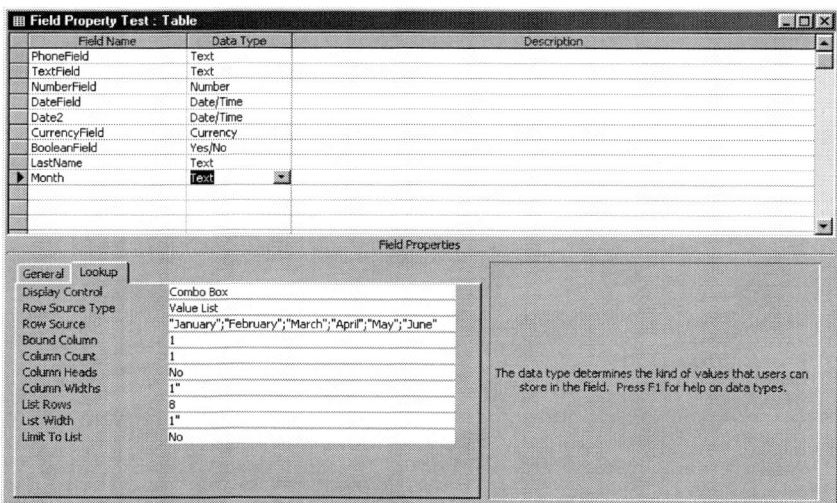

The wizard entered this information, but you could easily figure out what you would have to enter to create a lookup list by hand.

View

9 Click the **View** button to change to Datasheet view, saving your changes.

10 Adjust the column widths so that you can see all the fields, by dragging the vertical bars between columns in the header.

11 Click in the **Month** field of a record, and then click the down arrow to display the list, which looks like this:

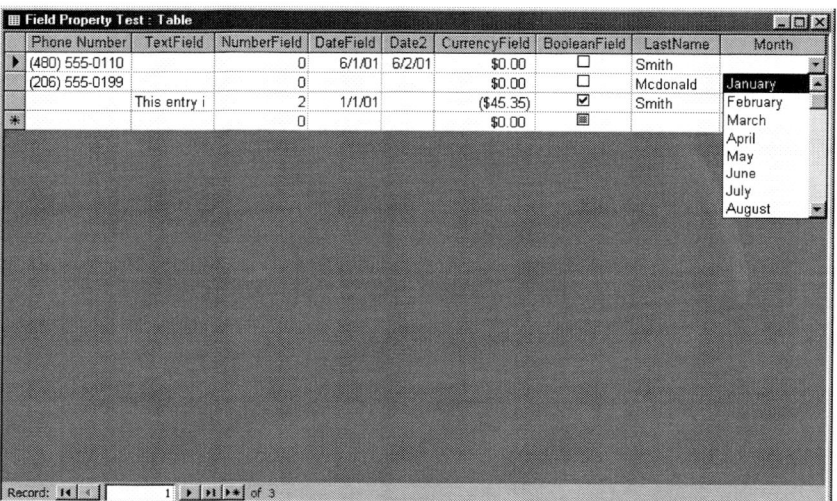

12 Click **February** to enter it in the field.

13 Click in the next **Month** field, type **Jan**, and press ⌈ Enter ⌋.

As soon as you type the *J*, the combo box displays *January*. If you had typed *Ju*, the combo box would have jumped to *June*.

14 In the next **Month** field, type **jly**, and press ⌈ Enter ⌋.

The entry is accepted just as you typed it. Although there might be times when you want to allow the entry of information other than the items on the list, this isn't one of those times.

15 Return to Design view.

The last property on the **Lookup** tab is **Limit To List**. It is currently set to **No**, which allows people to enter information that isn't on the list.

16 Change **Limit To List** to **Yes**.

17 Save the table, return to Datasheet view, type **jly** in a new **Month** field, and press ⬚Enter⬚.

Access informs you that the text you entered is not on the list, and refuses the entry.

18 Click **OK**, press ⬚Esc⬚ to close the list, remove your entry, and then return to Design view.

A list of the names of months is convenient for people, but if your computer has to deal with this information in some mathematical way, a list of the numbers associated with each month is easier for it to use. There is a solution that will work for both humans and machines.

19 Create a new field named **Month2**, and again set the data type to **Lookup Wizard**.

20 Click **I will type in the values that I want**, and click **Next**.

21 Type **2** to add a second column, and then click in the **Col1** box.

22 Enter the following numbers and months in the two columns, pressing ⬚Tab⬚ to move from column to column:

Number	Month	Number	Month
1	January	7	July
2	February	8	August
3	March	9	September
4	April	10	October
5	May	11	November
6	June	12	December

The wizard now looks as shown on the next page.

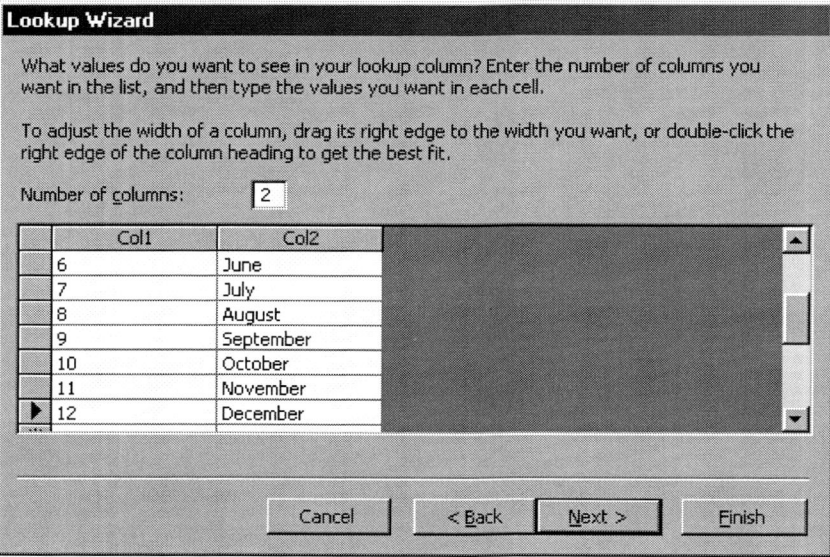

23 Click **Next** to move to the next page.

24 Accept the default selection of **Col1** as the column whose data you want to enter when a selection is made from the list, and click **Finish**.

You return to the table, with the **Field Properties** section displaying the **Lookup** information, like this:

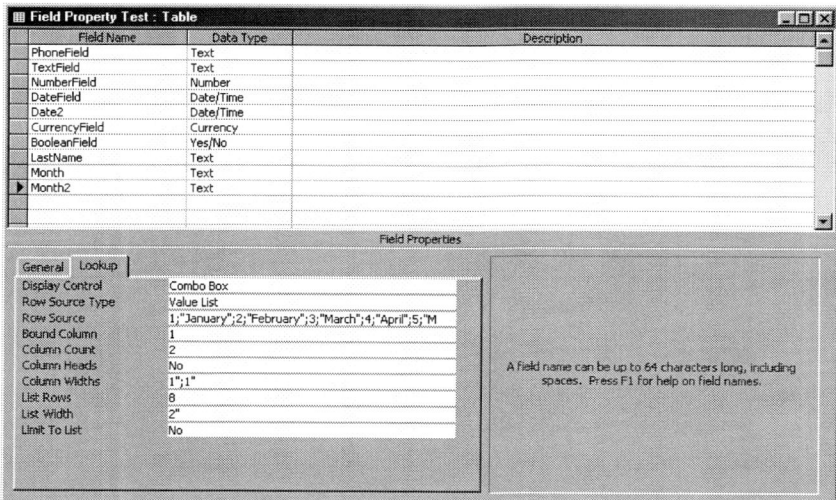

The wizard has inserted your column information into the **Row Source** box and set the other properties according to your specifications.

25 Change **Limit To List** to **Yes**.

26 Save your changes, switch to Datasheet view, and then click the down arrow in a **Month2** field to display this list:

27 Click **January**.

Access displays the number *1* in the field, which is useful for the computer. However, people might be confused by the two columns and by seeing something other than what they clicked or typed.

28 Switch back to Design view, and in the **Column Widths** box, change the width for the first column to **0"** to prevent it from being displayed.

29 Save your changes, return to Datasheet view, and as a test, set **Month2** to **February** in two records and to **March** in one record.

Only the name of the month is now displayed in the list, and when you click a month, that name is displayed in the field. However, Access actually stores the associated number from the list's first column.

30 Right-click in the **Month2** column, click **Filter For** on the shortcut menu, type **2** in the box, and press ⌐Enter⌐.

Only the two records with *February* in the **Month2** field are now displayed.

Remove Filter

▽

31 Click the **Remove Filter** button, and then repeat the previous step, this time typing **3** in the box to display the one record with *March* in the **Month2** field.

32 Close the **Field Text** database, clicking **Yes** when prompted to save your changes.

33 Close the database.

Deleting Information from a Table

Ac2002-5-1
Ac2002e-3-4

Over time, some types of information in a database can become obsolete. The Products table in The Garden Company database, for example, maintains a list of all the products the company currently offers for sale or has sold in the past. When a product is no longer available for sale, for whatever reason, a check mark is placed in the Discontinued field. Discontinued products aren't displayed in the catalogue or pushed by salespeople, but they are kept in the database for a while in case it becomes practical to sell them again. A similar situation could exist with customers who haven't placed an order in a long time or who have asked to be removed from a mailing list but might still place orders.

Eventually, the time comes to clean house and discard some records. You could do this by scrolling through the tables and deleting records by hand, but if all the records to be deleted match some pattern, you can use a **delete query** to quickly get rid of all of them.

important

Keep in mind several things when deleting records from a database. First, there is no quick recovery of deleted records. Second, the effects of a delete query can be more far-reaching than you intend. If the table where you are deleting records has a relationship with another table and the **Cascade Delete Related Records** option for that relationship is set, records in the second table will also be deleted. Sometimes this is what you want, but sometimes it isn't. For example, you don't want to delete the records of previous sales just because you're deleting discontinued products. There are two solutions to this problem: back up your database before deleting the records; or create a new table (perhaps named *Deleted<file name>*), and then move the records you want to delete to the new table.

GardenCo

In this exercise, you will create a delete query to remove all discontinued products from the Products table of the GardenCo database. The working folder for this exercise is *\SBS\Access\Accurate\QueryDel*. Follow these steps:

1   Open the **GardenCo** database located in the working folder.

2   On the **Objects** bar, click **Queries**.

3   Double-click **Create query in Design view** to open both the query window and the **Show Table** dialog box.

4   Double-click **Products** to add that table to the list area of the query window, and then click **Close** to close the **Show Table** dialog box.

5   Double-click the asterisk at the top of the list of fields to include all the fields in the query.

    Products.* appears in the **Field** row of the first column of the design grid, and **Products** appears in the **Table** row.

tip

Clicking the asterisk in the field list is a quick way to move all the fields in the table to the query, without having each field appear in its own column. However, then you can't set **Sort**, **Show**, and **Criteria** values for individual fields. To set these values, you have to add the specific fields to the design grid, thereby adding them twice. To avoid displaying the fields twice, clear the check mark in the **Show** row of the duplicate individual fields.

6   Scroll to the bottom of the field list, and double-click **Discontinued** to copy it to the next available column in the design grid.

7   On the **Query** menu, click **Delete Query** to convert this select query to a delete query.

In the design grid, the **Sort** and **Show** rows have disappeared, and a **Delete** row has been added. In the first column, which contains the reference to all fields in the Products table, the **Delete** row contains the word *From*, indicating that this is the table from which records will be deleted. When you add individual fields to the remaining columns, as you did with the Discontinued field, the **Delete** row displays *Where*, indicating that this field can include deletion criteria.

8   Type **Yes** in the **Criteria** row under **Discontinued**.

The Discontinued field is set to the **Boolean** data type, which is represented in the datasheet as a check box that has a check mark to indicate **Yes** and no check mark to indicate **No**. So to locate all discontinued products, you need to identify records with the Discontinued field set to **Yes**.

View

9   To check the accuracy of the query, click the **View** button.

Access displays a list of 18 discontinued products that will be deleted, but it hasn't actually changed the table yet. Scroll to the right to verify that all records display a check in the Products.Discontinued field.

10   Click the **View** button to return to Design view, confident that you have identified the correct records.

tip

Before actually deleting records, you might want to display the Relationships window by clicking **Relationships** on the **Tools** menu. If the table you are deleting from has a relationship with any table containing order information that shouldn't be deleted, right-click the relationship line, click **Edit Relationship** on the shortcut menu, and make sure that **Enforce Referential Integrity** is selected and **Cascade Delete Related Records** is *not* selected.

Run

11   Click the **Run** button to run the delete query.

Access displays a warning to remind you of the permanence of this action.

12   Click **Yes** to delete the records.

Access displays another warning, stating it can't delete two of the records due to key violations. This is because two discontinued products have been ordered, and so are in the Order Details table. This table has a one-to-many relationship with the Products table, and **Enforce Referential Integrity** is set between the two tables.

13   Click **Yes** to run the query, and then click **View** to see the two discontinued products that were not deleted.

Save

14   If you think you might want to run the same delete query in the future, click the **Save** button and provide a name to save it. Then close the query.

tip

If you are concerned that someone might accidentally run a delete query and destroy records you weren't ready to destroy, change the query back to a select query before saving it. You can then open the select query in Design view and change it to a delete query when you want to run it again.

15   Close the query, and then close the database.

16   If you are not continuing on to the next chapter, quit Access.

Quick Quizzes

●   How do you delete records from a table?

●   What is an input mask?

●   What does Validation do ?

LESSON 7: Working with Reports

After completing this chapter, you will be able to:

✔ *Create a report using a wizard*

✔ *Add a subreport to a report*

✔ *Preview and print a report*

People generally think of **reports** as summaries of larger bodies of information. For example, The Garden Company's database might hold detailed information about thousands of orders. If you want to edit those orders or enter new ones, you do so directly in the table or via a form. If you want to summarize those orders to illustrate the rate of growth of the company's sales, you use a report.

Like a book report or the annual report of a company's activities, a report created in Microsoft Access is typically used to summarize and organize information in order to express a particular point of view to a specific audience. When designing a report, it is important to consider the point you are trying to make, the intended audience, and the level of information they will need.

In many ways, reports are like forms. You can use similar wizards to create them, and the design environment is much the same. Just as with a form, you can add label, text box, image, and other controls, and you can set their properties. You can display information from one or more records from one or more tables or queries, and you can have multiple sets of headers and footers.

Forms vs. Reports

Forms and reports have one purpose in common: to give people easy access to the information stored in a database. The main differences between forms and reports are the following:

- ■ Forms are used to enter, view, and edit information. Reports are used only to view information.

- ■ Forms are usually displayed on the screen. Reports can be previewed on the screen, but they are usually printed.

- ■ Forms generally provide a detailed look at records and are usually for the people who actually work with the database. Reports are often used to group and summarize data and are often for people who don't actually work with the database but who use its information for other business tasks.

Forms and reports are sufficiently alike that you can save a form as a report when you want to take advantage of additional report refinement and printing capabilities.

In this chapter, you will learn how to generate and print reports that extract specific information from a database and format it in an easy-to-read style. You will be working with the GardenCo database files that are stored in the following subfolders of the *SBS\Access\Reports* folder: *RepByWiz*, *Modify*, *ByDesign*, *Subreport*, and *Print*.

Creating a Report Using a Wizard

Ac2002-7-1
Ac2002e-4-1
Ac2002e-4-3

The content of an Access report can be divided into two general categories: information derived from records in one or more tables, and everything else. The *everything else* category includes the title, page headers and footers, introductory and explanatory text, logo, background and graphics, and calculations based on database content.

You can use a wizard to get a jump-start on a report. The wizard creates a basic layout, attaches styles, and adds a text box control and its associated label for each field you specify. Depending on the report you want to produce, you might be able to do almost all the work in the wizard, or you might have to refine the report in Design view.

GardenCo

In this exercise, you will use the **Report Wizard** to create a simple report that displays an alphabetical list of The Garden Company's products. The working folder for this exercise is *SBS\Access\Reports\RepByWiz*. Follow these steps:

The use of grouping levels allows you to highlight certain fields.

1   Open the **GardenCo** database located in the working folder.

2   On the **Objects** bar, click **Tables**, and then click the **Products** table to select it.

tip

If you select a table or query before starting the **Report Wizard**, that table or query becomes the basis for the report.

3   On the **Insert** menu, click **Report** to display the **New Report** dialog box.

Notice that **Products** is already selected as the table on which to base the new report.

4   Double-click **Report Wizard** to open the **Report Wizard**.

You use this page of the wizard to select the fields to be included in the new report.

tip

You can also click **Report Wizard** in the **New Report** dialog box that appears when you click **Report** on the **New Object** button's list; or click the **New** button on the database window's toolbar; or double-click **Create report by using wizard** in the **Report** pane of the database window.

5   Double-click **ProductName, QuantityPerUnit,** and **UnitsInStock** to move them to the **Selected Fields** list.

tip

Fields appear in a report in the same order they are listed in the wizard's **Selected Fields** list. You can save yourself the effort of rearranging the fields on the report if you enter them in the desired order in the wizard.

6   Select **Tables:Categories** in the **Tables/Queries** list to display the fields from the Categories table.

7   Click **ProductName** in the **Selected Fields** list to select it.

The next field you add will be inserted below the selected field.

8   Double-click **CategoryName**.

The **Report Wizard** now looks as shown on the next page.

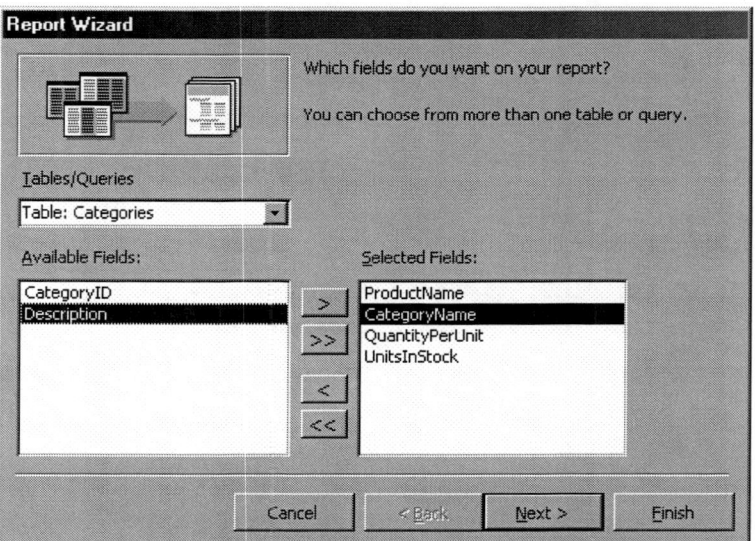

tip

If you are using more than two tables in a form or report, or if you will be using the same combination of tables in several places, it is more efficient to create a query based on those tables and use that query as the basis for the form or report.

9   Click **Next** to move to the wizard's second page, which looks like this:

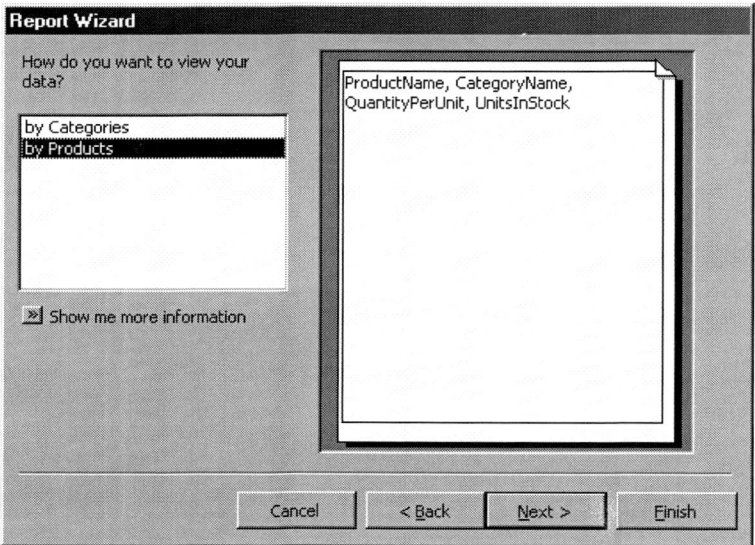

When you include more than one table in a report, the wizard evaluates the relationships that exist between the tables and offers to group the records in any logical manner available. In this case, you can choose to group them by category or product. You can click either option to see it depicted in the right pane.

important

If the relationships between the tables aren't already established in the Relationships window, you have to cancel the wizard and establish them now.

10 Accept the default to group **By Products**, and click **Next**.

On this page you can specify any fields you want to use to establish **grouping levels**. You want to group by the first letter of the product names.

11 Double-click **ProductName** to move it to the top of the simulated report on the right.

12 Click the **Grouping Options** button at the bottom of the page to open this dialog box:

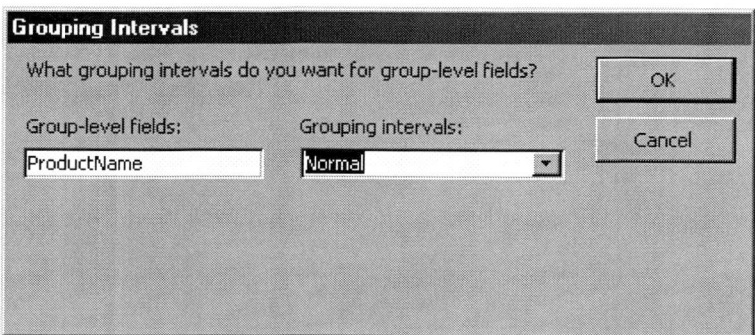

13 Display the **Grouping intervals** drop-down list, click **1st Letter**, and then click **OK**.

The wizard now looks like this:

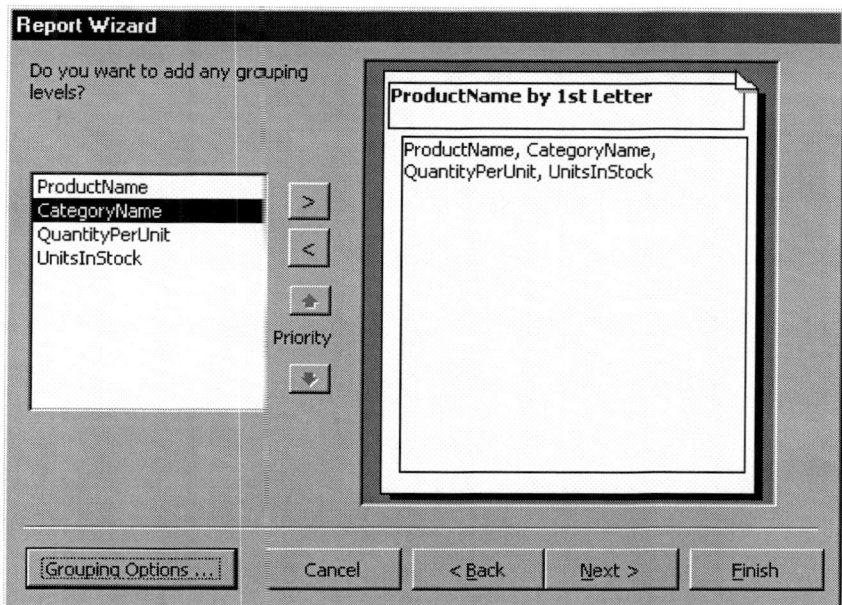

14 Click **Next** to display a page where you can specify the sort order and summary options.

15 Specify **ProductName** as the first **Ascending** sort field.

You can use this page to specify up to four fields on which to sort. If any fields include numeric information, the **Summary Options** button becomes available. You can click it to display a list of the numeric fields, each with **Sum**, **Avg** (average), **Min** (minimum), and **Max** (maximum) check boxes. The only numeric field in this report is UnitsInStock, and there is no need to summarize it.

16 Click **Next** to display the next page of the wizard.

On this page, you can click the options in the **Layout** group to see what each one looks like. None of them is exactly what you are looking for, but **Outline 1** is close.

17 Click **Outline 1**, leave **Portrait** orientation selected, and then click **Next** to display a list of predefined styles.

18 Click **Compact**, and then click **Next** to display the wizard's final page.

19 Type **Alphabetical List of Products** as the title, and click **Finish** to preview the report, which looks like this:

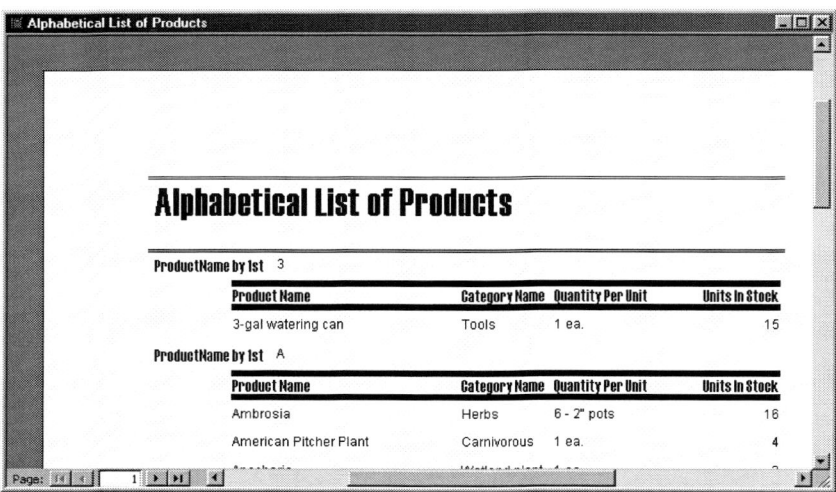

20 Close the report window, and then close the database.

Adding a Subreport to a Report

Ac2002-7-2
Ac2002e-4-2

You can use a wizard to quickly create a report that is bound to the information in one table or in several related tables. However, reports often include multiple sets of information that are related to the topic of the report but are not necessarily related to each other. A report might, for example, include charts, spreadsheets, and other forms of information about several divisions or activities of a company. Or it might include information about production, marketing, sales, compensation, and the company's 401(K) plan. All these topics are related to running the business, but they don't all fit nicely into the structure of a single Access report.

One solution to this problem is to create separate reports, print them, and put them in one binder. But an easier solution is to use **subreports**. A subreport is simply a report that you insert in a subreport control that you have placed in another report. You can create the subreport as you would any other report and then use a wizard to insert it, or you can use a wizard to insert a subreport control in the main report and then let the wizard guide you through the process of creating the subreport in the control. In either case, you end up with both the main report and the subreport listed as objects in the **Reports** pane of the database window.

Often you will use queries as the basis for reports that require summary calculations or statistics. But you can also enhance the usefulness of both regular reports and subreports by performing calculations in the reports themselves. By inserting **unbound** controls and then using the Expression Builder to create the expressions that tell Access what to calculate and how, you can make information readily available in one place instead of several.

tip

Assuming that the correct relationships have been established, you can quickly add an existing report as a subreport by opening the main report in Design view and then dragging the second report from the **Reports** pane to the section of the main report where you want to insert it.

GardenCo

In this exercise, you will add a subreport to a main report. This subreport will display the total sales for each of the products in the category that is selected on the main report, as well as a calculated control for the total sales for the category. The working folder for this exercise is *SBS\Access\Reports\Subreport*. Follow these steps:

1   Open the **GardenCo** database located in the working folder.

2   Open the **Sales by Category** report in Design view.

Subform/Subreport

3   Click **Subform/Subreport** in the toolbox, and then click a point even with the left edge of the Product label and about two grid intervals below it.

Access opens a blank, unbound subreport on the main report and displays the first page of the **SubReport Wizard**, shown on the next page.

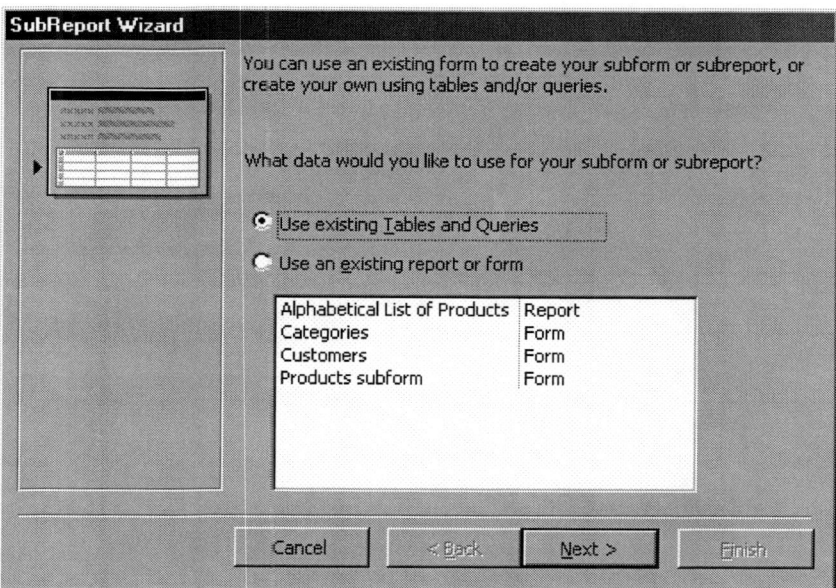

4   With **Use existing Tables and Queries** selected, click **Next**.

5   Select **Query: Sales by Category** from the **Tables/Queries** list.

6   Double-click **CategoryID**, **ProductName**, and **ProductSales** to move them to the **Selected Fields** list, and then click **Next**.

7   Accept the default **Choose from a list** selection by clicking **Next**.

8   Accept the suggested name, *Sales by Category subreport*, and click **Finish**.

The **Sales by Category** subreport takes the place of the unbound subreport in the main report.

9 If the **Properties** dialog box for the subreport isn't displayed, click the subreport control and press [F4] to display the dialog box.

10 On the **Format** tab, change the width of the subreport to **4"** and the height to **1"**. Then press [Enter].

11 In the subreport, right-click the **Report Header** section selector, and click **Report Header/Footer** on the shortcut menu to delete the header and footer. Click **Yes** in the alert box.

12 In the subreport, right-click the **Page Header** section selector, click **Page Header/ Footer** on the shortcut menu, and click **Yes** in the alert box.

The subreport now has only a **Detail** section.

13 In the **Detail** section, delete the **CategoryID** text box.

14 Click the **ProductName** text box, and change its width to **2.125"**.

15 Click the **ProductSales** text box, and change its **Left** property to **2.3"** and its **Width** property to **1"**.

16 On the main report, click the partially hidden **Sales by Category** subreport label, and delete it.

tip

If you accidentally delete something, press [Ctrl] + [Z] to undo the deletion.

The subreport now looks like this:

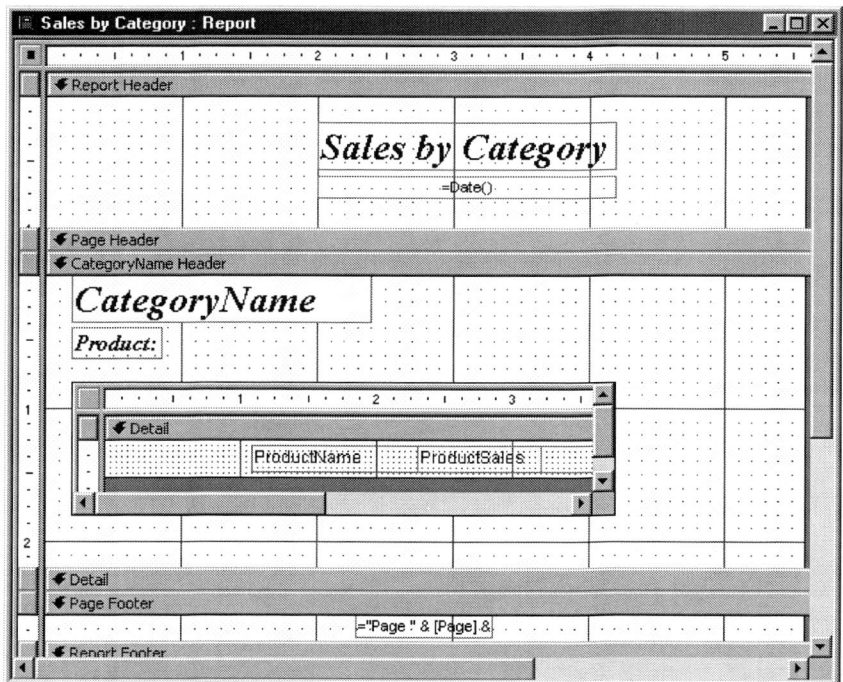

17 Now you'll add a section in which to calculate the total product sales for each category. Click the selector in the upper left corner of the subreport, and then click **Report Header/Footer** on the **View** menu to display those sections.

Text Box
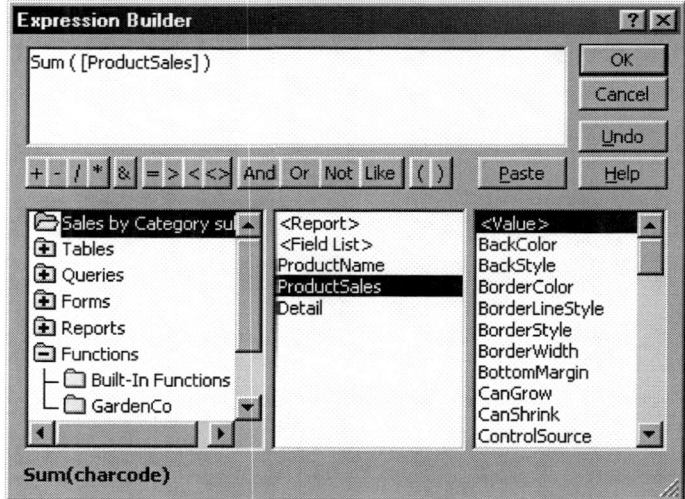
ab|

18 Scroll the subreport to display the **Report Footer** section, click the **Text Box** control in the toolbox, and then click anywhere in the footer grid.

Access inserts an unbound control and its label. You will use this control to perform the calculation.

19 Change the label's text to **Total:**, and set the **Font Name** property to **Arial**, the **Font Size** property to **9**, and the **Font Weight** property to **Bold**.

20 Now click the text box control, click the **Data** tab in the **Properties** dialog box, and click the button to open the **Expression Builder**.

21 Double-click **Functions**, and click **Built-In Functions** in the first column. Then scroll the third column, and double-click **Sum**.

Access displays *Sum (<<expr>>)* in the expression box.

22 Select <<**expr**>>, click **Sales by Category subreport** in the first column, and double- click **ProductSales** in the second column.

The Expression Builder now looks like this:

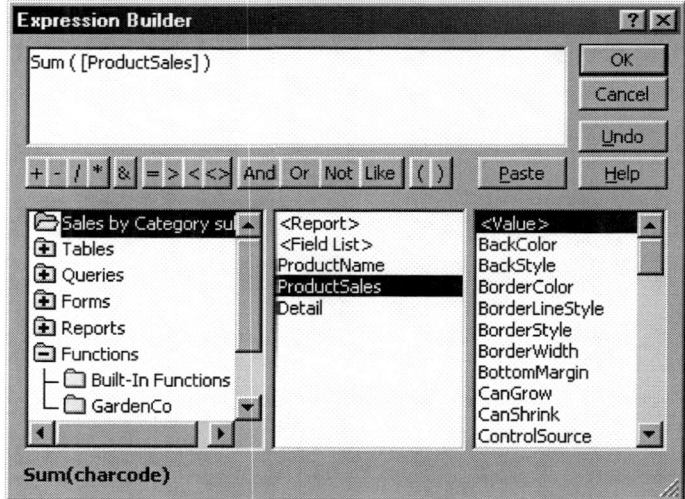

23 Click **OK** to close the **Expression Builder**, and then press
[Enter] to enter the calculation in the unbound text box.

24 Click the **Format** tab of the **Properties** dialog box, and format the control as **Arial**, **9**, and **Bold**. Then click the **Format** property, and click **Currency** in the drop-down list.

Now the results of the calculation will be displayed as currency.

25 Position and size the calculated control and its label to match those in the **Detail** section above.

Your report now looks like this:

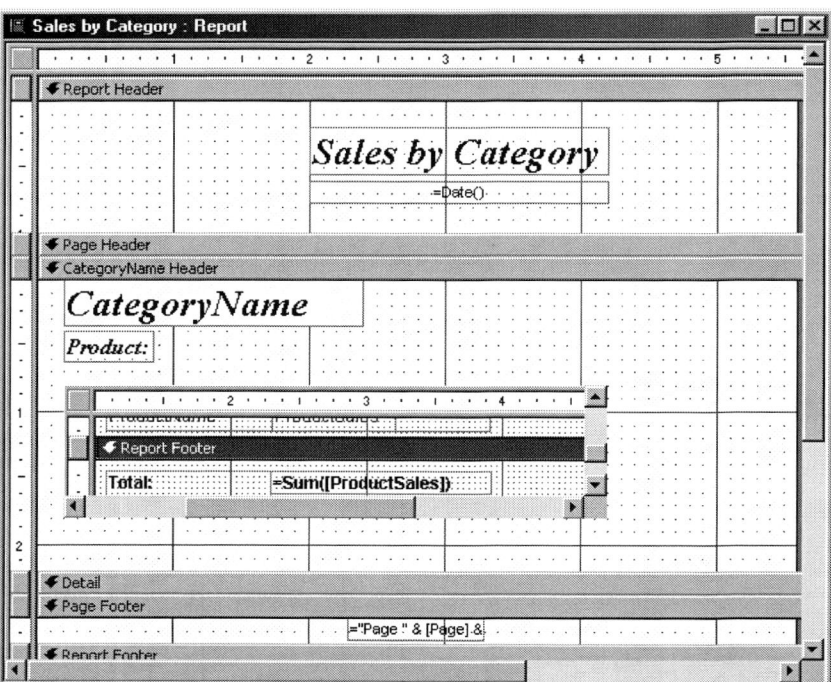

26 Save your changes, and switch to Print Preview to see these results:

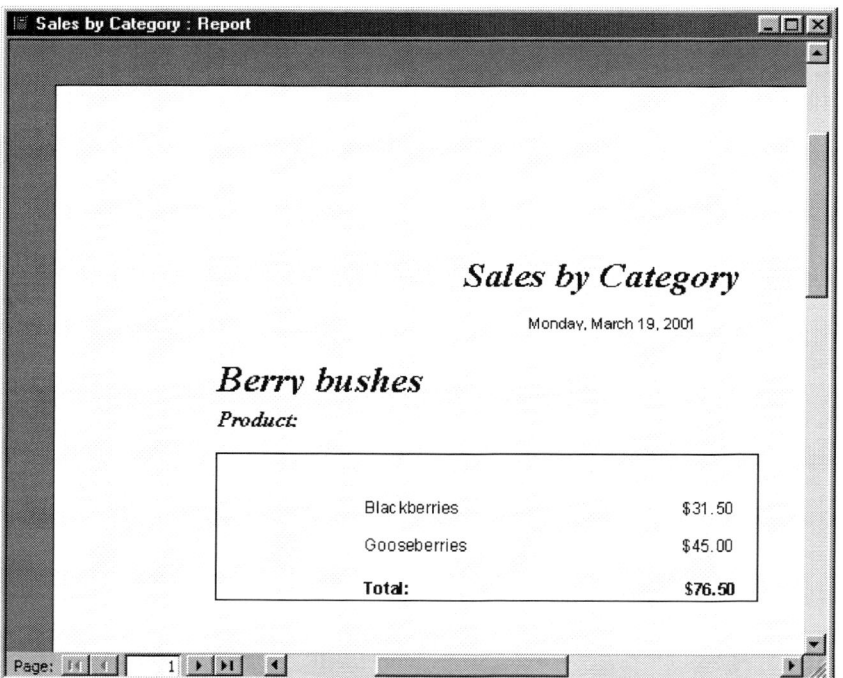

This looks pretty close to what you want, but to make the report look cleaner, you need to remove the border around the subreport.

27 Return to Design view, and click the subreport to select it.

28 On the **Format** tab of the **Properties** dialog box, change the **Border Style** property to **Transparent**.

tip

Several factors affect the layout of the subreport on the main report when it is displayed in Print Preview. The width of the subreport sets the width of the space available for the display of text. The height of the subreport sets the minimum height of the area where product information is displayed (because the **Can Shrink** property for the subreport is set to **No**). The maximum height of the product display area is the length of the list (because the **Can Grow** property is set to **Yes**) plus the space between the bottom of the subreport and the bottom of the **Detail** section.

29   Save your changes, preview the report, and then close it.

30   Close the database.

Previewing and Printing a Report

Ac2002-7-3

Print Preview in Access is very similar to Print Preview in other Microsoft Office products. If you check out your reports carefully in Print Preview, you won't be in for any major surprises when you print them. But Access also provides a "quick and dirty" preview option called Layout Preview that displays only enough of the report for you to see all the elements. This view often produces a shorter report that provides just enough information to help you refine the layout but is faster to print.

GardenCo

Most people don't spend a lot of time studying the preview and print options, so in this exercise you will review them, in case there are a few you haven't tried yet. Then you'll print a report. The working folder for this exercise is *SBS\Access\Reports\Print*. Follow these steps:

1   Open the **GardenCo** database located in the working folder.

2   Open the **Alphabetical List of Products** report in Design view.

View

3   Click the **View** button's arrow to display this list of possible views:

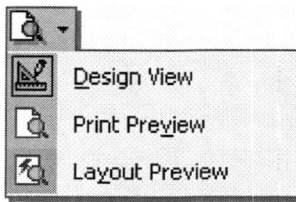

Each of the three choices-Design view, Print Preview, and Layout Preview-has an associated icon. The Design view icon has a border, indicating it is the current view. The Print Preview icon is duplicated on the **View** button, indicating that it is the default view if you simply click the button rather than display this menu and choose a view. When you are in Design view, both Print Preview and Layout Preview are available.

4   Click **Print Preview**.

In the preview environment, the Formatting and Report Design toolbars are hidden, the toolbox is hidden, and an image of how the report will look when it is printed is displayed, along with the Print Preview toolbar, as shown here:

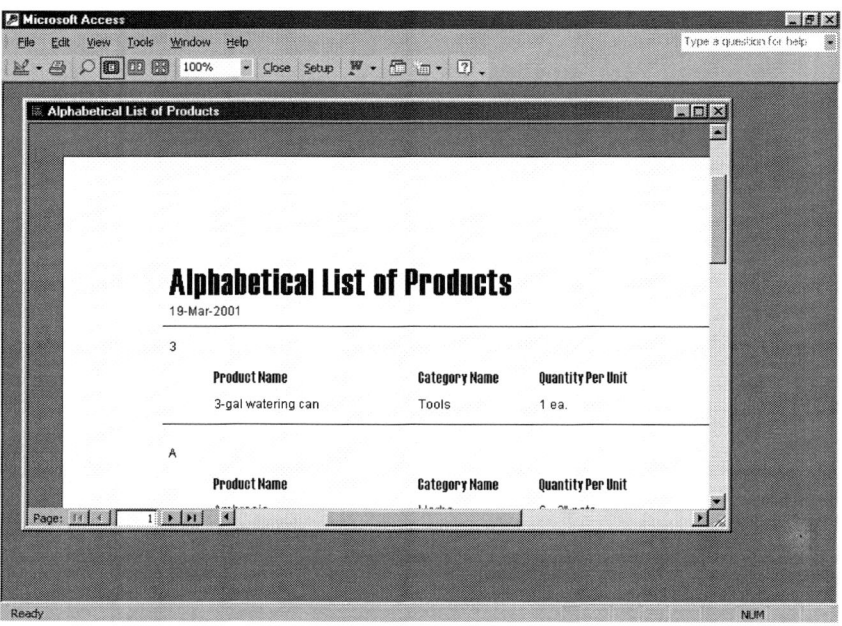

Zoom

5   Click the **Zoom** button to toggle the page magnification so that an entire page fits in the report window.

Next Page

6   Repeatedly click the **Next Page** button on the Navigation bar to view each of the 10 pages of this report.

7   Move the pointer over a page, and when the pointer changes to a magnifying glass with a plus sign in it, click to zoom in for a closer look.

The plus sign changes to a minus sign, meaning that you can click to zoom out again.

8   Click the **Close** button on the Print Preview toolbar.

9   Display the **View** button's arrow, and click **Layout Preview** in the list.

The same Print Preview toolbar is displayed, and the report looks similar to the way it does in Print Preview. However, not all products are listed in each group. (If you can't see the page clearly, zoom in.)

10   Click the **Next Page** button.

In Layout Preview, the report has only two pages.

11   Click the **Close** button to return to Design view.

12   On the **File** menu, click **Print** to display the **Print** dialog box:

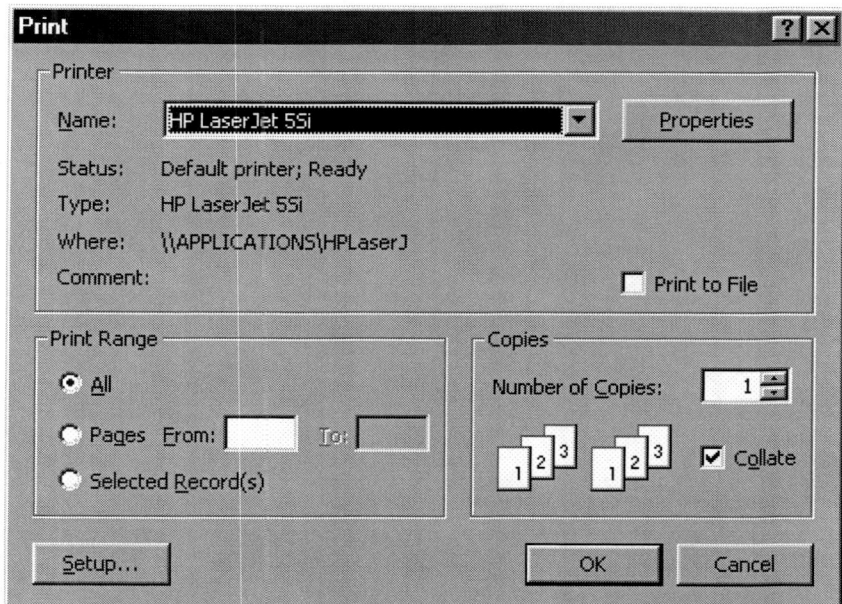

A fast way of opening the **Print** dialog box from the Report Preview is to press

Ctrl + P

This is a standard Microsoft Windows **Print** dialog box. You can click the **Setup** button to open the **Page Setup** dialog box, or **Properties** to open a dialog box where you can set properties specific to the printer specified in the **Name** box. You can also specify which pages to print and the number of copies of each.

13   Click **Cancel** to close the **Print** dialog box.

14   Close the report and the database.

15   If you are not continuing on to the next chapter, quit Access.

Quick Quizzes

●   What is a report?

●   What is a subreport?

●   Can you create calculated controls in a report?

●   How do you specify which pages of a report are to be printed?

LESSON 8: Working with Pages and Modules

After completing this chapter, you will be able to:

✓ *Create dynamic Web pages for modifying data on the Web.*

The World Wide Web is the largest public clearinghouse of information in the world. It has become *the* place to publish and distribute books, software, and data of all types. If your organization has an Internet presence, you will want to take advantage of features in Microsoft Access that can be used to publish your database information so that it is accessible via an intranet or the Internet.

important

This discussion assumes that you are already familiar with the Internet, the World Wide Web, Internet service providers, and methods of placing HTML pages on a Web site for publication. If this is not the case, you should still be able to follow along and work through the exercises, but you might need help moving your files to the Web.

Information on the Web is viewed with a **Web browser**. The two most popular Web browsers are Microsoft Internet Explorer and Netscape Navigator; however, these browsers are available in many versions, and other browsers are also available. All browsers are capable of viewing files based on a simple set of **Hypertext Markup Language (HTML)** tags. Newer versions of the popular browsers also recognize non-standard HTML tags and other file formats, such as **Dynamic Hypertext Markup Language (DHTML)** and **Extensible Markup Language (XML)**.

important

If you intend to place database information on the Web, give careful thought to what operating system and browser will be used by people viewing your site. If you would like your site to be available to the general public, then you will have to forgo cutting- edge technology, such as data access pages, in favour of static Web pages or Active Server Pages (ASP).

You can use Access to create two types of Web pages:

■ **Static HTML pages,** which provide a snapshot of some portion of the database contents at one point in time. These pages can be viewed by any modern browser and can be stored on a server running any server software.

■ **Dynamic Web pages**, which are created in response to some action on the part of each user.

There are two main types of dynamic Web pages:

■ **Data access pages** allow users to directly manipulate data in your database. You can allow users to add, edit, and delete records, and change their view of the data, in much the same way as they would in a form. To take full advantage of data access pages, users must be running Internet Explorer version 5.0 or later.

■ **Active Server Pages** are stored on a **network server** and generate different views of the data in response to choices users make on a Web page. The pages can be viewed with any modern browser, but the server where the pages are stored must be running Microsoft Windows NT 4 or Microsoft Windows 2000. Although Access can export a form or report as an Active Server Page, you will not do that in this chapter. Search for *ASP* in Access online Help for more information.

In this chapter, you will create static and dynamic Web pages. You will get an overview of Microsoft Visual Basic for Applications (VBA) and see how VBA procedures stored in Access modules can be used to create Web pages. You will also add controls to data access pages to allow other people to view your data, add and edit records, make projections, and analyze your data. You will be working with the GardenCo database files and several other sample files that are stored in these subfolders of the *SBS\Access\PgsMods* working folder: *Static*, *VBA*, *AutoPage*, *Wizard*, and *Analyze*.

Creating Static Web Pages

The most basic form of an HTML page is a static page. If you want any Web browser that supports HTML 3.2 or later to be able to view your data, you should display the data in static HTML pages. Static pages are downloaded and displayed in their entirety; the user can't edit them, and there are no tricky bits that pop up or change format as users move through the page.

Access can export tables, queries, forms, and reports as static HTML pages. Exported tables, queries, and forms are displayed in datasheet format. (If you have a lot of data, the Web page might be very long.) Exported reports are displayed on a series of short pages, similar to reports in Access.

GardenCo

In this exercise, you will export the Alphabetical List of Products report from the GardenCo database to a set of static HTML pages. The working folder for this exercise is *SBS\Access\PgsMods\Static*. Follow these steps:

1   Open the **GardenCo** database located in the working folder.

2   On the **Objects bar**, click **Reports**.

3   Open the **Alphabetical List of Products** report in Print Preview, just to see what it looks like.

4   Close the report.

5   On the **File** menu, click **Export** to display the **Export** dialog box.

6   Browse to the *SBS\Access\PgsMods\Static* folder, type **AlphaProd** in the **File name** box, select **HTML Documents** as the **Save as type** setting, select the **Autostart** check box, and then click **Export**.

7   In the **HTML Output Options** dialog box, make sure the **Select a HTML Template** check box is not selected, and then click **OK**.

Access displays its progress as it exports the report to HTML pages. Because you clicked **Autostart**, when the export process is complete, the first HTML page opens in your Web browser. (It may appear as a blinking button on the taskbar.)

8   If you don't see the HTML page, click **Alphabetical List of Products** on the taskbar to display it.

The first HTML page looks like this:

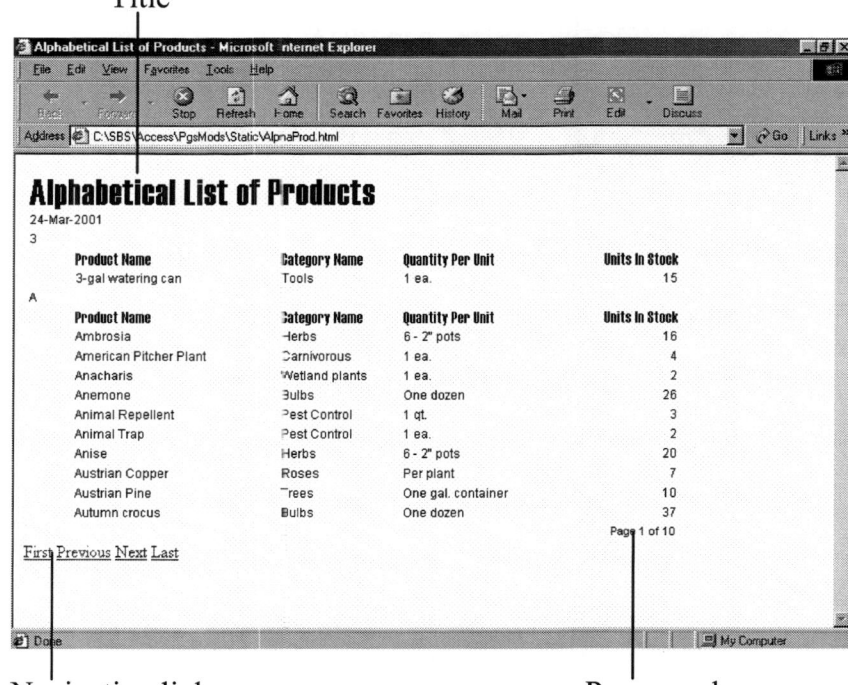

Title

Navigation links   Page number

When Access created these pages, it placed a title in the title bar, put the data in the body of the page, and added navigation links and a page number at the bottom.

9   Start Microsoft Windows Explorer, and browse to the working folder.

Access created a file named *AlphaProd*, which is the first page of the report, and nine more files named *AlphaProd2* through *AlphaProd10*, which are the remaining pages.

10 Return to the HTML page, and repeatedly click the **Next** hyperlink to scroll through the 10 pages of the report.

tip

If you are interested in seeing the HTML code that makes this page look the way it does, you can view it in Internet Explorer by right-clicking the body of the page and clicking **View Source**. If you are running Netscape Navigator, click **View Document Source** or **View Page Source** on the **View** menu, depending on the version of Netscape you are using.

11 Close the HTML report and the **GardenCo** database.

Creating a Data Access Page with AutoPage

Ac2002-8-3

If you are confident that everyone who will need to access your data on the Internet or an intranet will be using Internet Explorer version 5.0 or later, and that they will have Microsoft Office XP Web Components installed, you can take advantage of the special capabilities of **data access pages**. (Office XP Web Components is a set of ready-made controls that allow you to work interactively with information in a data access page.)

If you create a data access page while the database is open, a link to the page is displayed in the database window.

A data access page is similar to a form, in that it can be used to view, enter, edit, or delete data from a Microsoft Access or a Microsoft SQL Server database. Like a form, a data access page is an Access object. Unlike a form, a page is not stored as part of your database: it is an external HTML file that is linked to your database in such a way that it makes the information in the database available over an intranet or the Internet. The window displayed when you click **Pages** on the **Objects** bar contains shortcuts to any pages you have created, and each page contains code that connects it to the appropriate database when the page is opened in Internet Explorer.

In Design view, a data access page looks somewhat like a form or report in Design view, but there are several differences.

In a form or report, the entire object is contained within the sections. In a data access page, the sections contain and control data that is **bound** to the database. The space above and below the sections is also part of the page, and you can place text and other controls in it.

The Field List for a form or report displays only the fields in the specific table or query to which the object is bound. The Field List for a data access page displays fields from all available tables and queries.

You can view a data access page in Access or in Internet Explorer. For example, suppose The Garden Company's head buyer is visiting suppliers and she wants to check the store's stock of particular kinds of gardening tools. She can connect to the Internet, start Internet Explorer, open an Inventory data access page, check current stock levels, and change the On Order field to show the number of items she is about to order from the supplier.

important

In order to interact with and use the full functionality of a data access page, users must have Office XP installed on their computers. If they don't, they can view the data but they can't add, delete, or edit data.

There are four ways to create a data access page: in Design view, from an existing Web page, with the **Page Wizard**, or with AutoPage. AutoPage is the simplest method. Like AutoForm and AutoReport, AutoPage creates a simple page using all the available fields and minimal formatting.

GardenCo

In this exercise, you will create a data access page that allows people to update entries in the Employees table in the GardenCo database via the Internet. The working folder for this exercise is *SBS\Access\PgsMods\AutoPage*. Follow these steps:

1   Open the **GardenCo** database located in the working folder.

2   Click **Pages** on the **Objects** bar.

3   Click the **New** button on the database window's toolbar to display this **New Data Access Page** dialog box:

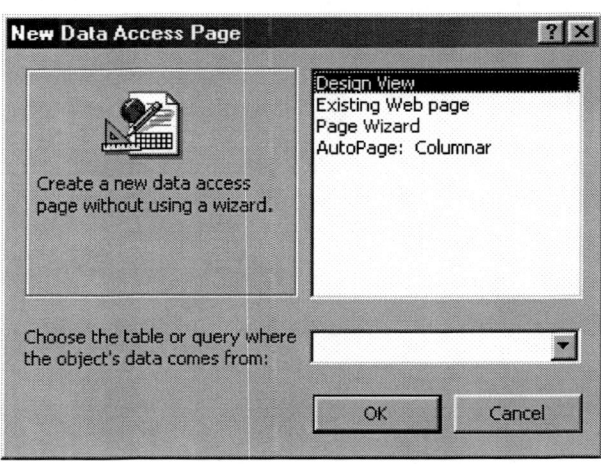

4   Click **AutoPage: Columnar**, select **Employees** from the list of tables and queries, and then click **OK**.

This simple data access page is created and displayed in Page view:

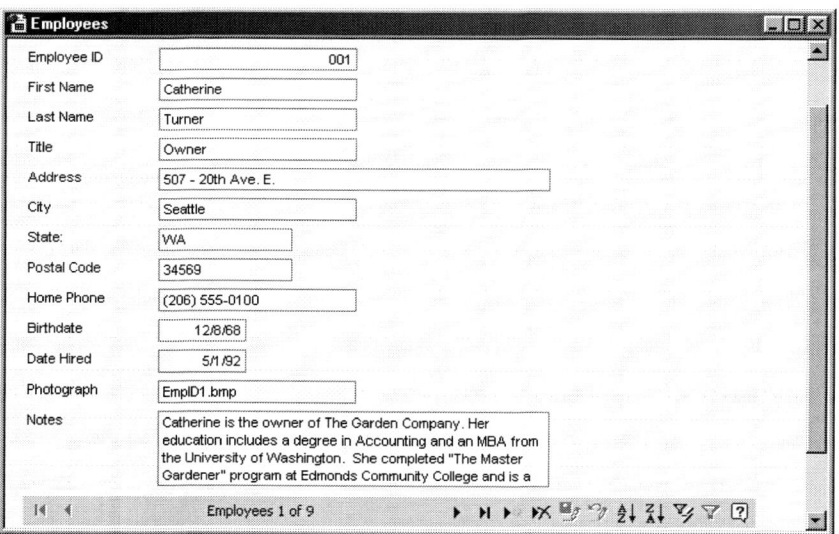

Every field in the underlying Employees table, along with its caption, is listed in one column. (AutoPage creates only columnar pages.) Below the **fields** is a navigation bar, which is included by default in all data access pages. (You might have to increase the size of the window to see this bar.)

5   Click the **Save** button on the toolbar to save your new page.

6   In the **Save As Data Access Page** dialog box, click **Save** to save the file in the *SBS\Access\PgsMods\AutoPage* folder with the suggested name of *Employees*.

7   If Access warns that the connection string for this page uses an absolute page, click **OK** to dismiss the message.

Since you are using a file on your own computer and not a network computer, a **UNC path** is not appropriate.

Next

8   Hold the pointer over each navigation button until a ScreenTip displays the name of the button.

9   Click the **Next** button on the navigation bar to move to the next record.

Lost Database or Data Access Page?

A data access page is an HTML file that is connected to a **data source** - in this case, an Access database. The data source can be located on the same computer as the data access page or on some other computer on an intranet or the Internet. Where it's located is not important as long as the data access page can locate and open the database.

The page's **ConnectionString** property, which is stored in the HTML file, includes a path to the data source and other information that allows it to connect to the source. If you create a data access page while you have the data source open on your own computer, the **ConnectionString** property includes a path to your hard drive, in the usual C:\ path format. When the page is opened on another computer, the page is downloaded to that computer. The **ConnectionString** information is read, the computer attempts to follow the path to the data source, and the attempt fails. Using a UNC path ensures that the data source can be found because it specifies the computer on which the data source is stored, as well as the drive and folders.

Just as you can "lose" a data source, you can also "lose" data access pages. If you create a data access page and later move it or rename the folder where it is stored, you will get an error when you attempt to open it in either Access or Internet Explorer. To fix this problem, try to open the page in Page view. When you see the message that the file can't be found, click the **Update Link** button, and locate the HTML file. You will then be able to open the page, but you will get another error stating that the page can't find the database. Switch to Design view, click the title bar to select the page, and then click **Properties** on the **View** menu to open the **Properties** dialog box for the page. On the **Data** tab, click **ConnectionString**, and then click its button. In the **Data Link Properties** dialog box, click the **Connection** tab, edit or browse to the correct path in the first box, and then click **OK**.

Help

10 Click the **Help** button.

Access online Help opens to the topic *About data access pages*.

11 Close Help.

12 In Windows Explorer, browse to the *SBS\Access\PgsMods\AutoPage* folder, and open **Employees** in Internet Explorer by double-clicking it.

The page should look and function identically to the way it did in Access.

tip

You can view data access pages only in Internet Explorer 5.0 or later. (You must also have Internet Explorer 5.0 or later installed on your computer to create data access pages.) These exercises were developed using Internet Explorer 5.5. If you are using Internet Explorer 5.0, you might notice slight differences in the screens and in the options available.

Sort Ascending

13 Click the **Last Name** field, and then click the **Sort Ascending** button on the navigation bar.

The records are sorted in ascending order, based on the last name.

View

14 Minimize Internet Explorer (don't close it). Then click the **View** button on the Access window's toolbar to view the Employees page in Design view.

Your screen looks like this:

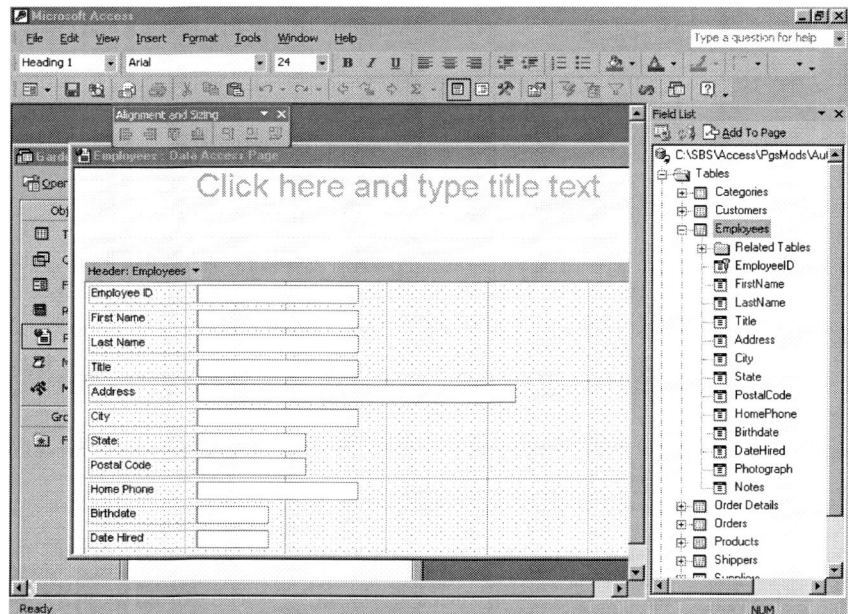

15 Click the **Close** button in the upper right corner of the Field List so that you can see the entire page window.

16 Click where you see *Click here and type title text*, and type **Employee List**.

As you can see in the **Style** box on the Formatting toolbar, the words you typed are styled as Heading 1.

17 Press the ⬇ key to move to the line below the heading.

The **Style** box shows that this paragraph is styled as Normal.

18 Type the following:

> **While viewing this page, you can:**

Bullets

19 Press Enter , click the **Bullets** button on the Formatting toolbar, and type the following lines, pressing Enter after each:

> **Click Next or Previous to scroll records.**
>
> **Edit information.**
>
> **Click a field, and click one of the Sort buttons to sort records.**
>
> **Click Help for more information about using this page.**

Here are the results:

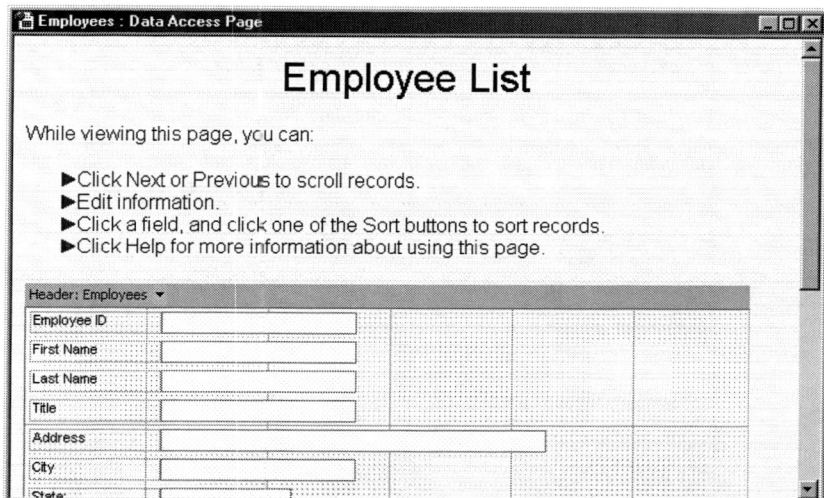

Bold

B

20   Double-click the word *Next* in the first bulleted item, and click the **Bold** button on the Formatting toolbar.

21   Do the same for the words *Previous*, *Sort*, and *Help*.

22   Scroll down the page, click below the navigation bar, and type:

Copyright 2001, The Garden Company.

tip

You can add a © symbol by clicking where you want the symbol to appear, and then with [Num Lock] turned on, holding down the [Alt] key and typing **0169** on the numeric keypad. When you release the [Alt] key, the copyright symbol is inserted.

23   Select the line you just typed, click the down arrow next to the **Font Size** box on the Formatting toolbar, and click **8**.

The size of the text changes to 8 points.

24   Save the page, and then click the **View** button.

The bottom part of the page now looks like this:

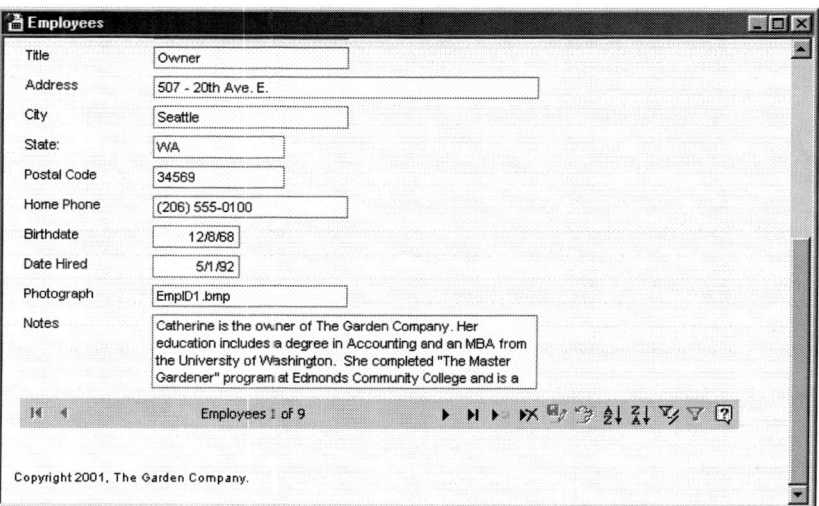

25 Return to Design view.

26 Delete the **Last Name** label, drag the **LastName** text box to the right, and then drag both the **FirstName** text box and its label down until the text box is in line with the **LastName** text box.

27 Double-click the **First Name** label, click the **Other** tab to open its **Properties** dialog box, and change the **InnerText** property to **Name**.

As you have just seen, the process for changing the layout and properties of a data access page is almost identical to that for a form or report.

tip

You can also view the properties for an element of a data access page by clicking it and then clicking **Properties** on the **View** menu, or by right-clicking it and clicking **Properties** on the shortcut menu. Pressing ⌐F4⌐ doesn't toggle the display of properties for data access pages as it does with other objects.

28 Click the **View** button to change to Page view.

29 Select the **Employee ID** number, and press ⌐Tab⌐ three times.

The order in which the insertion point moves through the fields is determined by the **TabIndex** property.

30 Switch back to Design view.

31 Click the navigation bar at the bottom of the data access page.

The entire bar is selected, and its properties appear in the **Properties** dialog box.

Delete

32 Click the **Delete** button on the navigation bar.

Now only that button is selected, and its properties are displayed.

33 In the **Properties** dialog box, click the **Format** tab to display the following properties:

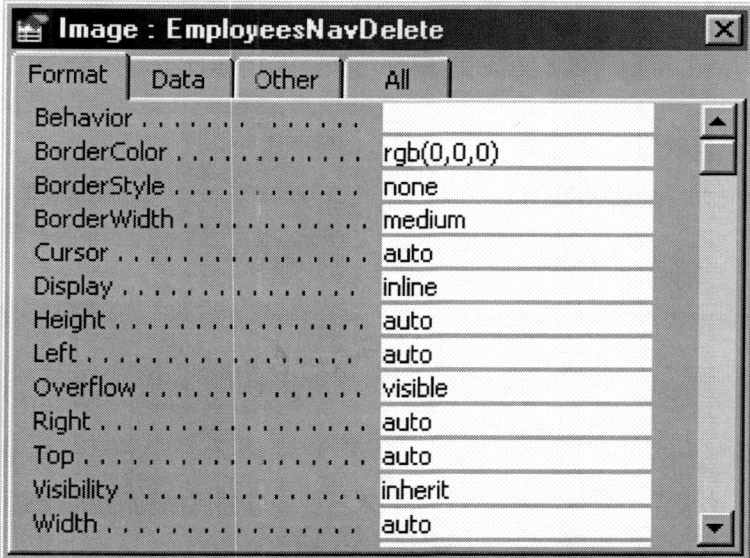

34 Click the **Visibility** property, and then select **hidden**.

This will prevent viewers from deleting records.

35 Click the **View** button on the toolbar to change to Page view.

The page is displayed, and the **Delete** button no longer appears on the navigation bar.

36 Click the **Save** button on the toolbar.

37 Return to Internet Explorer, and click the **Refresh** button.

When the browser reloads the Web page, the **Delete** button is no longer available.

38 Close the browser, close the **Employees** page, and close the **GardenCo** database.

Creating a Data Access Page with the Page Wizard

Ac2002-8-3
Ac2002e-6-1

You can create an independent data access page by doing the following: Close the database, choose **New** from the **File** menu and then select **Blank Data Access Page** from the **Task Pane.**

GardenCo

Using AutoPage is a quick way to create a simple data access page in columnar format. But if you want more control over the content and layout, you should use the **Page Wizard**. With this wizard, you can select the initial fields to include on the data access page, create groups, and pick a theme from the dozens of those available. The theme you select is applied to the page when viewed in Access or Internet Explorer.

In this exercise, you will use the **Page Wizard** to create a data access page based on the Products by Category query in the GardenCo database. The working folder for this exercise is *SBS\Access\PgsMods\Wizard*. Follow these steps:

1 Open the **GardenCo** database located in the working folder.

2 Click **Pages** on the **Objects** bar.

3 Click the **New** button at the top of the database window.

4 In the **New Data Access Page** dialog box, click **Page Wizard**, select **Products by Category** from the list of tables and queries, and then click **OK**.

You then see the wizard, page shown on the next page, which is the same as the one displayed when you are creating a form or report.

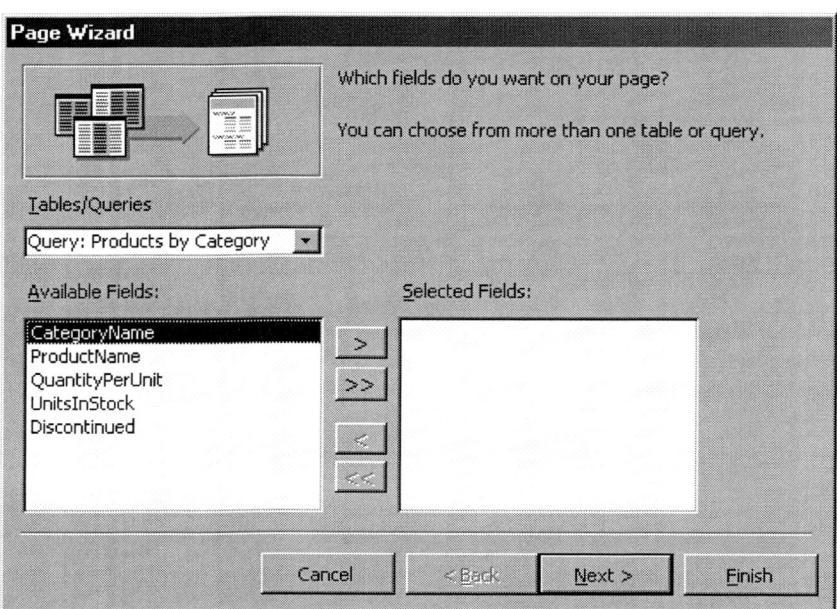

5 Click the **>>** button to move all the fields to the **Selected Fields** list, and then click **Next** to display this page, in which you can set grouping levels:

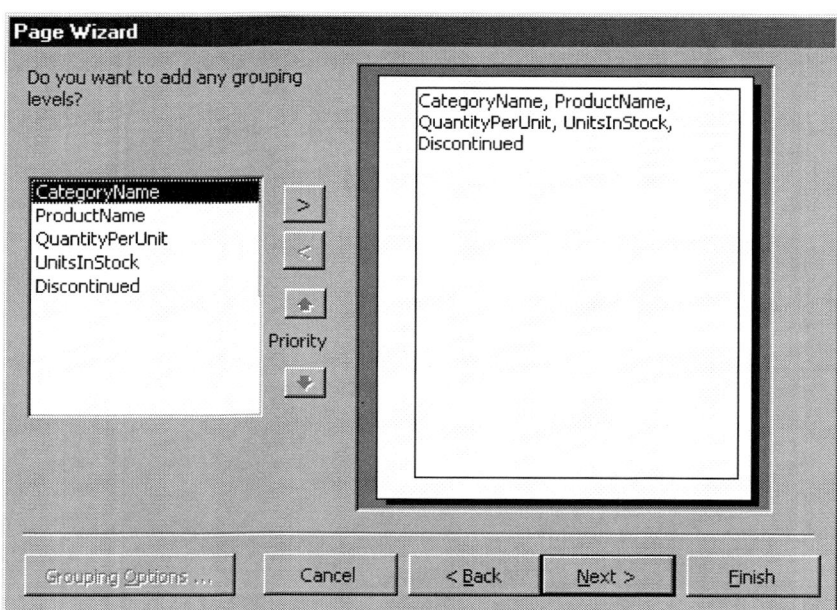

6 Double-click **CategoryName**, and then click **Next**.

You use this page to set the order in which the records will initially be displayed.

7   Select **ProductName** in the first sort box, and click **Next**.

8   Select the **Do you want to apply a theme to your page** check box, and click **Finish**.

Access creates the page, opens it in Design view, and displays this **Theme** dialog box:

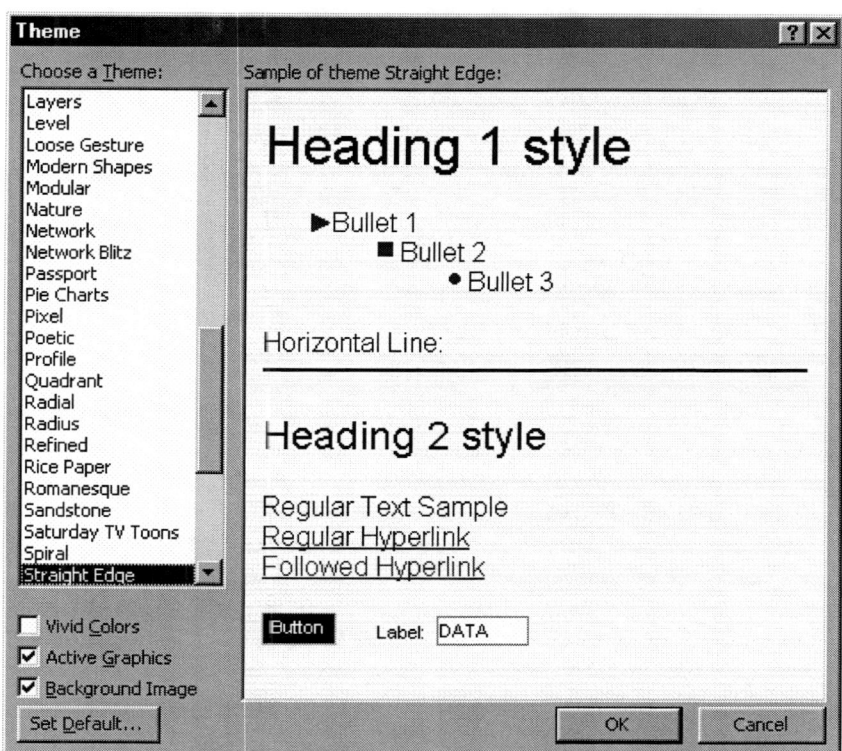

You can click the name of any theme to see a sample. You can also use the check boxes at the bottom of the dialog box to modify the theme, and you can set the selected theme as the default for all new pages.

9   Scroll to the bottom of the list, select **Willow**, and then click **OK**.

The new page appears in Design view.

10   If necessary, close the **Properties** dialog box, and then scroll to the top of the page.

11   Click the placeholder title text at the top of the page, and type **Products by Category**.

View

12   Click the **View** button to change to Page view, where the page looks like the graphic shown on the next page.

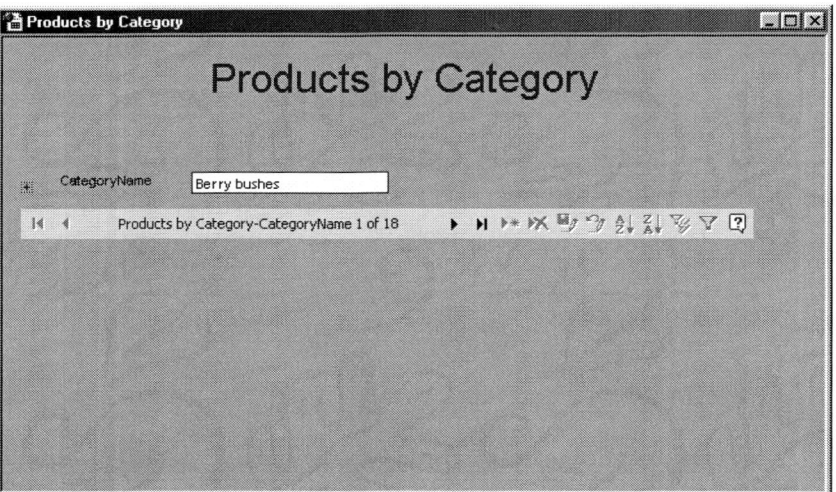

Next

13   Click the **Next** button on the navigation bar to move to the next category.

14   Click the ➕ button to the left of **CategoryName**.

The display expands to show a product record under the category name, and a second navigation bar is displayed under the first, as shown here:

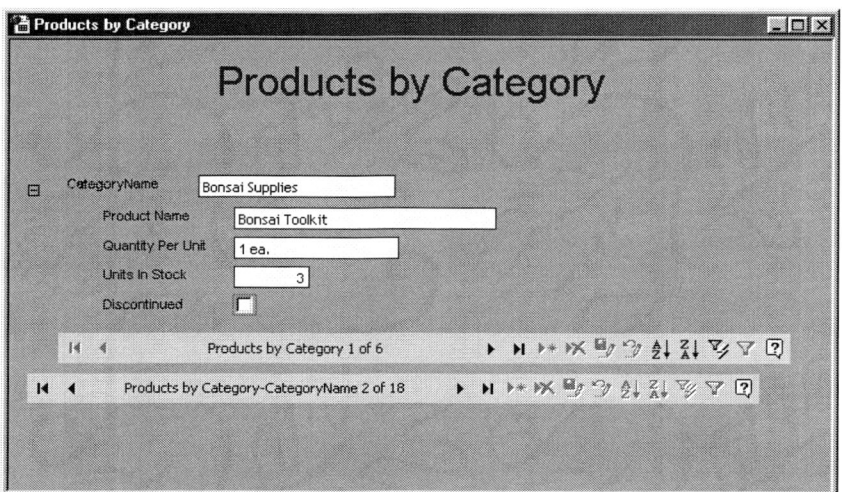

15   Click **Next** on the upper navigation bar to view the next product record in that category.

16   Click **Next** on the lower navigation bar to move to the next category.

The next category name is displayed, and the Products section disappears. You don't want to have to click the + button to display the section every time you move to a new category, so you need to make a change.

17   Switch to Design view, right-click the top header (**Products by Category- CategoryName**), and click **Group Level Properties** on the shortcut menu.

Access opens the **GroupLevel Properties** dialog box.

18   Double-click the **ExpandedByDefault** setting to change it to **True**.

19   Return to Page view, and click the **Next** button on the lower navigation bar several times.

The Product section now remains expanded as you move from category to category.

20   Close the page without saving it, and then close the **GardenCo** database.

Quick Quizzes

●   What are ASP pages?

●   What does ASP mean?

●   What is a control label?

Quick Reference

Lesson 1:   Getting to Know Microsoft Access 2002

To view details about objects listed in the database window

Details

● Click the Details button on the toolbar at the top of the database window.

To hide command shortcuts in the database window

1 On the **Tools** menu, click **Options**.

2 On the **View** tab, clear the **New object shortcuts** check box, and click **OK**.

To open a table, query, form, or report

1 With the database open, click **Tables, Queries, Forms, or Reports** on the **Objects** bar.

2 Make your selection from the options available, and then click the **Open** button at the top of the database window.

Lesson 2:   Creating a New Database

To change the default storage location

1 When a database file is open, click **Options** on the **Tools** menu.

2 On the **General** tab, enter a new path in the **Default database folder** box, and then click **OK**.

To create an empty database structure

New

1 Click the **New** button on the toolbar to display the **New File** task pane.

2 In the **New** section of the task pane, click **Blank Database**.

3 Navigate to the storage location you want for the file, type a name for the new database, and click **Create**.

To switch views of a database object

View

● Click the View button on the toolbar.

● Click the View button's down arrow, and click an option in the drop-down list.

To set the primary key field

1   Display the table in Design view.

2   Select the field that you want to be the primary key field in the top portion of the window.

3   On the **Edit** menu, click **Primary Key**.

To set a field's data type

1   Display the table in Design view.

2   Click in the **Data Type** cell for the field you want to change, and then click the down arrow to display a list of all possible data types.

3   Click the type you want.

To assign a caption (a column header that is different from the field name)

1   Display the table in Design view.

2   Click the field to which you want to assign a caption.

3   Click the **Caption** box, and type the caption text.

To set a text field's size

1   Display the table in Design view.

2   Click the field whose size you want to change.

3   Click the **Field Size** box, and type the number of characters you want to allow in the field.

Lesson 3:   Getting Information Into and Out of a Database

To import data from a delimited or fixed-width text file

1   On the **File** menu, point to **Get External Data**, and then click **Import**.

2   In the **Files of type** list, click **Text Files**.

3   Navigate to the storage location of the file you want to import, click the file name, and then click **Import**.

4   Follow the instructions of the **Import Text Wizard**, click **Finish** on the wizard's last page to import the text file into the appropriate location, and then click **OK** to close the message box.

To import data from an Access database

1   On the **File** menu, point to **Get External Data**, and then click **Import**.

2   If necessary, select **Microsoft Access** in the **Files of type** list.

3 Navigate to the storage location of the file you want to import, click the database name, and then click **Import**.

4 Click the **Options** button to select any import options you want.

5 Select the objects you want to import, or click **Select All** to import all objects, and then click **OK**.

To import data from an HTML file

1 On the **File** menu, point to **Get External Data**, and then click **Import**.

2 In the **Files of type** list, click **HTML Documents**.

3 Navigate to the storage location of the file you want to import, click the file name, and then click **Import**.

4 Follow the instructions of the **Import HTML Wizard**, click **Finish** on the wizard's last page to import the data, and then click **OK** to close the message box that appears.

To import XML data

1 On the **File** menu, point to **Get External Data**, and then click **Import**.

2 In the **Files of type** list, click **XML Documents**.

3 Navigate to the storage location of the file you want to open, click the file name, and then click **Import.**

4 Click the **Options** button to select any import options you want, and then click **OK** twice.

To export information to another application

1 In the database window, click the object you want to export.

2 On the **File** menu, click **Export**.

3 Navigate to the folder where you want to store the exported file, select the appropriate **Save as type** option, type a name for the file, and click **Export**.

Lesson 4: Simplifying Data Entry with Forms

To edit form properties

1 Display the form in Design view.

2 Use the buttons and boxes on the **Formatting** toolbar to change the formatting of labels and controls.

3 To change the properties of a control, right-click the control, and click **Properties** on the shortcut menu.

4 Make your changes in the **Properties** dialog box.

To add a graphic to a form

Toolbox

1   Display the form in Design view.

2   If necessary, click the **Toolbox** button to open the toolbox.

Image

3   Click the **Image** control in the toolbox, and then drag a rectangle the height and width that you want in the desired location on the form.

4   In the **Insert Picture** dialog box, navigate to the storage location of the file you want to use, and double-click it.

To add a control to a form

1   Display the form in Design view.

Toolbox

2   If necessary, click the **Toolbox** button to open the toolbox.

3   Click the appropriate control button in the toolbox, and then drag a rectangle in the desired location on the form.

4   If necessary, display the control's **Properties** dialog box, and make changes.

To copy the formatting of one form control to another

1   Display the form in Design view.

2   Click the control that contains the formatting you want to copy.

Format Painter

3   Click the **Format Painter** button on the toolbar, and then click the control to which you want to copy the formatting.

To create a form using an AutoForm

1   On the **Objects** bar, click **Forms**.

2   On the database window's toolbar, click the **New** button.

3   Click the option you want in the list, select the table on which you want to base the form, and then click **OK**.

Save

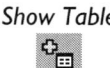

4   Click the **Save** button, enter the name you want for the form in the **Save As** dialog box, and click **OK**.

To define a relationship between tables

Relationships

1   With the database open, click the **Relationships** button on the toolbar to open the Relationships window.

Show Table

2   If the **Show Table** dialog box isn't displayed, click the **Show Table** button on the toolbar. Double-click the tables you want to work with in the list displayed, and then close the **Show Table** dialog box.

3   Drag a field from one table so that it is on top of the corresponding field in the other table.

4   Select the options you want in the **Edit Relationships** dialog box, and then click **Create**.

5 Close the Relationships window, clicking **Yes** when prompted to save its layout.

To edit or delete a table relationship

Relationships

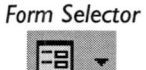

1 With the database open, click the **Relationships** button on the toolbar to open the Relationships window.

2 Right-click the line representing the relationship you want to edit or delete, and click the appropriate command on the shortcut menu.

To add a subform to a form

Toolbox

1 Open the form in Design view.

2 If the toolbox isn't displayed, click the **Toolbox** button.

Control Wizards

3 Make sure the **Control Wizards** button in the toolbox is active (has a border around it).

4 Click the **Subform/Subreport** button, and drag a rectangle in the desired location of the form.

Subform/ Subreport

5 Follow the instructions of the **Subform Wizard**, and click **Finish** on the wizard's last page to complete the process.

6 Adjust the size and location of the objects on your form as necessary.

To adjust a subform's properties

1 Display the form that contains the subform in Design view.

2 If necessary, open the **Properties** dialog box.

Form Selector

3 Click the **Form Selector** button in the upper left corner of the subform twice.

4 Make the changes you want in the **Properties** dialog box.

Lesson 5:   Locating Specific Information

To sort information in a table

Sort Ascending

1 With the table open in Datasheet view, click anywhere in the column of the field on which you want to base the sort, and then click the **Sort Ascending** button or the **Sort Descending** button. (To sort on more than one column of information, arrange them so they are side-by-side in the order you want to sort them, select the columns, and then use the **Sort** buttons.)

Sort Descending

2 To reverse the sort order, click the opposite **Sort** button.

To filter a table based on a selection

1 Open the table in Datasheet view.

Filter By

2 Select the information you want to use as the filter criteria.

Selection

3 Click the **Filter By Selection** button.

4 If necessary, repeat steps 2 and 3 to filter the information further.

Remove Filter

5 **Click the Remove Filter** button to redisplay all of the table's records.

To filter a table based on text you type

1 Open the table in Datasheet view.

2 Right-click any field in the appropriate column, and click **Filter For** on the shortcut menu.

3 Type the criteria you want to use as the filter, and press [Enter]. (You can use wildcards and simple expressions as the filter criteria.)

To filter a table excluding a selection

1 Open the table in Datasheet view.

2 Right-click the appropriate field in any record, and click **Filter Excluding Selection** on the shortcut menu.

To filter by form to locate information

1 Open the table or form you want to work with in either Datasheet or Form view.

Filter By Form

2 Click the **Filter By Form** button on the toolbar.

3 Click the field box in which you want to create the filter, type the filter criteria you want, and press [Enter]; or select the criteria from the list of options. (Repeat this step for any other fields you want to filter.)

Apply Filter

4 To add additional filter criteria for a particular field, click the **Or** tab and enter the criteria as necessary.

5 Click the **Apply Filter** button.

To save a query created in the Advanced Filter/Sort window

1 Click **Save As Query** on the **File** menu.

2 Name the query, and click **OK**.

To create a select query

1 On the **Objects** bar, click **Queries**.

2 Double-click **Create query in Design view**.

3 In the **Show Table** dialog box, double-click the tables you want to use in the query, and then close the dialog box.

4 To include fields in the query, drag them from the lists at the top of the window to a column in the design grid. To copy all fields to the grid, double-click the title bar above the field list to select the entire list, and then drag the selection over the grid.

Run

5 Click the **Run** button to run the query and display the results in Datasheet view.

To add an expression to a query

1 With the query window displayed, right-click the appropriate cell in the design grid, and click **Build** on the shortcut menu.

2 Double-click the **Functions** folder in the first column of the elements area, and then click **Built-In Functions**.

3 Click the function type you want in the second column. Then double-click the function you want in the third column.

4 Build the expression, and then click **OK**.

5 Press ⌊ Enter ⌋ to move the insertion point out of the field, which completes the entry of the expression.

6 To rename the expression, double-click **Expr1**, and then type the name you want.

To turn off the display of a field in a query

1 Display the query in Design view.

2 Clear the **Show** check box for any fields you don't want displayed.

3 Switch to Datasheet view to see the results.

Lesson 6:   Keeping Your Information Accurate

To create a table from scratch

1 Click **Tables** on the **Objects** bar, and double-click **Create table in Design view**.

2 Click the first **Field Name** cell, type the field name you want, and press ⌊ Tab ⌋ to move to the **Data Type** cell.

3 Continue to fill in the necessary information for each field in the new table.

Save

4 Click the **Save** button, enter a name for the table, and click **OK**.

5 If necessary, assign a field as the primary key, or click **No** to have no primary key field.

To create a custom input mask

1   Open the table in Design view.

2   Select the field to which you want to apply a special format.

3   In the **Field Properties** section, click **Input Mask**, type the mask you want, press `Enter`, and then save your changes.

To create a field validation rule

1   Open the table in Design view.

2   Select the field you want to add a rule to, and then click in the **Validation Rule** box.

3   Click the **...** button at the right end of the **Validation Rule** box to open the Expression Builder, or type an expression and press `Enter`.

4   To state the rule, type some explanatory text in the **Validation Text** box, and then save the table.

5   If Access warns you that data integrity rules have changed, click **Yes** to apply the rule or **No** to cancel it.

To test validation rules for a table

●   Right-click the title bar of the table, and click Test Validation Rules on the shortcut menu.

To create a table validation rule

1   Open the table in Design view.

2   Right-click the table window, and click **Properties** on the shortcut menu.

3   Click in the **Validation Rule** box, type the expression for the rule you want, and press `Enter`.

4   In the **Validation Text** box, type the explanatory text, close the dialog box, and then save the table.

5   If Access warns you that data integrity rules have changed, click **Yes** to apply the rule or **No** to cancel it.

To create a delete query

1   Use any method to create a query that displays the information you want.

2   In Design view, click the **Query** menu, and click **Delete Query**.

3   Type the text you want in the **Criteria** row under the appropriate field.

Run

4 Click the **Run** button to run the delete query.

5 Click **Yes** in the warning box to delete the records, and then save the query, if necessary.

Lesson 7: Working with Reports

To add a subreport to a report

Toolbox

1 Open the report to which you want to add a subreport in Design view.

2 If the toolbox isn't displayed, click the **Toolbox** button on the toolbar.

Subform/ Subreport

3 Click **Subform/Subreport** in the toolbox, and then click where you want the subreport to appear.

4 Follow the **SubReport Wizard's** instructions, and click **Finish** on the wizard's last page to see the subreport.

To modify a subreport

1 Display the report that contains the subreport you want to modify in Design view.

2 If the **Properties** dialog box isn't displayed, press F4 to display it.

3 If necessary, select the subreport in the **Objects** list at the top of the **Properties** dialog box.

4 Use the options in the **Properties** dialog box to make the necessary changes.

5 Save your changes, and switch to Print Preview to see the results.

To add a border to a subreport

1 Display the report that contains the subreport you want to modify in Design view.

2 If the **Properties** dialog box isn't displayed, press F4 to display it.

3 On the **Format** tab of the **Properties** dialog box, change the **Border Style** property to the option you want.

To preview a report

View

1 With the report open in Design view, click the **View** button to switch to Print Preview.

Next Page

2 To move through the pages of the report, click the **Next Page** button on the navigation bar.

Close

3 Click the **Close** button on the Print Preview toolbar.

To preview the layout of a report

1   With the report open in Design view, click the **View** button's down arrow, and click **Layout Preview**.

2   Click the **Close** button to return to Design view.

Lesson 8:   Working with Pages and Modules

To use AutoPage to create a data access page

1   With the database open, click **Pages** on the **Objects** bar.

2   Click the **New** button at the top of the database window.

3   Click the **AutoPage** option you want, display the list of tables and queries, click the table or query you want, and then click **OK**.

Save

4   Click the **Save** button on the toolbar to save your new page.

5   In the **Save As Data Access Page** dialog box, browse to the folder where you want to save the file, type the name you want for the file, and click **Save**.

6   If Access warns that the connection string for this page uses an absolute page, click **OK** to dismiss the message. (A UNC path is appropriate if you are using a file on a network computer.)

7   Use the buttons on the navigation bar to view different records and perform other tasks.

To update links when you move a data access page

1   Try to open the data access page in Page view.

2   When you see the message that the file can't be found, click the **Update Link** button, and locate the HTM file.

3   When you get another error stating that the page can't find the database, switch to Design view, and open the **Page Properties** dialog box.

4   On the **Data** tab, click **ConnectionString**, and then click its `...` button.

5   Click the **Connection** tab, edit or browse to the correct path in the first box, and then click **OK**.

To hide buttons on the navigation bar in a data access page

1   Display the data access page in Design view.

2   Click the button on the navigation bar that you want to hide.

3   In the **Properties** dialog box, click the **Format** tab, click the **Visibility** property, and then select **hidden**.

To create a data access page from scratch

1   With the database open, click **Pages** on the **Objects** bar.

2   Double-click **Create data access page in Design view** to open a blank data access page.

Save

3   **Click the** Save button, browse to the folder where you want to save the file, type the name you want for the page, and click **Save.**

Index

ITS-Feda Ltd

ITS-Feda Ltd is proud to present the Microsoft© Access 2002 Core Skills Student Guide as part of the Microsoft© Office Specialist XP Courseware Series.

The original self-paced training materials created by Online Training Solutions, Inc., have, thanks to the work of a team of dedicated training professionals and writers, become Microsoft© Office Specialist XP Courseware for Instructor Led, classroom training. This courseware maintains the standards of excellence you have come to expect from ITS-Feda Ltd and Microsoft Press®

The book's straightforward approach and easy to read format provides both the Instructor and the students with the training tool they need to gain the maximum benefit from using Microsoft© Office XP products. The books focus on developing both essential skills and the skills required to pass the Microsoft© Office Specialist Certification Exams.

ITS-Feda Ltd would like to acknowledge the team at TESI Automazione s.r.l. and Microsoft Press® who's hard work has made the production of these materials possible.

For further information please visit our web site at www.itservices.org.uk.

The following materials are also available as part of this range from ITS-Feda Ltd:

Title	ISBN NO.
Word 2002	
Step by Step Courseware: Word Version 2002 Core Skills Student Guide	1-904644-00-7
Step by Step Courseware: Word Version 2002 Expert Skills Student Guide	1-904644-01-5
Step by Step Courseware: Word Version 2002 Instructor Guide	1-904644-02-3
Excel 2002	
Step by Step Courseware: Excel Version 2002 Core Skills Student Guide	1-904644-03-1
Step by Step Courseware: Excel Version 2002 Expert Skills Student Guide	1-904644-04-X
Step by Step Courseware: Excel Version 2002 Instructor Guide	1-904644-05-8
Outlook 2002	
Step by Step Courseware: Outlook Version 2002 Core Skills Student Guide	1-904644-06-6
Step by Step Courseware: Outlook Version 2002 Expert Skills Student Guide	1-904644-07-4
Step by Step Courseware: Outlook Version 2002 Instructor Guide	1-904644-08-2
Access 2002	
Step by Step Courseware: Access Version 2002 Core Skills Student Guide	1-904644-09-0
Step by Step Courseware: Access Version 2002 Expert Skills Student Guide	1-904644-10-4
Step by Step Courseware: Access Version 2002 Instructor Guide	1-904644-11-2
PowerPoint 2002	
Step by Step Courseware: PowerPoint Version 2002 Student Guide	1-904644-12-0
Step by Step Courseware: PowerPoint Version 2002 Instructor Guide	1-904644-13-9

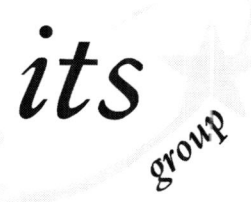

Microsoft Access 2002
Core Exercises
Student

Version 1.0

Table of Contents

SCENARIO FOR EXERCISES

You and three friends have invented a new PC based computer game. You are about to embark on a business venture to get the new game out into the market place. The following are tasks that you have to complete before the bank will grant you a business loan to be able to market the new game.

Important

It is important to complete the exercises in the order of the instructions, as in the exam environment you will be marked down if you complete a question in a different order.

Microsoft Access 2002 Core Chapter 1
Consolidation Exercise

Ac2002-1-2   Open database objects in multiple views

1. Open the database called **Competition Winners.mdb**, which can be found in the **C:\SBS\Access\Consolidation\Core** folder.

2. View the table called **tbl-entries** as a datasheet.

3. View the query called **qry-entries to competition** as a datasheet.

4. View the design of the **tbl-winners names** table.

5. Open the form called **Competition**.

6. Preview the **Winners Names** report.

7. Change from the preview of the open report to the design view of the report.

8. Close the database.

Ac2002-5-3   Sort records

1. Open the database called **Competition Winners.mdb**, which can be found in the **C:\SBS\Access\Consolidation\Core** folder.

2. Open the **tbl-entries** table.

3. Sort the information by **Last Name**.

4. Close the datasheet and save the layout changes.

5. Close the database.

Ac2002-5-4   Filter records

1. Open the database called **Competition Winners.mdb**, which can be found in the **C:\SBS\Access\Consolidation\Core** folder.

2. Open the table called **tbl-entries**.

3. Filter the records to show all entrants from Kent.

4. Save the filter as Kent entries.

5. Show all data.

6. Close the database.

Ac2002-7-3   Preview and print reports

1. Open the database called **Competition Winners.mdb**, which can be found in the **C:\SBS\Access\Consolidation\Core** folder.

2. Preview the **Winners Names** report.

3. Print the report to the default printer.

4. Close the database.

Microsoft Access 2002 Core Chapter 2
Consolidation Exercise

Ac2002-1-1 Create Access databases

1. Create a new blank database in a **C:\SBS\Fantasy Games\Orders** folder called **Orders.mdb**.

2. Close the new database.

3. Create a new database using the expenses template that will store your company's expenses. Accept all default settings.

4. Save the new database as **Expenses.mdb** to a **C:\SBS\Fantasy Games\Accounts** folder.

5. Close the new database.

Ac2002-1-3 Move among records

1. Open the database called **Competition Winners.mdb**, which can be found in the **C:\SBS\Access\Consolidation\Core** folder.

2. Open the table called **tbl-entries**.

3. Go to the last record in the table.

4. Go to the first record in the table.

5. Move to the fifth record.

6. Close the datasheet.

7. Close the database.

Ac2002-1-4 Format datasheets

1. Open the database called **Competition Winners.mdb**, which can be found in the **C:\SBS\Access\Consolidation\Core** folder.

2. Open the table **tbl-competitions** in a datasheet format.

3. Resize the following columns:

    a. Competetion Name

    b. Winners Name

4. Rename the Competetion Name column to be **Competition Name**.

5. Close the datasheet and save your changes.

6. Close the database.

Ac2002-2-1 Create and modify tables

1. Open the **Expenses.mdb** database, which can be found in the **C:\SBS\Fantasy Games\Accounts** folder.

2. Modify the design of the employees table as follows:

   a. Delete the following fields:

      i. Country/Region

      ii. Work Phone

   b. Change the following field names:

      i. StateorProvince to **Town**

      ii. Region to **County**

      iii. SocialSecurityNumber to **NI Number**

   c. Move the **Town** field to be above the **City** field.

   d. Save and close the table.

3. Create a new table called **VAT** with the following fields and properties:

   a. **VATID** field

      i. Autonumber

      ii. Primary Key

   b. **VAT CODE** field

      i. Text

      ii. Characters always in capitals

   c. **VAT RATE** field

      i. This must have 2 decimal places.

      ii. Formatted as a percentage.

4. Save and close the new table.

5. Close the database.

Ac2002-2-4   Modify field properties

1. Open the **Expenses.mdb** database, which can be found in the **C:\SBS\Fantasy Games\Accounts** folder.

2. Modify the design of the employees table as follows:

   a. Change the following field properties:

      i. Size of the **NI Number** field should be a maximum of 15.

      ii. The format for the **NI Number** field should always be capitals.

      iii. Replace the caption for the **NI Number** field with the same text as the field name.

   b. Add a new field at the end of the table field list called **Photo** with an **OLE Object** data type.

3. Save the changes to the table and close it.

4. Close the database.

Ac2002-5-1   Enter, edit and delete records

1. Open the database called **Competition Winners.mdb**, which can be found in the **C:\SBS\Access\Consolidation\Core** folder.

2. Open the **tbl-entries** table.

3. Add a new record and add your own details as the competition entrant.

4. Close the datasheet.

5. Close the database.

Microsoft Access 2002 Core Chapter 3
Consolidation Exercise

Ac2002-8-1   Import data into Access

1. Open the database called **Orders.mdb**, which can be found in the **C:\SBS\Fantasy Games\Orders** folder.

2. Create a new table by importing the **Order List.xls** file, which can be found in the **C:\SBS\Access\Consolidation\Core** folder. Use the following settings when importing:

   a. Use the named range **Orders**.

   b. The first row is your column headings.

   c. Let Access create a primary key.

   d. Save the table as **tbl-Orders**.

5. Look at the design for the **Orders** table modify it as follows:

   a. Delete the total cost field.

   b. Format the date of the order to be a short date.

   c. The maximum number of character in the postcode field will be 15 and they will always display as capitals.

   d. The maximum number of characters for all other text fields is 50.

6. Save the changes to the table.

7. Close the table.

8. Close the database.

Ac2002-8-2   Export data from Access

1. Open the database called **Competition Winners.mdb**, which can be found in the **C:\SBS\Access\Consolidation\Core** folder.

2. Export the table called **tbl-winners names** to an Excel v97-2002 workbook.

3. Save the Excel file as **Design competition winners names.xls** in a new folder called **C:\SBS\Fantasy Games\Competitions**.

4. Close the database.

Microsoft Access 2002 Core Chapter 4
Consolidation Exercise

Ac2002-4-1   Create and display forms

1. Open the database called **Orders**, which can be found in the **C:\SBS\Fantasy Games\Orders** folder.

2. From the **tbl-orders** table, create a new form called **Order Form**, which has the following properties:

    a. Columnar.

    b. All fields except the **ID** field.

    c. Expedition style.

3. Close the form.

4. Close the database.

Ac2002-4-2   Modify form properties

1. Open the database called **Orders**, which can be found in the **C:\SBS\Fantasy Games\Orders** folder.

2. Open the form called **Order Form**.

3. Modify the form so that the **ID** field is on the form, but not visible.

4. Add a new field to the bottom of the form that will calculate the total cost of the order.

Note: The total cost of the order is the **Quantity** multiplied by **£49.99**, and the **Postage** added.

5. Call the new field **TotalCost** and change the format to be **Currency**.

6. Save the changes on the form.

7. Close the form.

8. Close the database.

Ac2002-6-1   Create one-to-many relationships

1. Open the database called **Competition Winners.mdb**, which can be found in the **C:\SBS\Access\Consolidation\Core** folder.

2. Create a One to Many relationship between the winners name table and the entries table.

3. Save changes and close the relationship window.

4. Close the database.

Microsoft Access 2002 Core Chapter 5
Consolidation Exercise

Ac2002-3-1   Create and modify select queries

1. Open the database called **Orders**, which can be found in the **C:\SBS\Fantasy Games\Orders** folder.

2. Using the Simple Query Wizard create a new query that has the following properties:

   a. Display the following fields:

      i. Date of Order

      ii. Quantity

      iii. Postage

   b. Calculates the average postage cost.

   c. Calculates the total, average minimum and maximum of the quantity field.

   d. Counts the records in this table.

   e. Group the dates by **Month**.

   f. Query name **qry-summary of orders**.

3. Close the query.

4. Close the database.

Ac2002-5-2   Create queries in design view

1. Open the database called **Orders**, which can be found in the **C:\SBS\Fantasy Games\Orders** folder.

2. Create a new query from the orders table with the following properties:

   a. Fields and order of fields in the datasheet:

      i. Name

      ii. Address 1

      iii. Town

      iv. County

      v. Postcode

      vi. Date of Order

      vii. Quantity

      viii. Postage

   b. Only orders where 5 or more games were ordered.

   c. Sorted ascending by date and then by name.

3. Save the query as **qry-large orders**.

4. Run the query.

5. Close the query.

6. Close the database.

Ac2002-3-2   *Add calculated fields to select queries*

1. Open the database called **Orders**, which can be found in the **C:\SBS\Fantasy Games\Orders** folder.

2. Change the **qry-large orders** query so that calculated fields are added which have the following properties:

    a.   Cost of items on the order

    b.   Total Cost

    c.   All calculated fields to be formatted as currency.

Note: The cost of items on order is calculated by multiplying the **Quantity** by £49.99. The total cost is the **Postage** plus the **cost of items on order**.

3. Save the query with the name **qry-large orders with calculations** and run it.

4. Close the query.

5. Close the database.

Microsoft Access 2002 Core Chapter 6
Consolidation Exercise

Ac2002-2-2   Add predefined input mask to field

1. Open the **Orders** database, which can be found in the **C:\SBS\Fantasy Games\Orders** folder.

2. Change the table design for the **tbl-Orders** table so that the **Order Date** field has in input mask that allows a short date only.

3. Save the changes to the table, and close it.

4. Close the database.

Ac2002-2-3   Create Lookup fields

1. Open the database called **Competition Winners.mdb**, which can be found in the **C:\SBS\Access\Consolidation\Core** folder.

2. Add a new field to the **tbl-Competitions** table that looks up the entries for the competition, and allows you to choose the winners name.

Note: Use the table called **tbl-Entries** as the data for your lookup.

3. Save the design changes.

4. View the table and select **Akasha Davis** as the winner for the design competition.

5. Close the table.

6. Close the database.

Ac2002-6-2   Enforce referential integrity

1. Open the database called **Competition Winners.mdb**, which can be found in the **C:\SBS\Access\Consolidation\Core** folder.

2. Edit the relationship between the winners name table and the entries table, to enforce referential integrity.

3. Cascade delete and cascade update this relationship.

4. Save changes and close the relationship window.

5. Close the database.

Microsoft Access 2002 Core Chapter 7 Consolidation Exercise

Ac2002-7-1   *Create and format reports*

1. Open the database called **Orders**, which can be found in the **C:\SBS\Fantasy Games\Orders** folder.

2. Create a report that shows all orders placed by **Oliver Judge**.

3. Include all fields except the **ID** field.

4. Save the report as **Orders from Games Galore**.

5. Modify the reports design so that Oliver's name and address details appear in the header of the report and only the order details appear in the details section.

6. Save the changes to the report.

7. Preview the report.

8. Close the report.

9. Close the database.

Ac2002-7-2   *Add calculated controls to reports*

1. Open the database called **Orders**, which can be found in the **C:\SBS\Fantasy Games\Orders** folder.

2. Create a report that will show the details for one order on one page.

3. Add calculated fields to the page footer of this report to show:

    a. Cost of items ordered   (Quantity * £49.99)

    b. Net Cost   (Cost of items ordered + postage)

    c. VAT   (Net cost * 17.5%)

    d. Total Cost   (Net Cost + VAT)

4. Format the calculated fields as Currency.

5. Save the report as **Invoice.**

6. Preview the report.

7. Close the report.

8. Close the database.

Microsoft Access 2002 Core Chapter 8
Consolidation Exercise

Ac2002-8-3   Create a simple data access page

1. Open the database called **Competition Winners.mdb**, which can be found in the **C:\SBS\Access\Consolidation\Core** folder.

2. Create a data access page based on the **Winners names** table.

3. The following fields are required:

   a. Title

   b. Last Name

   c. Town

   d. County

4. Sort the data by **Last Name**.

5. Title the page **Winners of the Design Competition 2003**.

6. Open the page when you have created it.

7. Look at the page.

8. Change the design of the page so the background colour is blue.

9. Save the changes.

10. Close the page.

11. Close the database.